I0500444

# The Land Knows
(me)

*Restoring*

*Prairie & Savanna, Wetlands, Woodlands & Wildlife*

*in Wisconsin's Northwest Sands Region*

(Station 1)

by

Damian A Vraniak

May, 2021

© Damian A. Vraniak (2021)

i

First Published in 2021 by Waubishmaa'ingan/Whitewolf Press

Copyright © by Damian A. Vraniak

All rights reserved. With the exception of quoting brief passages for the purposes of review, no part of this publication may be reproduced without prior permission from the Publisher.

The information in this book is true and complete to the best of our knowledge. All recommendations are made without any guarantee on the part of the author or Publisher, who also disclaim any liability incurred in connection with the use of this data or specific details.

Library of Congress Cataloging-in-Publication data

Vraniak, Damian A.
The Land Knows (me): Restoring Prairie & Savanna, Wetlands, Woodlands & Wildlife

   text by Damian A. Vraniak
      160 p. cm.
   Includes bibliographic references
   ISBN-13: 9780975090363 (softbound)
   ISBN-10: 0975090363   (softbound)
      1.   Environmental Education.  2. Literature.
      I. Vraniak, Damian A.  II. Title.  III. Series.
      BS2415   2018


Library of Congress Control Number:  2021938305



Printed in the USA
10 9 8 7 6 5 4 3 2 1

# Dedication

To my wife, Christina, my children, Brook Bock and Peter Vraniak, Anastasia Albert, Daybreak and Arendaki Vraniak, my grandchildren Talia and Emily Bock, Harper and Jacob Vraniak, and to those yet to come, I offer this brief view of the lands and living beings that is my home. May you come to love those where you live as I have cared for and loved these with whom I live, all these decades.

# Acknowledgements

I would like to express my appreciation to Robin Maercklin and Scott Weyenberg of the *National Park Service;* Carly Lapin, James Woodsford and Ryan Magana, (Tiffany Bougie, Austin Dixon and Cala Hakseth) of the *Wisconsin Department of Natural Resources;* Adrian Wydeven and Eric Olson of *Northland College*; James Reimer and Caitlin (Smith) Nagorka of the *U.S. Fish & Wildlife Serv*ice; Bill Schmelzer and Ed Haugen of the Hayward *Boy Scout Tro*op *70*; DJ Aderman of *SCOPE*; Karen Harden of the *LCO Boys & Girls Club*; Mike Heim of *LCO High School and College*; Jane Anklam of the *West Wisconsin Land Trust*; Eric Maki of *Midwest Timber*; Kristy Maki *Invasive Species Specialist*; Evanne Hunt and James Rogala of *The Prairie Enthusiasts*; Wendy Little of *The Friends of the Bird Sanctuary*; Chris Stein and Nate Orsburn (and his fire module team out of Indiana Dunes) of the *National Park Service*; Sue Menzel of *AmeriCorps*; Rick Hall of *Earth Partnership*; Diane Tremblay of the *Environmental Research Class of Hayward High School*; Jen Bos of the *Shell Lake High School Ag Class*; Virginia Kline of the *UW-Madison Arboretum*; Patrick Redig of the *U of Minnesota Raptor Research & Rehabilitation Program*; David Robinson of *Macalester College* and David Mech of the *International Wolf Center*; Sara Hotchkiss, Randy Calcote and Elizabeth Lynch of *UW-Madison, U of Minnesota and Luther College* respectively; Volker Radeloff and David Mladenoff of *UW-Madison Department of Forest Ecology and Management*; the *Wisconsin Environmental Education Board*; the *National Resources Foundation Besadny Conservation Grant Program*; the *Pri-Ru-Ta RC&D Council*; Kevin Schoessow of the *Spooner Area Agricultural Research Station*; Tom Frederickson of the *Washburn County Land & Water Conservation Department*; Keith Sengbusch and Ron Spiering of *USDA-NRCS & GLFWC*; Jessica Abbe of *POV Sacred Land Project PBS*; Dave Carlson of *Public Television Up North*; neighbors James Tobin (Roger and Janet) of *Yale University* and Spring Lake and Betty Cowie of *The Belwin Conservancy* in St. Paul and Spring Lake; fellow board members of *Prairie FEASSST, Stewards of the Tributaries of the Namekagon Ecological System, Friends of the Namekagon Barrens Wildlife Area, Namekagon River Partnership, and St. Croix River Association*; *Thompson Sand & Gravel*; and Greg Geller; Nick Eytcheson and Daniel Hubatch, for the assistance they have given enabling collaborative burning, mechanical brushing, seeding, wetland extension and management, invasives control, turtle nesting monitoring and protection, and a host of other restoration activities that have contributed significantly to the character and quality of this landscape and its wildlife; and to my grandfathers – Cyrus John Waggoner and Joseph Vraniak.

# Table of Contents

My friends, please allow me to welcome you formally to *Maa'inganagun*, this place that is our home.

*Aniin … Greetings.*

I am *Waubishmaa'ingan*.

For over four times four hundred years my *Dakota, (Nakota)* and *Hočąk* grandparents traveled and hunted these prairies, open pine and oak savannas and woodlands, upon this very land whereupon I greet you.

For a little over four hundred years my *Anishinabeg, (Ottawa, Menominee and Huron)* grandparents floated and fished the waters in this part of what is now called northwest Wisconsin.

For nearly two hundred years European relatives and friends lived and died here. This is where I have lived for most of seven decades and welcome you now, from this place that is the home of my family, the place that is my home.

When the Dakota and Hočąk first came here many centuries ago, the People were greeted by all living things in a special way. When the Anishinabeg (Ojibwe/Chippewa) were welcomed by the Dakota in the early 1600's, coming to Wisconsin for the first time, a formal greeting was offered by the Dakota in welcome to the new visitors. And much later when the *Oneida* were forced-marched to the area near Green Bay all the way from New York, the Ojibwe welcomed them with the same greeting. Long ago when visiting the Oneida community in Green Bay, I was offered this same welcoming, now a traditional Oneida greeting, which in Oneida involves important words that mean to "put it as one." So do we now welcome you in this Spirit:

*It is our way to acknowledge all parts of the world, the six directions, our ancestors and the Mystery and Spirit of all things.*

*Thus, my children, who are with me, greet your children, who are with you, now, here.*
*The families in my community, who have come with me, greet the families in your*
        *community, who have come with you.*
*And our clans, our groups and our communities of families, together come with*
        *us, in this place,*
*As we welcome one another as all parts of the whole.*

*And so I give condolences to your eyes, your ears and your throats;*
        *for our eyes get dusty and sore,*
        *our ears get worn and weary,*
        *and our throats get small and hoarse.*

*Therefore, we must clear our vision,*
> *so that the meanings we share with one another are like a long, clear, clean and refreshing drink of water,*

*And we must shape our ears like an eagle feather,*
> *so that our words are the wind that passes into and through us,*
> *smoothly lifting our hearts and thoughts,*

*And we must form our words like a soft doe-skin,*
> *so that we are warmly touched and comforted ...*

*For if our children have been hungry and thirsty,*
*And our families tired and torn,*
*And our clans and communities cold and wandering,*

*Then each of us must meet their needs by giving and providing what is needed,*
*you and I together must offer that which is of most benefit,*
*and all of us together must contribute, share, what would be most welcomed,*

*So that our gifts embrace one another in the very way that will put it as one*
*and make us one whole with our ancestors, all living beings and the great Mystery*
*and Spirit of all things.*

So, my friends, in this welcome you need not remember the words shared today that you do not understand. What good would that serve?

Such gifts within the stories shared with you that you *do* understand you may forget also, for if you have an open heart, they will be there for you when you need them. In the Dakota this is *chante ishta*, "seeing with the heart", and, in the Ojibwe, *muzhituming*, "to feel what you do not see".

This is how we begin to 'put it as one' - we bring all that is within us and in kindness and consideration we share these gifts in the voicing of our relationships, hoping to wrap our hearts and minds around the difficult challenges that exist for each of us and all of us together.

But this is not easy, for *information is not knowledge, knowledge is not wisdom and ideas are not relationships*. It is only in the care-filled *intimacy* that we bring all that is within us into and through our relationships. And what is it that we most importantly gift, what is this *mutual gifting* that in Ojibwe we call *meenidiwin*? It is the intimacy of caring for and with one another.

And that intimacy includes an active set of relations that involve care-taking of the land, its waters and wild life, illustrated in the following photos taken over the past forty years on the following pages.

*Please understand that this book is offered to family and guests who visit the land and/or may be used as a virtual tour of the land. It is about the restoration efforts that have been intended to increase the biodiversity in this particular place. It is a self-reflection and review of the successful and failed intentions, experiences and efforts that have gone into the restoration activities since 1975. The narrative and photos are arranged into four sections for each of twenty Stations:*

**Scenes** *- habitat descriptions for each of the Stations, relevant photos taken there.*
**Songs** *– a prosaic description for a focus species of each ecological community.*
**Stories** *– traditional ancestral stories, typically of one focus species for that habitat; and stories of the Vraniak family restoration efforts for that habitat.*
**Sacred** *– presentation and interpretation of spiritually informed verses for focus species, including personal experiences with those and other species.*

*The narrative crosses the boundaries of several conventions. There are aspects of the explorations, experiences and restorations that are science-based in nature. However, academic writing usually stays within disciplinary boundaries and typically does not incorporate the personal and interpersonal. Writing about biology is quite different than writing within psychology and sociology, let alone in the accepted terms of different theologies and spiritualities. Presenting material as an artist (photography), as an author (prose and poetry), as a scientist and educator (researcher and teacher), as a naturalist (ecological restorationist), as a community activist (not-for-profit administrator, board member of conservation organizations), or as a member of a faith community (spirituality), is usually done separately, not all at once, in one place.*

*Yet, this is part of the problem in our relationship with living beings and living systems – if it is not intimate and personal, if it is not sacred, then the relationship is often much more meager than it might be, less whole, and often damaging and destructive to everyone involved.*

*So, please know that entering and engaging this manuscript means moving quickly across such boundaries and conventions, humbly seeking more coherence, more wholeness, indeed, a more consecrated holiness, than is often typical. Thus, in character and quality, the narrative can vary between being quite intimately personal and profound, cerebral and caring, or objective and subjective, but hopefully, as captivating and consuming in the measure it has been for those who experienced it.*

*Even with this varied range of content and style, the attempt has been to form some structure so that if a reader prefers, s/he may jump from habitat description to habitat description (scenes), or from one detailed description of an animal to another (songs), or from the traditional ancestral stories and personal on-the-ground efforts we have made in our restoration efforts (stories), that are described at each of the twenty stations. Conversely, one can move sequentially through the pages as our family has experienced and expressed them, in a manner that offers all four of the elements (scenes, songs, stories, the sacred) at each individual station.*

# The Scenes

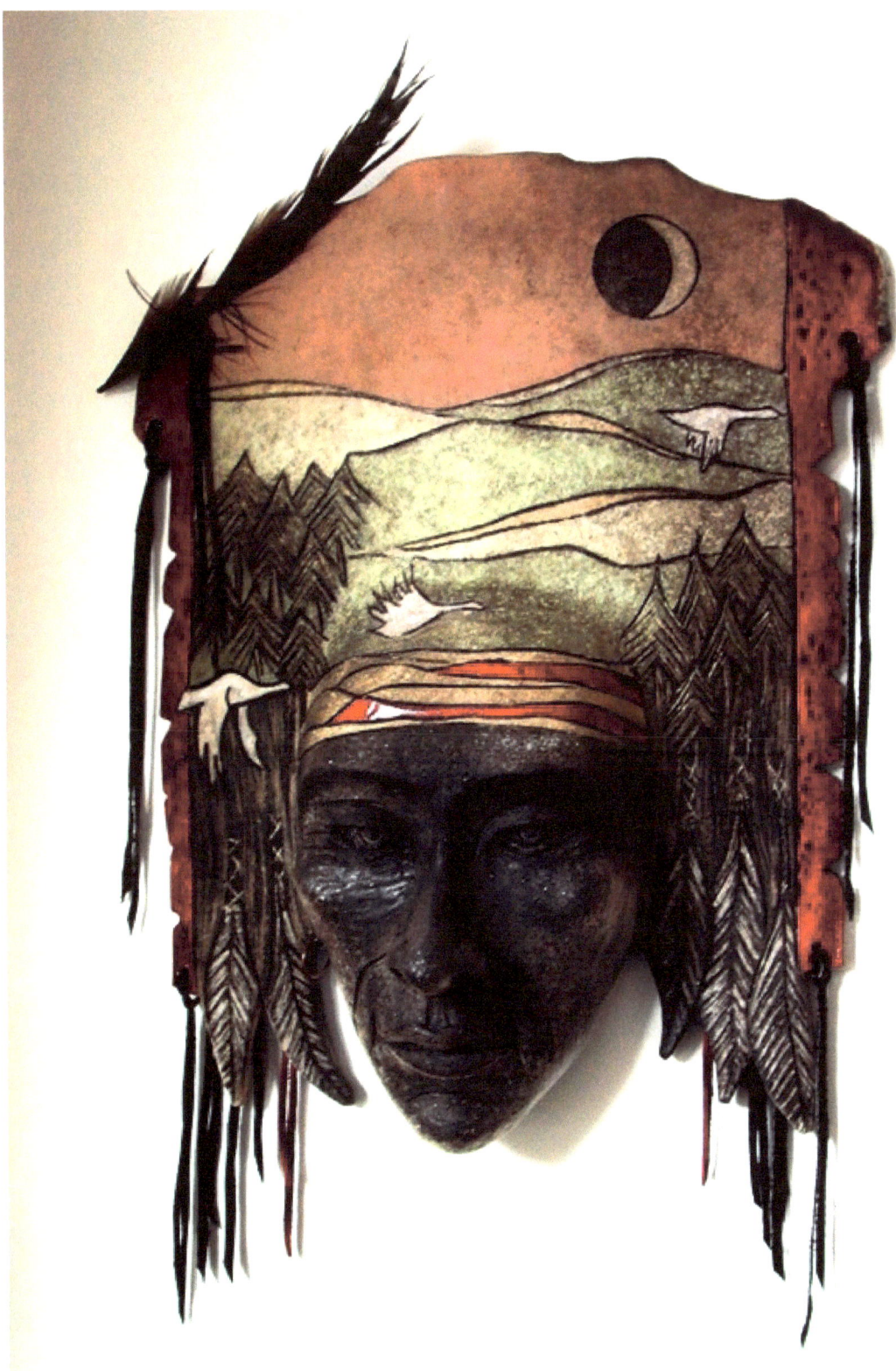

I have traveled from Montreal, Quebec to rest here, in this place.

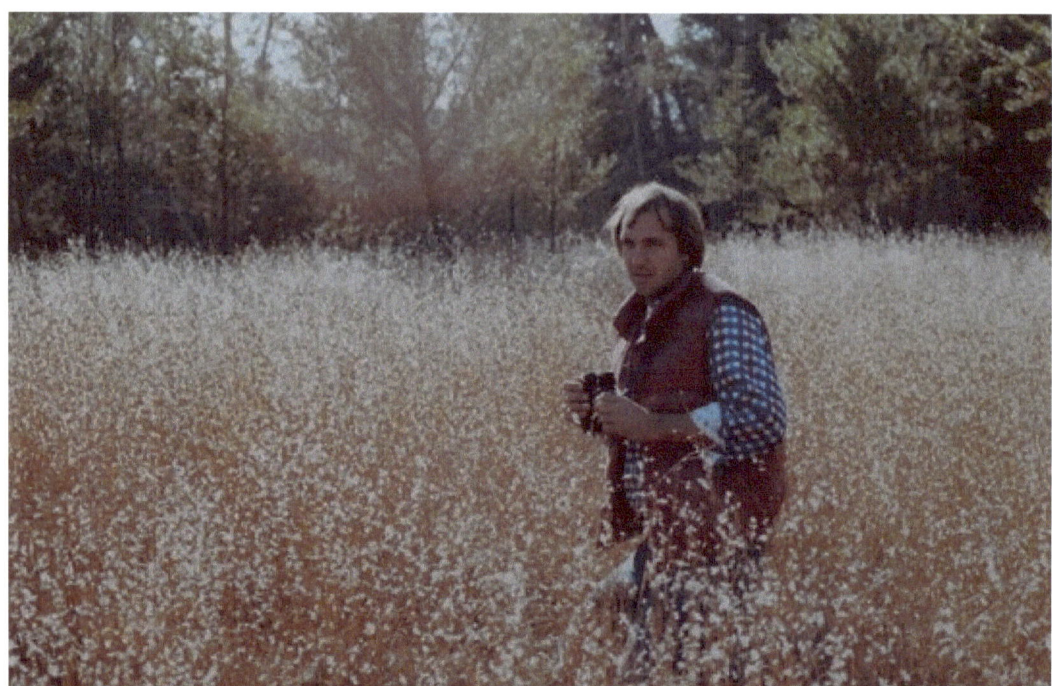

The author, Damian Vraniak, amidst little bluestem on the knoll, 1975.

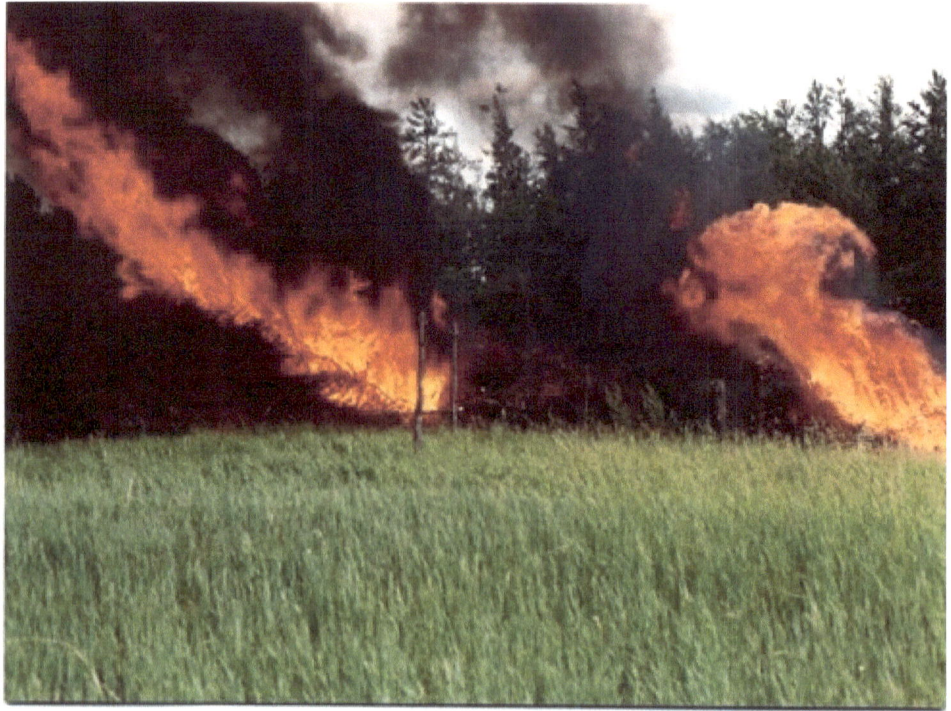

Fire on knoll, 1985.

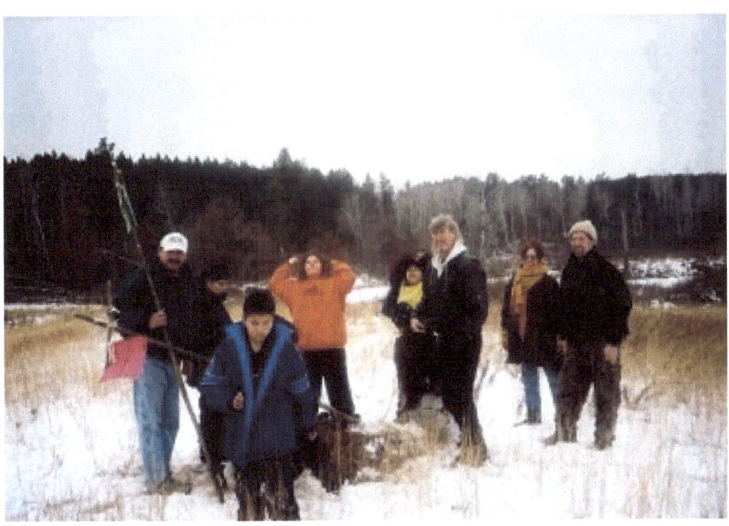

*Mashkawis* Program serving reservation children, 1995.

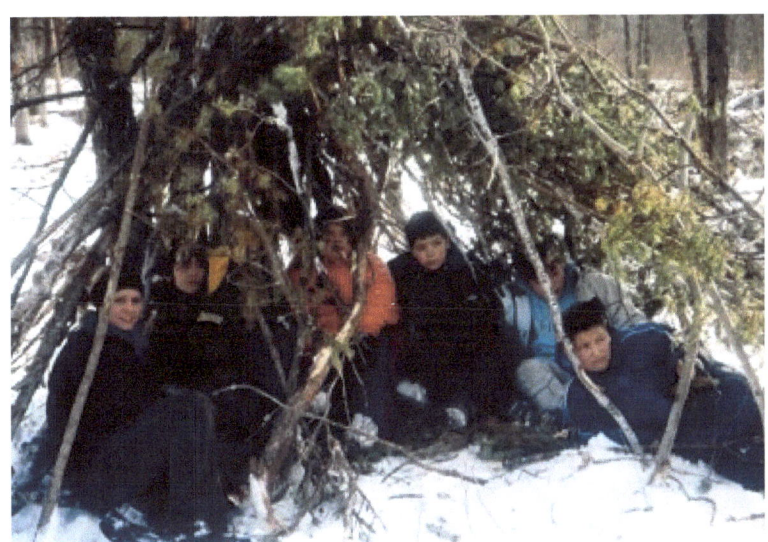

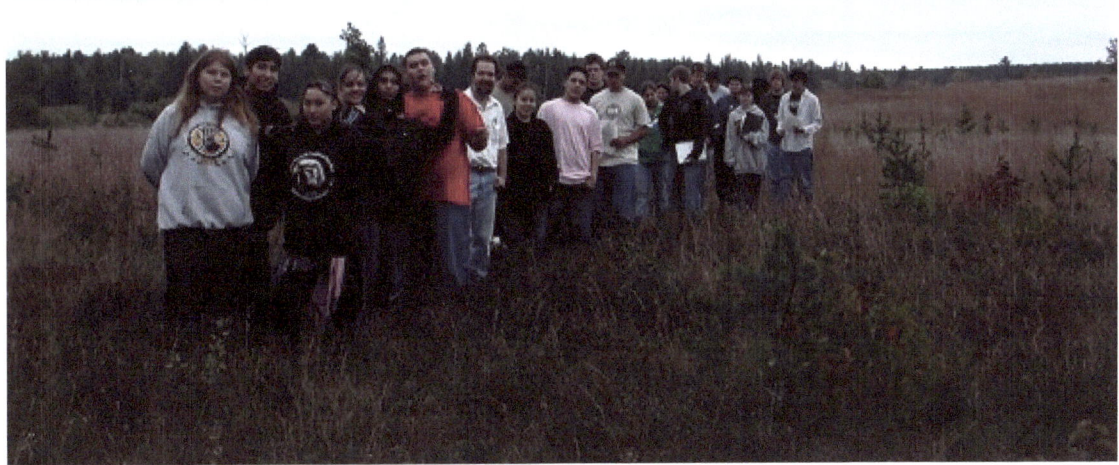

Lac Courte Oreilles Ojibwe High School Biology Class, 2005.

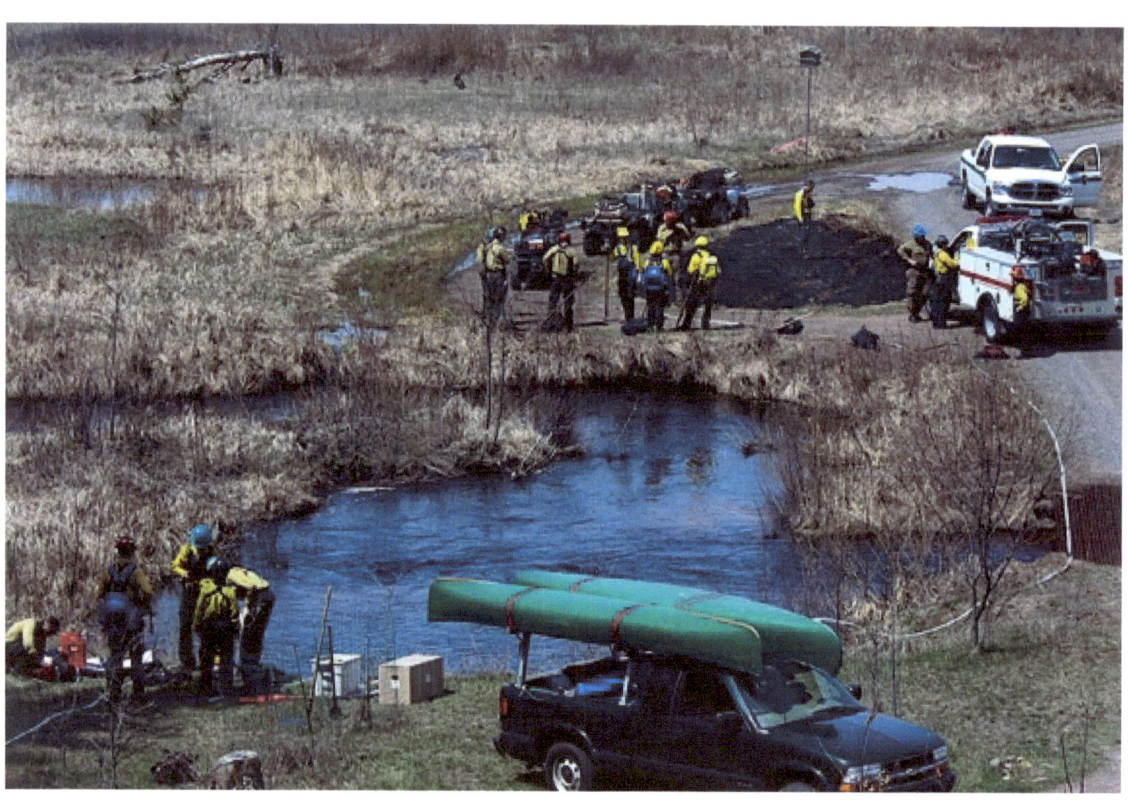

2008 Collaborative prescribed burn preparation by the National Park Service (NPS).

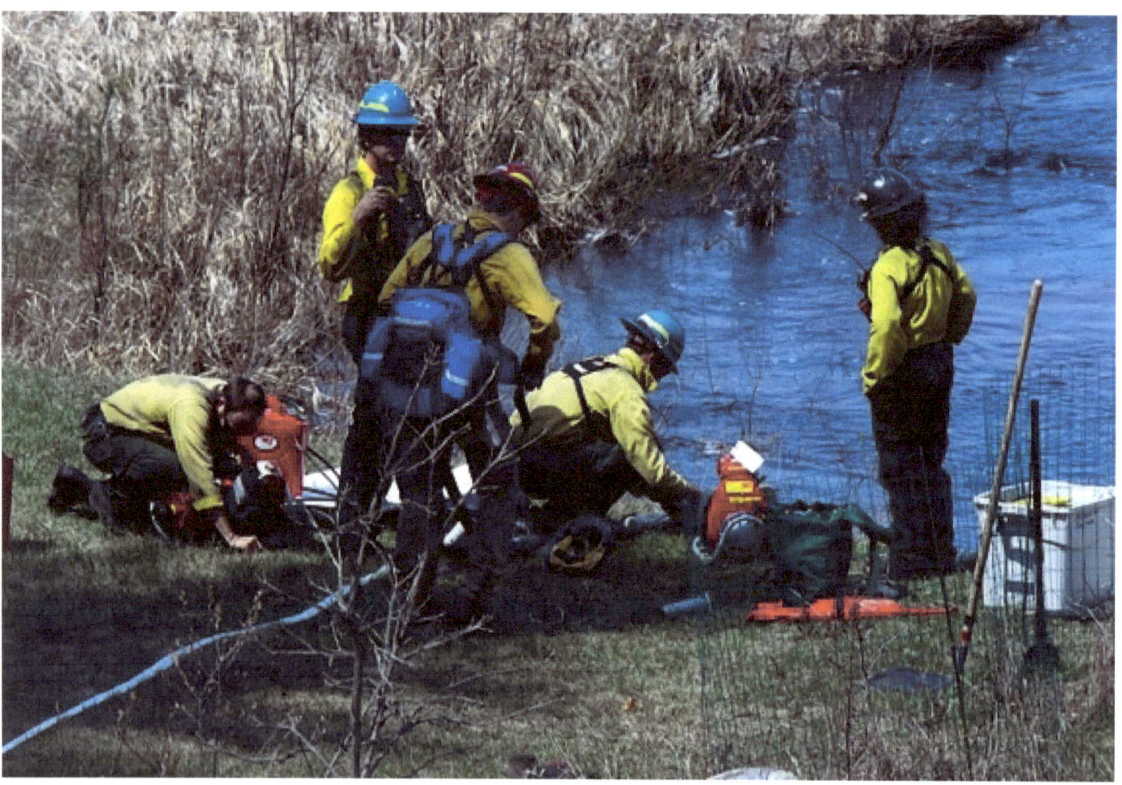

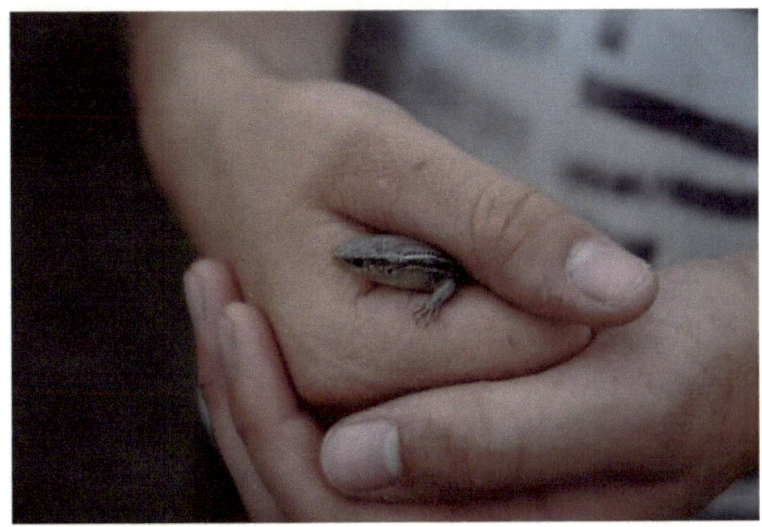

# 2013 Boy Scouts continuing
## *Paired-Learning*

5 years the Boy Scout Troop has been coming out every 4th Monday of the month

*Date June 24, 2013*

# History of Prairie FEASSST Efforts with Youth
## Leading to *MAGIIS* Outdoor Programming

- 1996-1999 WEEB, Pri-Ru-Ta restorations

- 1999-2000 Bremer-funded Family Intervention Team (FIT)

- 2000/2001-2010 Parenting Seminar, *Community Caring Awards*

- 2002 Community Forum on *Marriage*

- 2003-2007 LCO B&G Club - *Mashkawis*

- 2004 Boy Scouts, Girls Venture Crew

- 2006 Community Forum: *Boys to Men*

- 2007-2011 *123Mystery/PALMM* Training of 200+ Adults, Youth Leaders & Adult Small Group Facilitators

- 2009 Community Forum: *Girls to Women*

- 2009-2011 *Paired-Learning, Paired-Mentoring* Training of Teens, 1st-12th graders, Special Ed, Boy Scouts ... *River Elders/SEES/SEELS*

- 2009-2010 U of MN, Marquette, NYU Presentations on Paired-Learning

- 2011-2013 MAGIIS Outdoor Programming

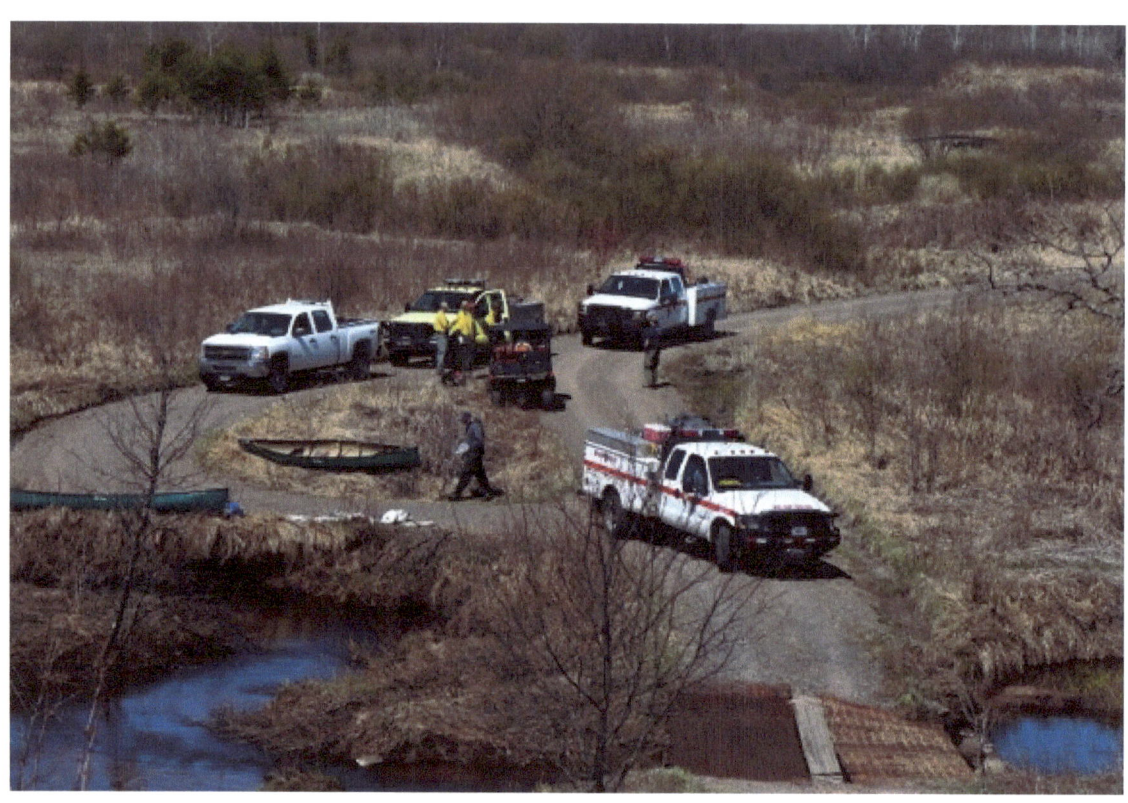

2015 burn preparation by NPS fire module teams from MN, WI and SD.

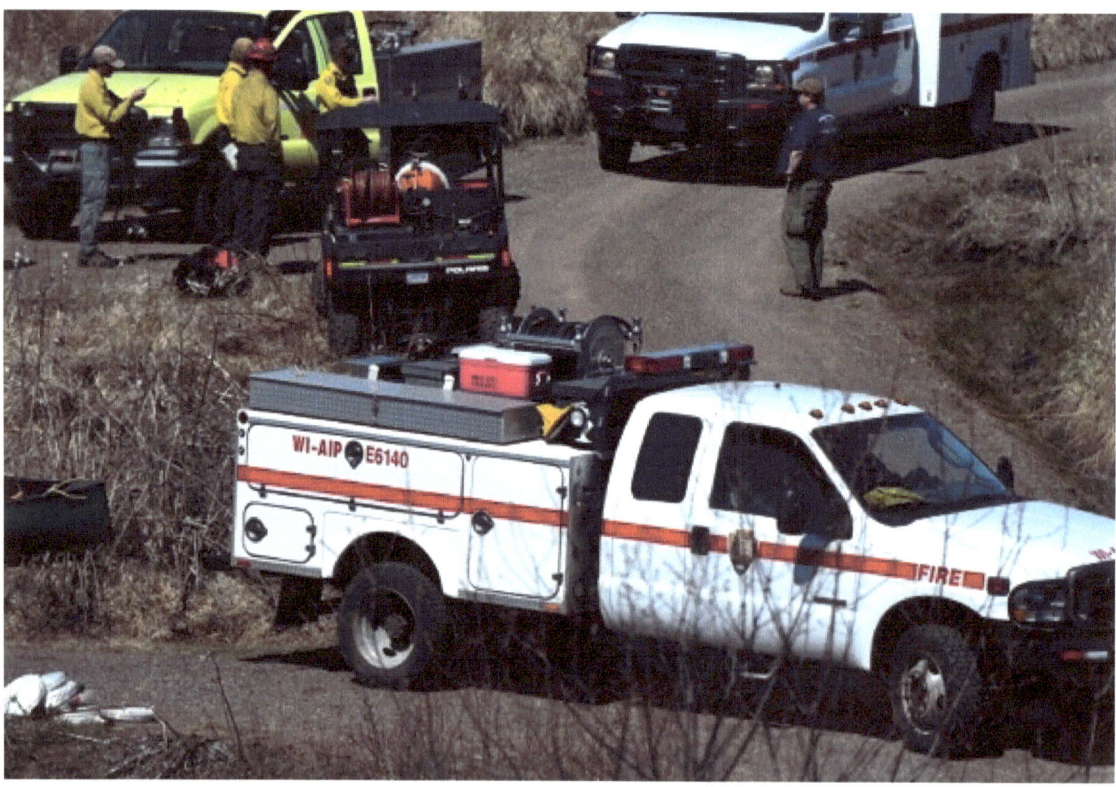

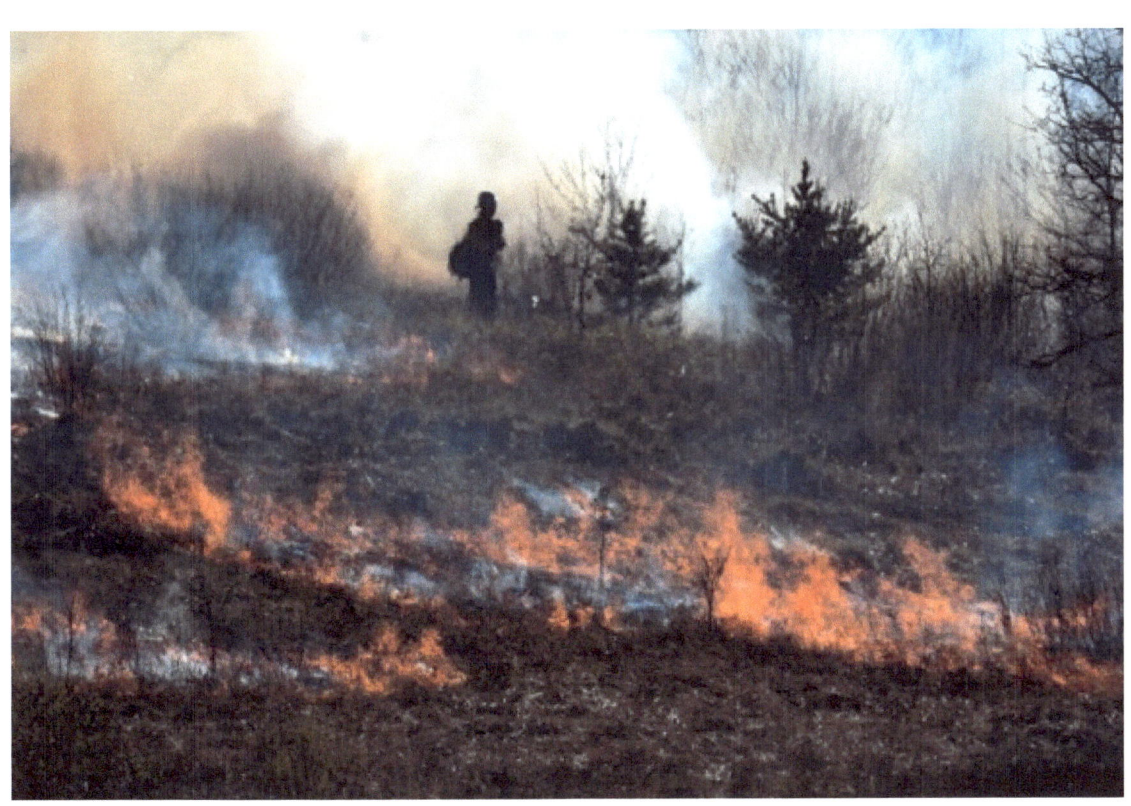

2016 collaborative prescribed burn with NPS.

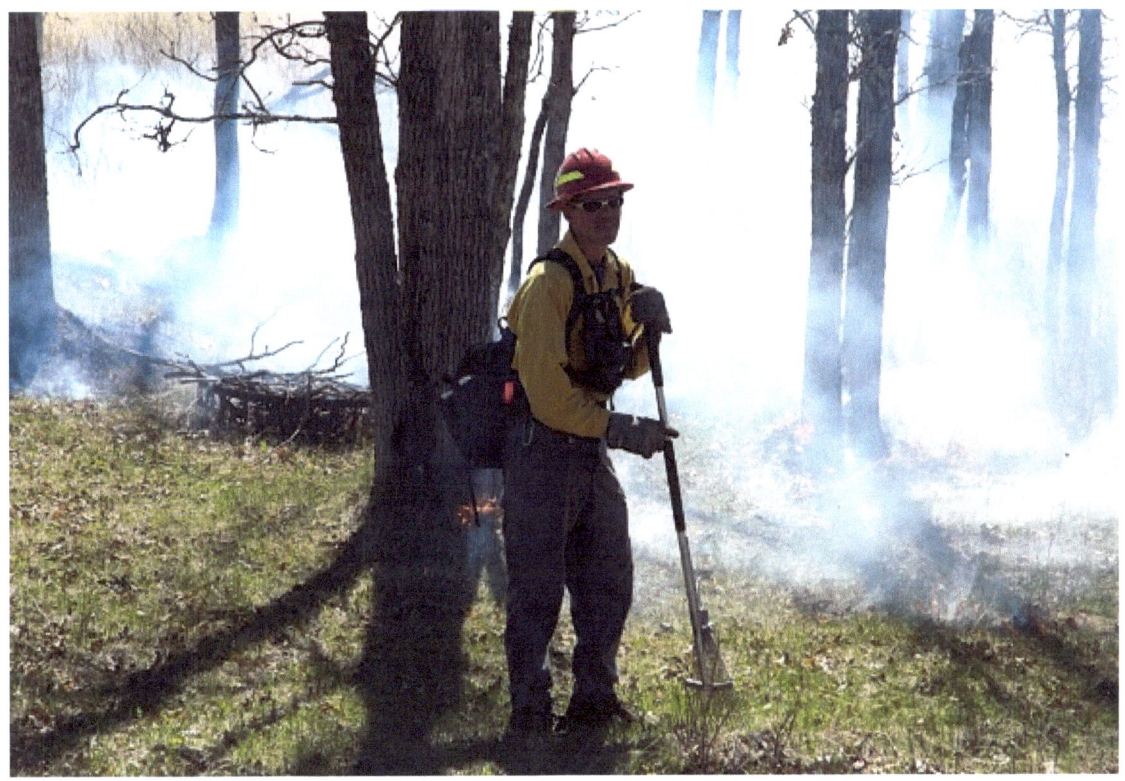

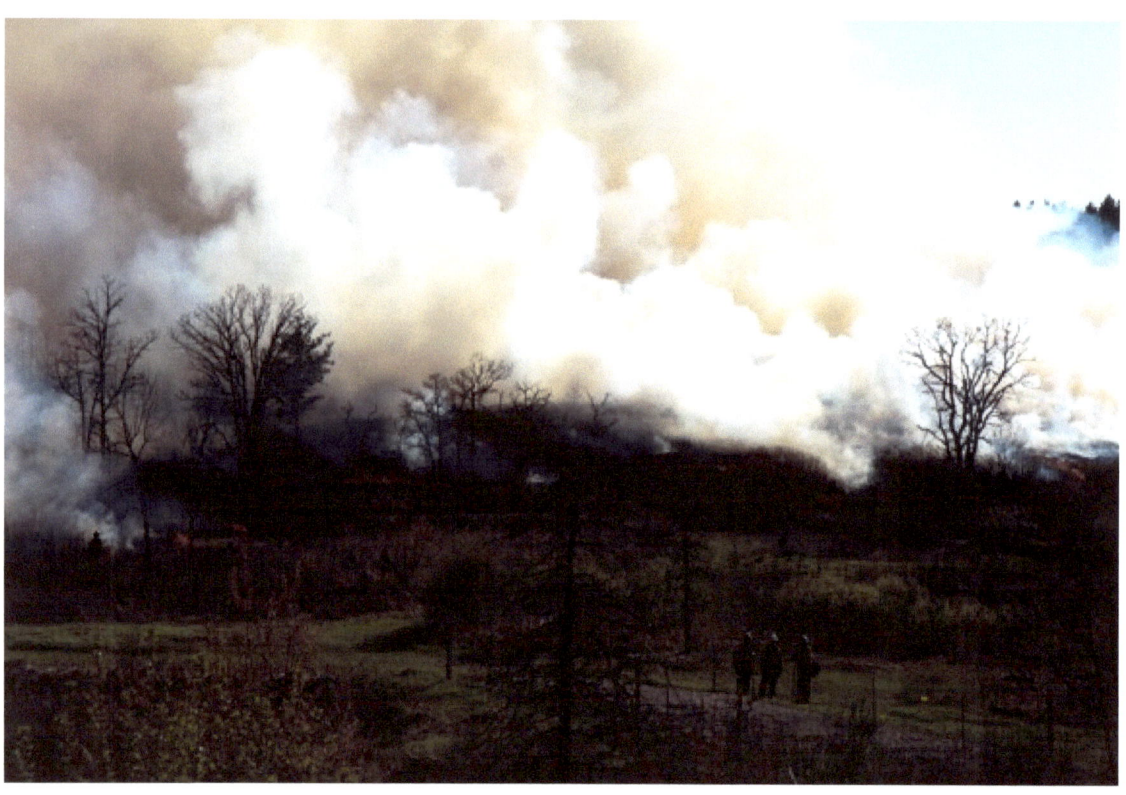

2016 collaborative prescribed burn with NPS.

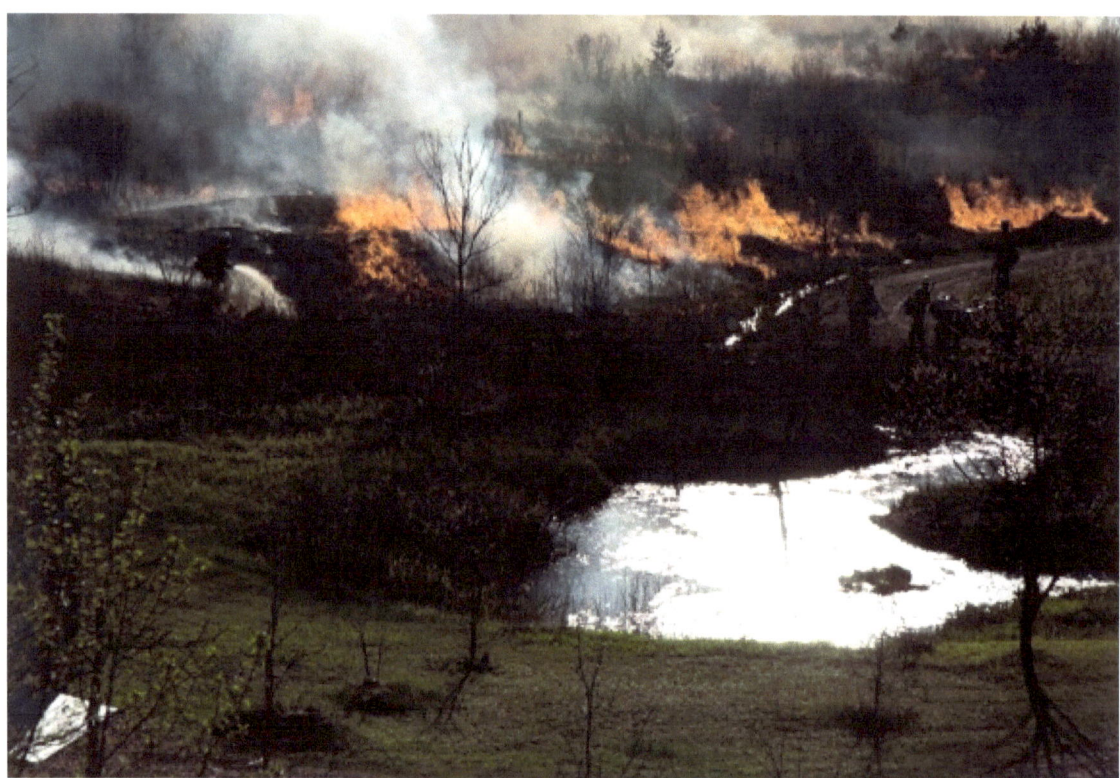

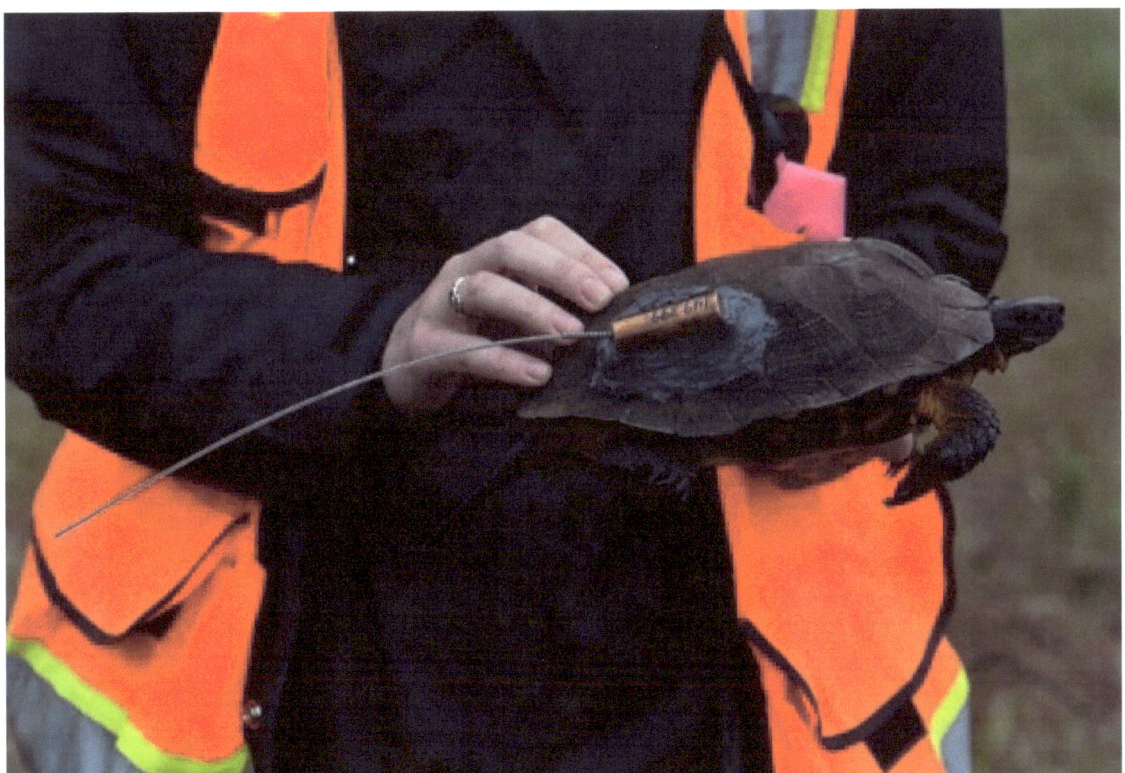

WI DNR staff placing telemetry devices on wood turtles (WI/MN/MI/IA: May, 2014).

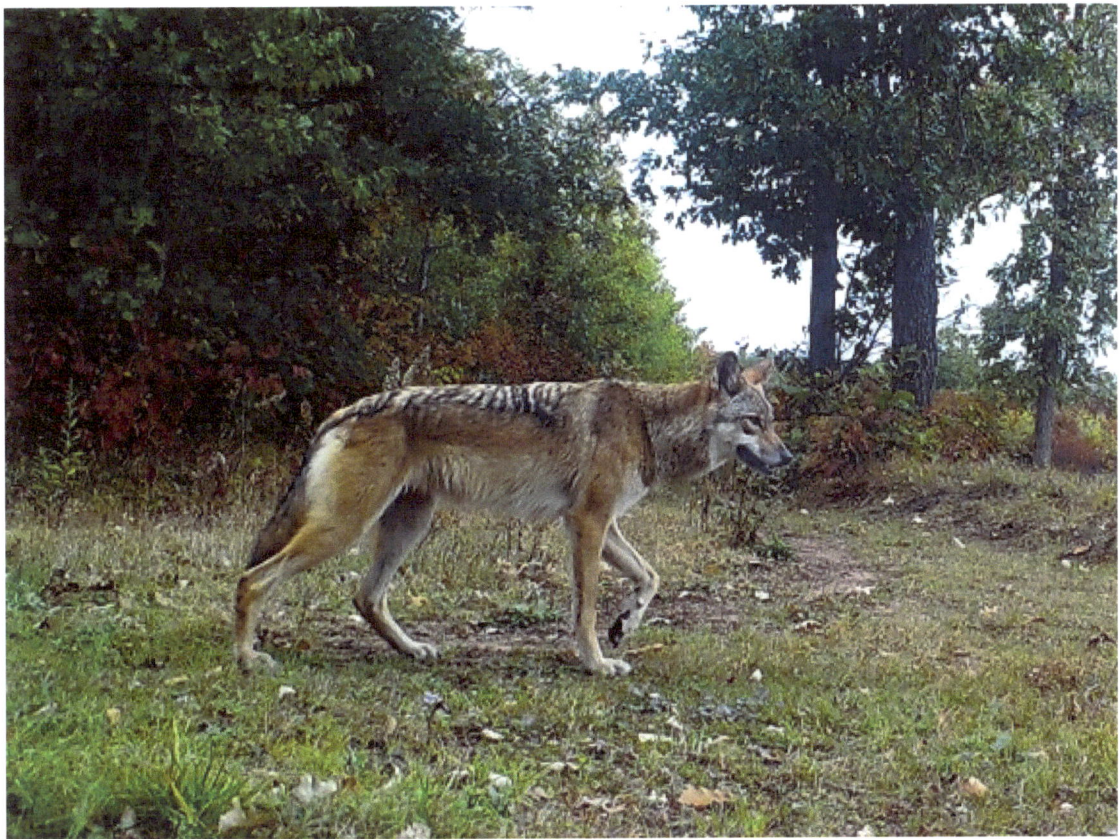

Wolf on the edge of the oak savanna (2019).

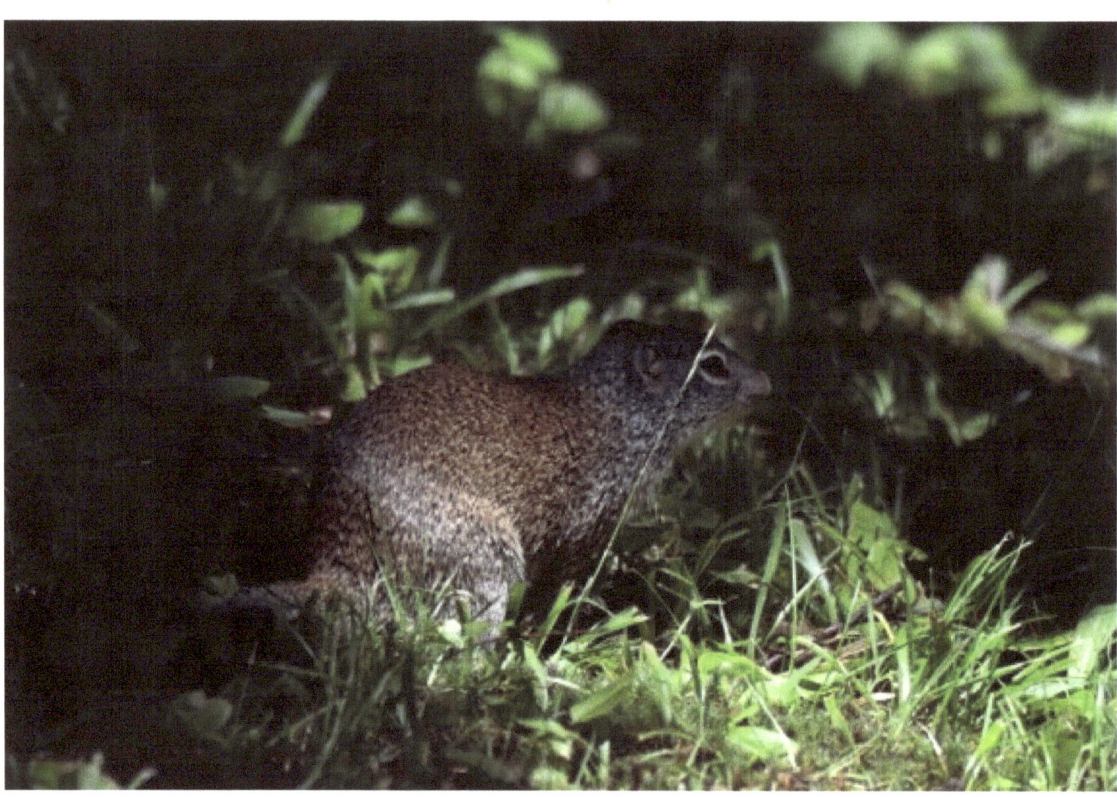

2019 Franklin Ground Squirrel Translocation Project.

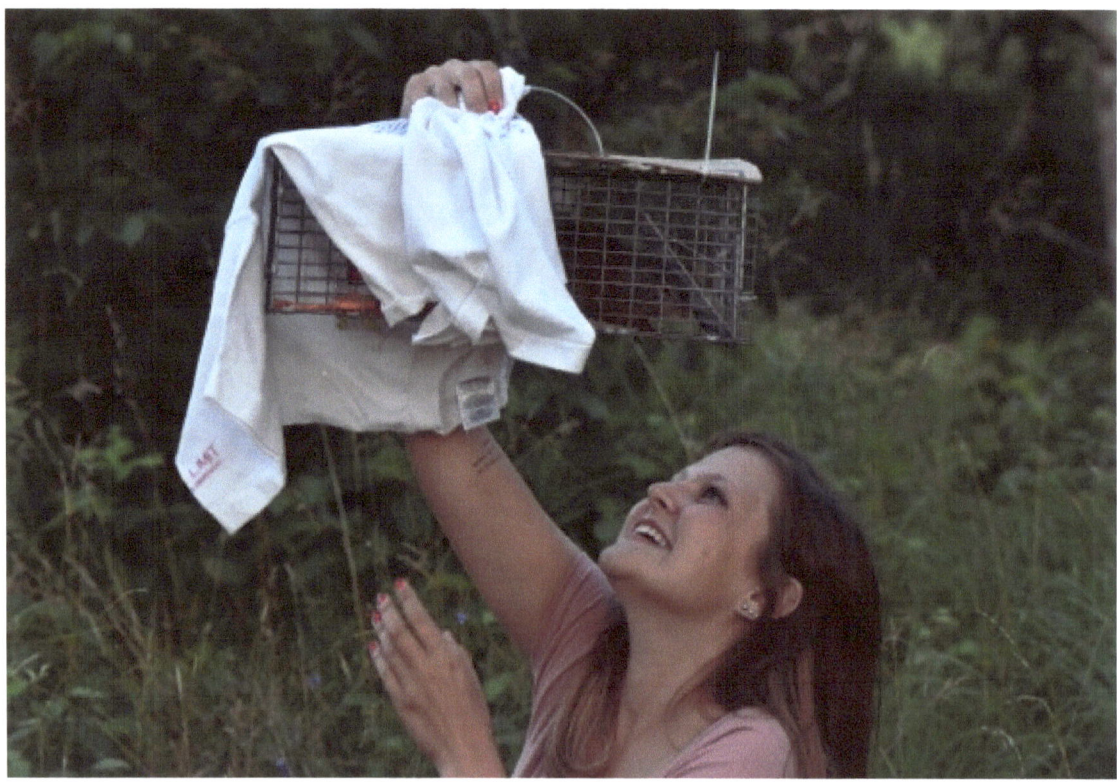

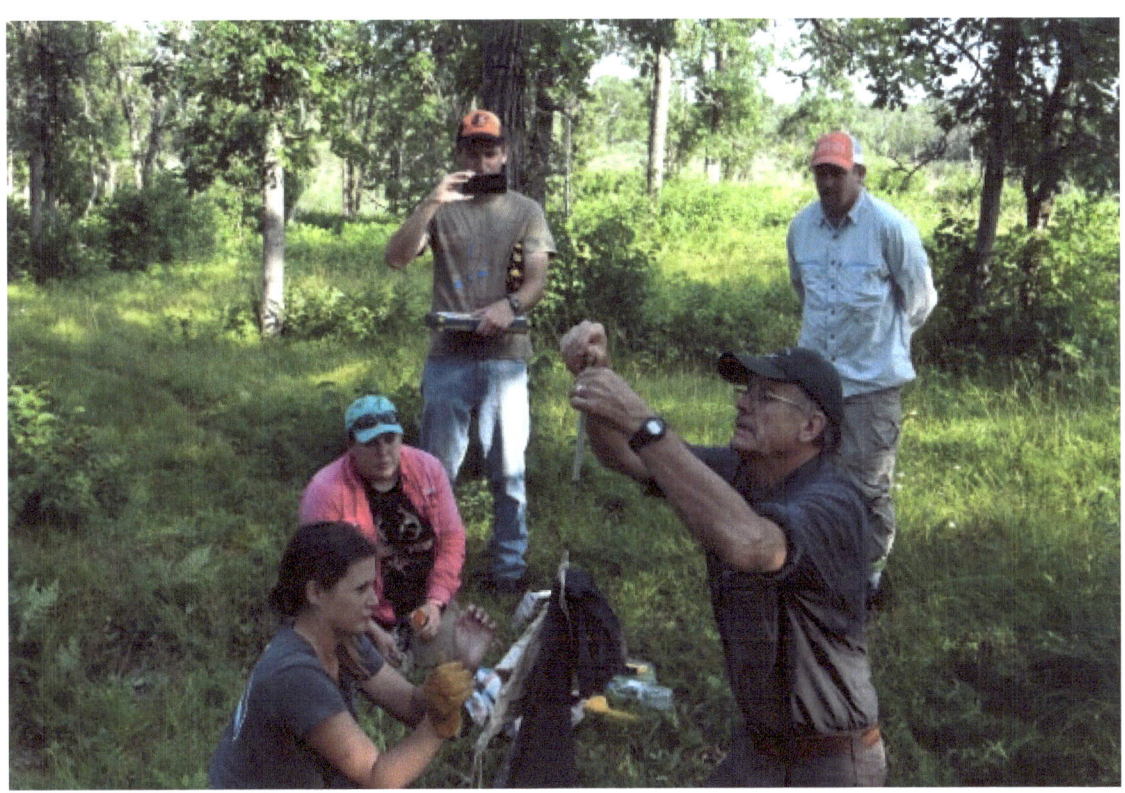

2019 Franklin Ground Squirrel Translocation Project (WI DNR, Northland College).

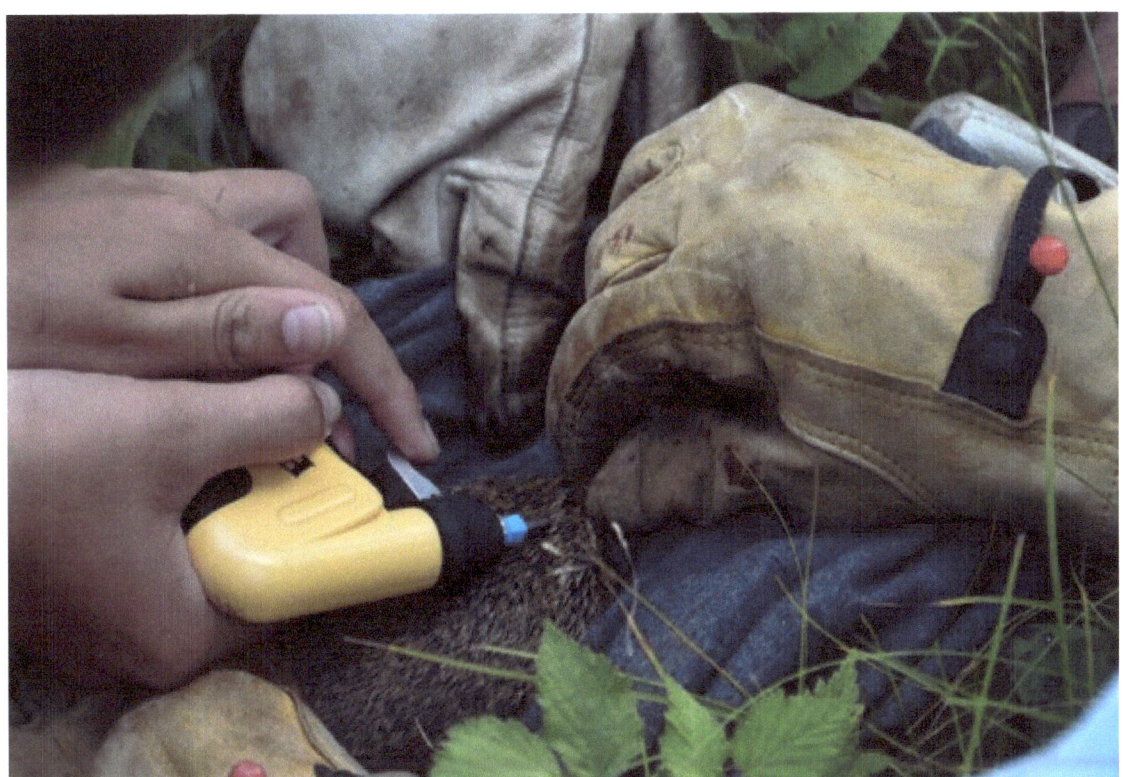

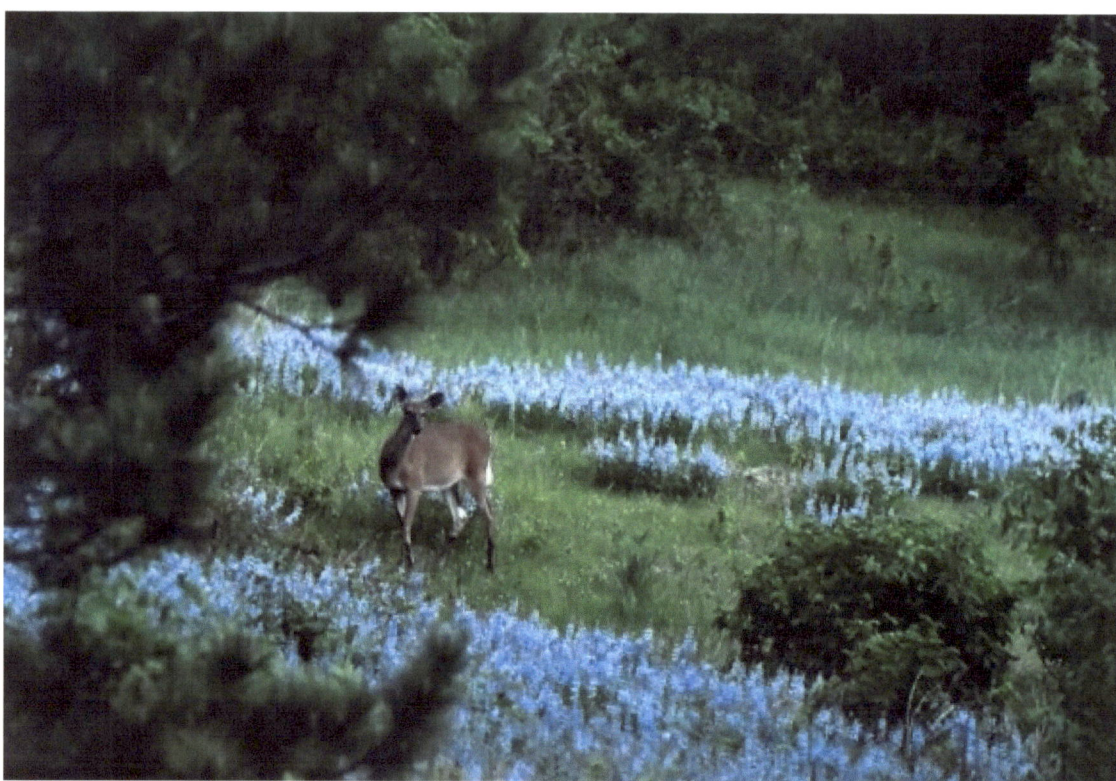

2020 Doe and lupine near the house on the hill in spring.

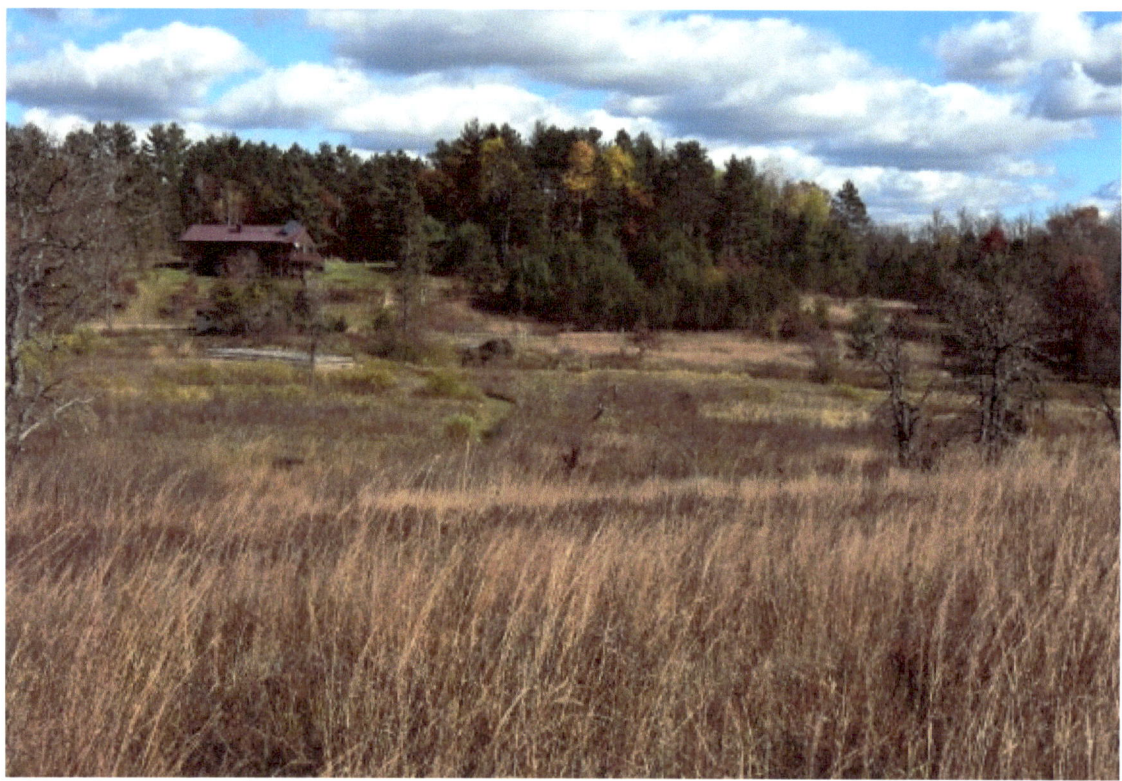

2020 Home & turtle protection structure along creek, from Burial Rock on the knoll.

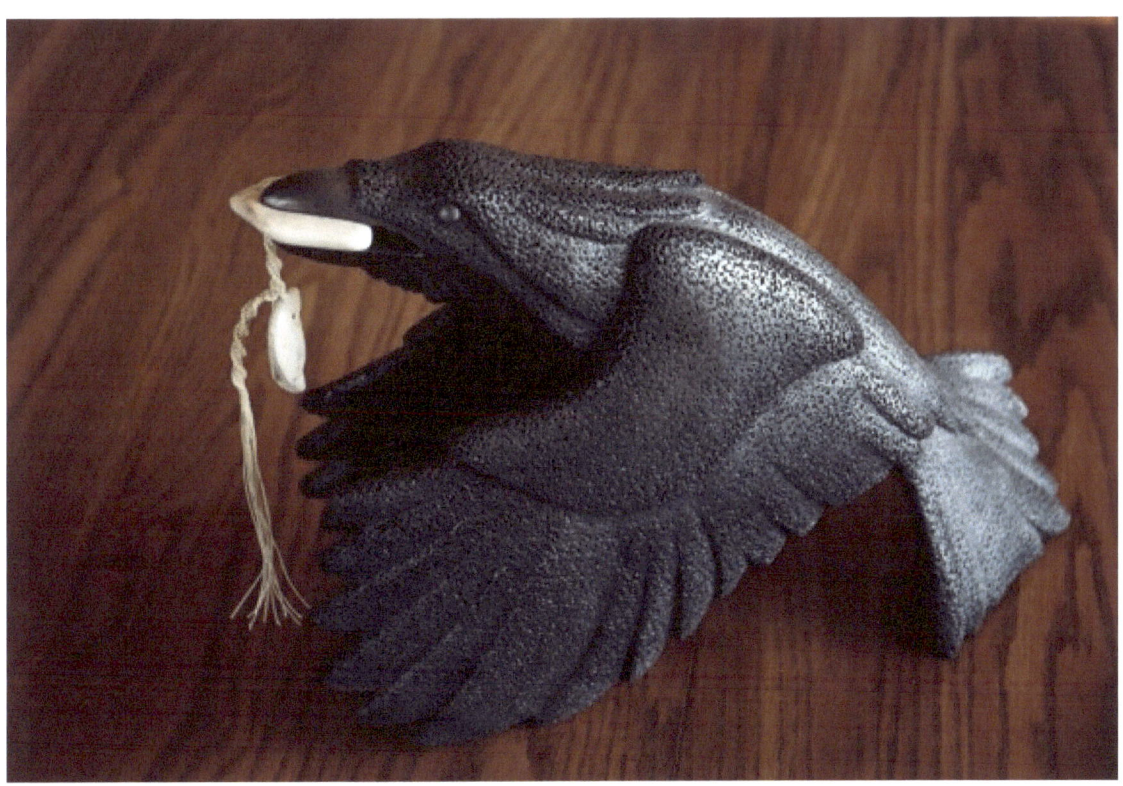

The young raven prematurely out of the nest, now visits regularly.

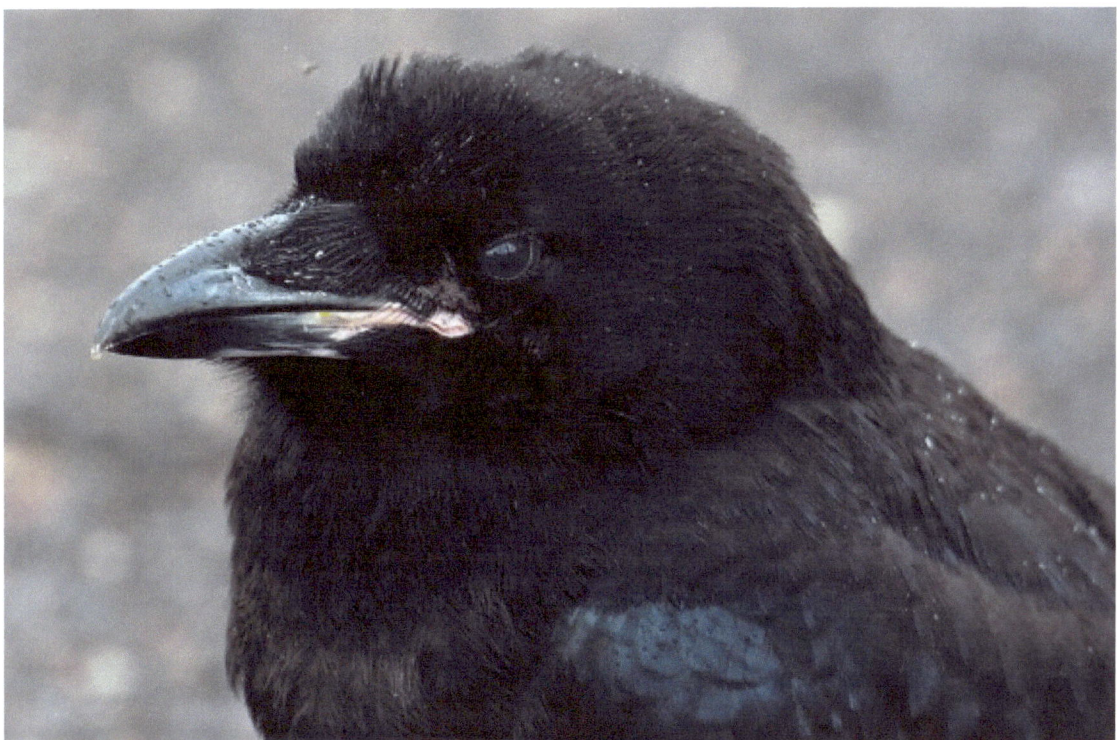

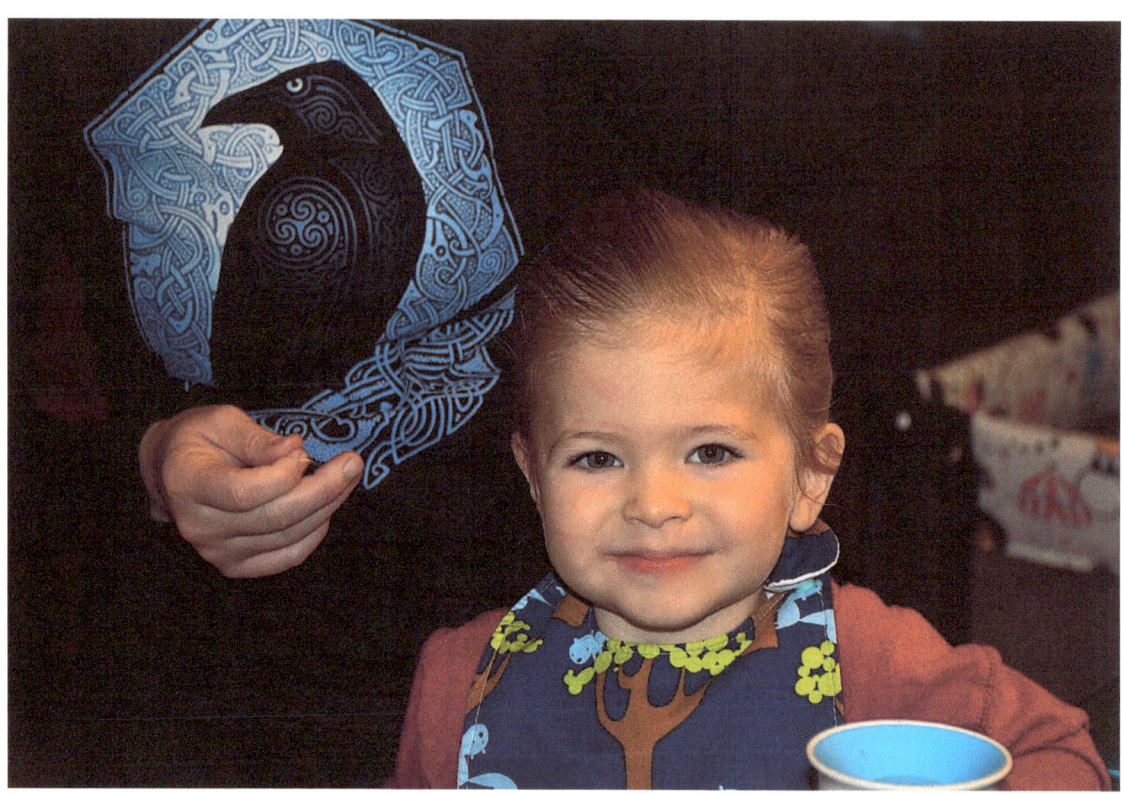

Sons Daybreak (5 years old) and Arendaki (3 years old)

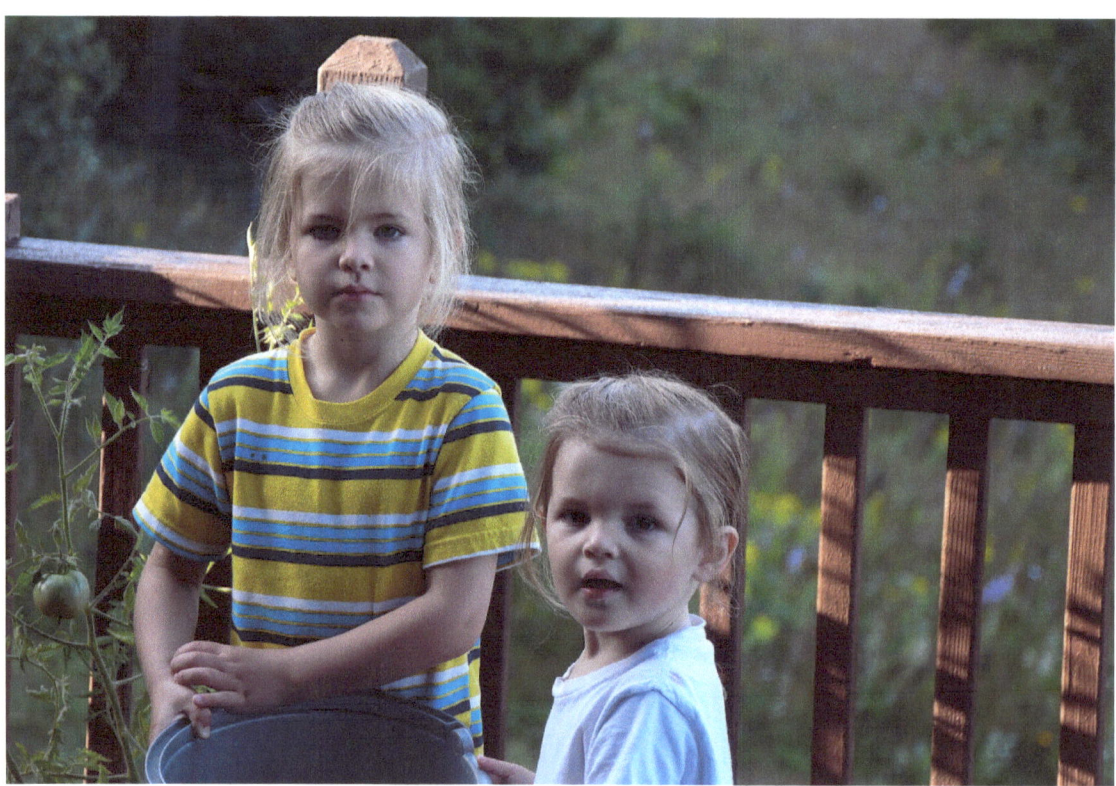

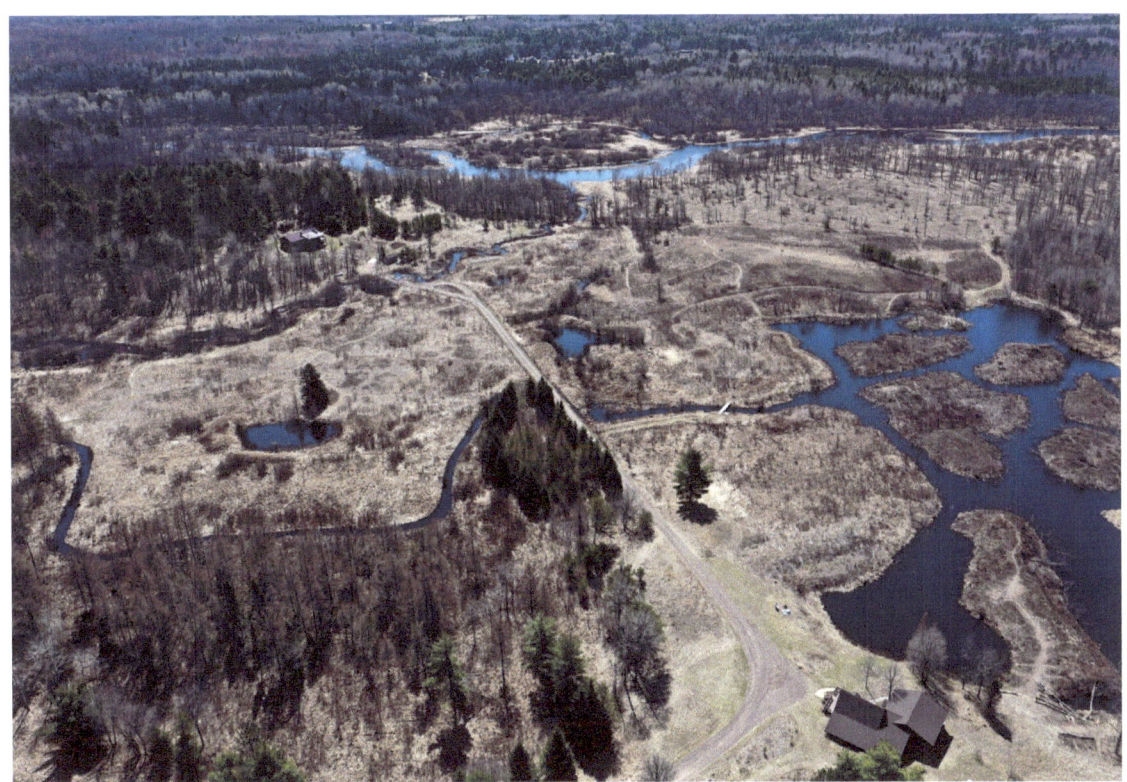

April 22, 2021 Before and after collaborative prescribed burn with the National Park Service, 137 acres.

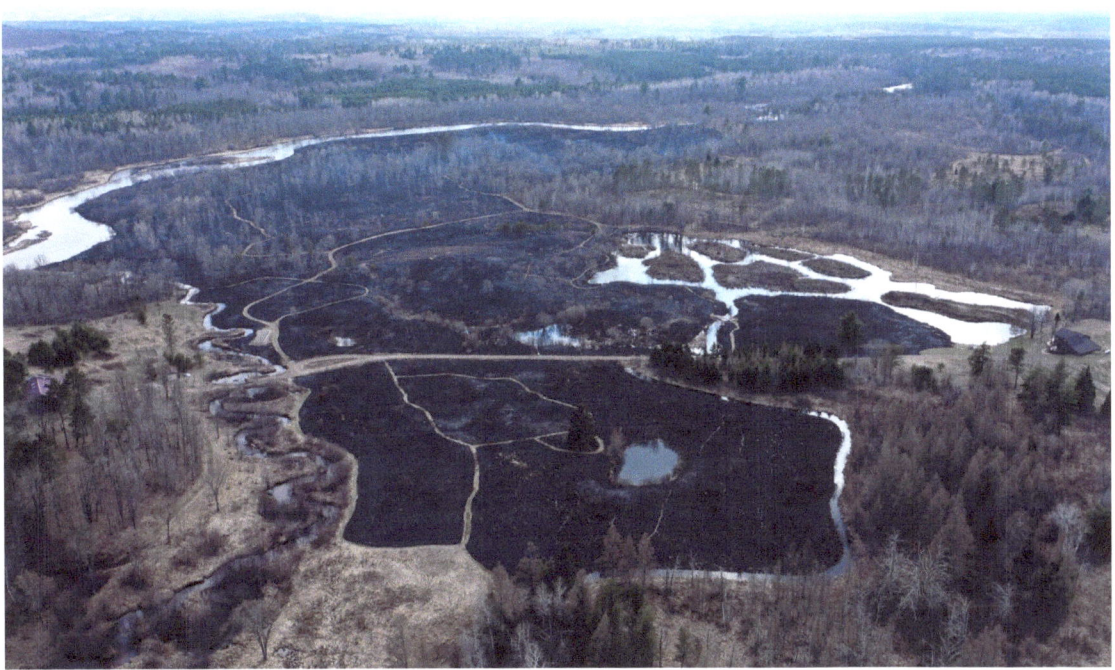

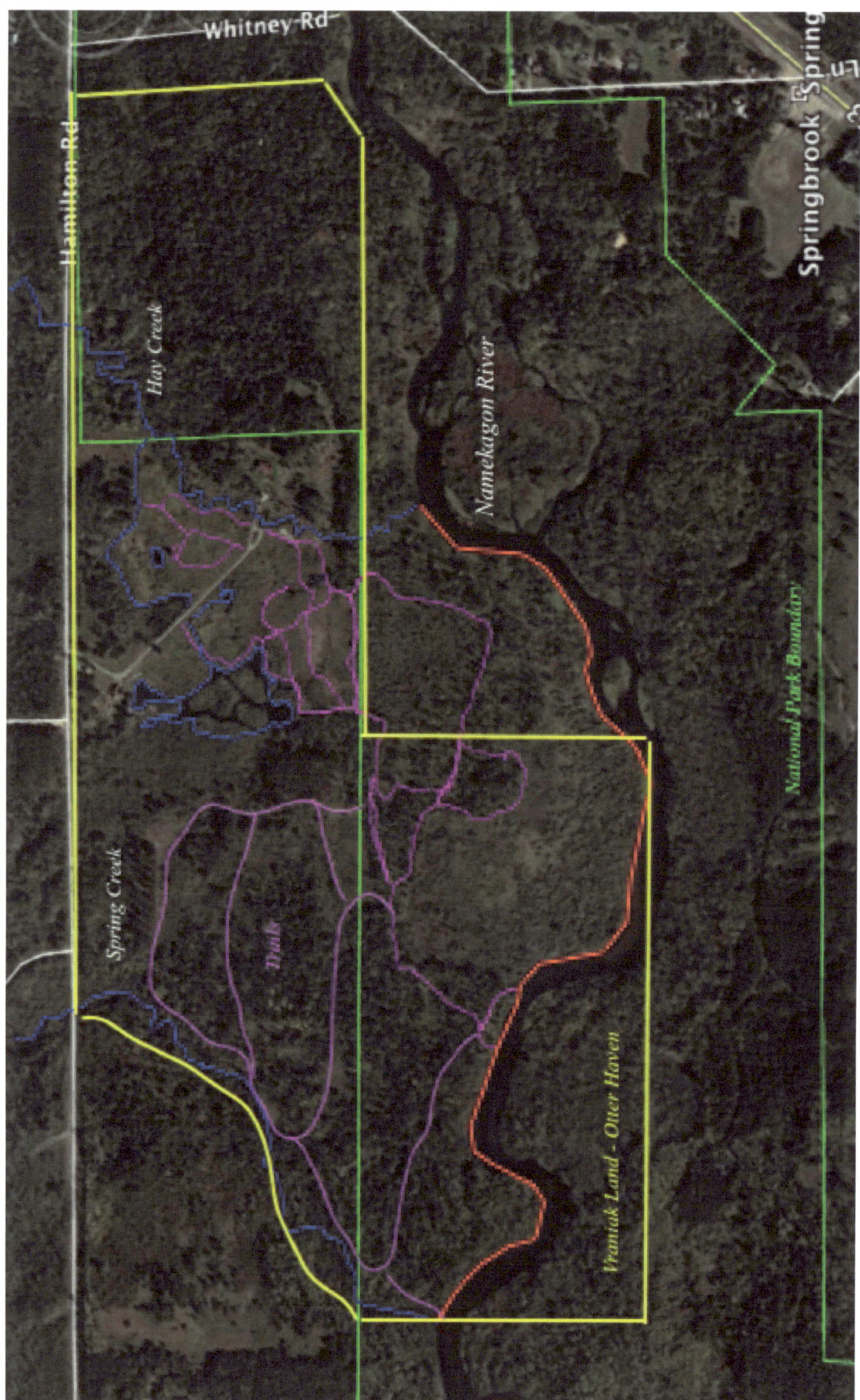

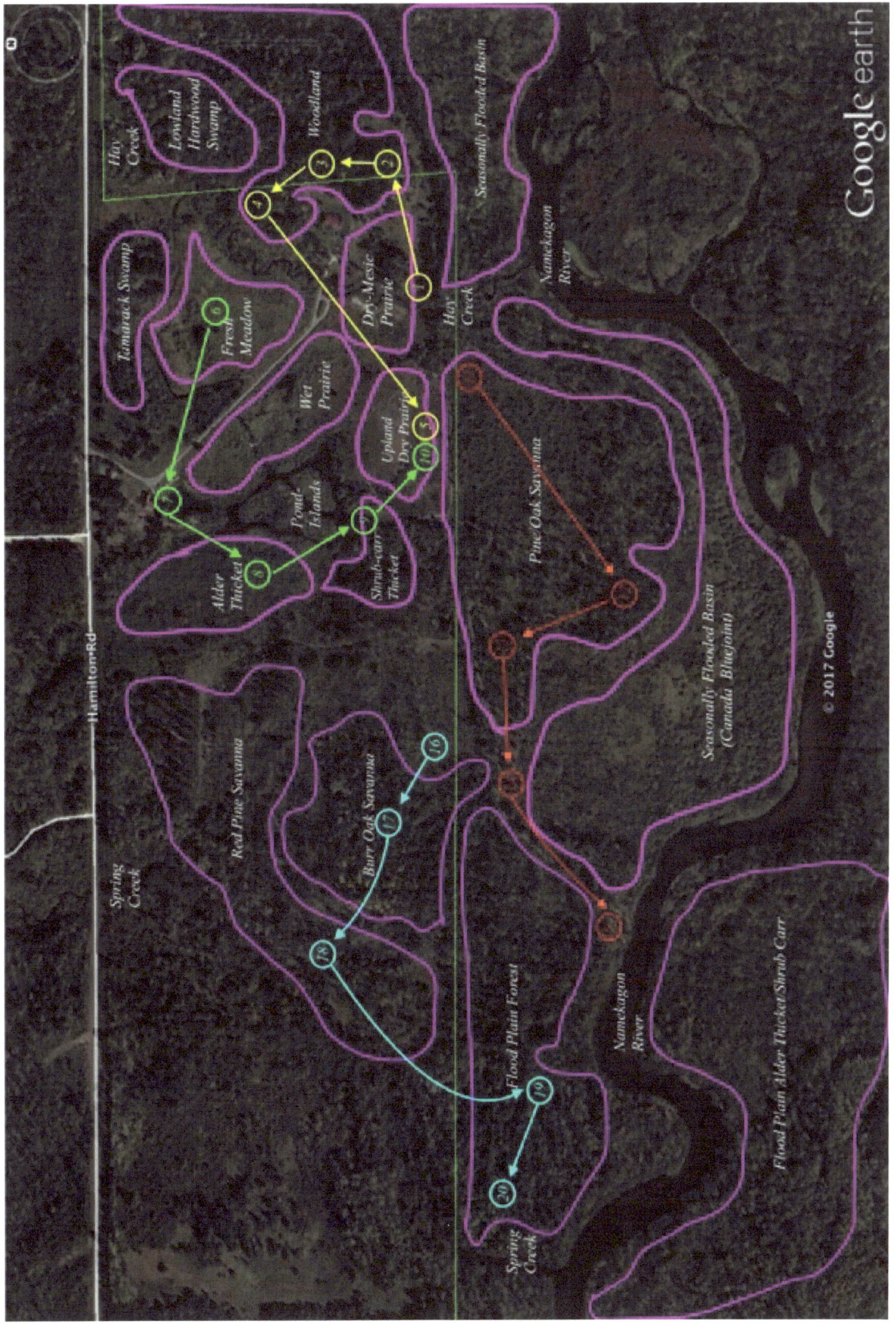

# The Songs

In the circle of abundant gifting that has embraced us here on this landscape, our family offers you a slightly different perspective, using a different narrative vehicle we call a 'song', which attempts to shift our human-centric viewpoint. We hope you enjoy the eyes and voices of Raven and Dove below, as well as other creatures that try out their voices in the following pages, for they have spoken to us directly quite often.

*Voice of the Raven … Eye of the Dove*

Leonardo da Vinci spoke forcefully to me (as he always did to anyone and anything that had his passionate focus, even and especially his pen), *"Dimmi!"* and then *"Dimmi tutu!"* (tell me, tell me all!). And so I demonstrated to him the importance of wind shear to dynamic soaring, which he included in his *Codex on the Flight of Birds* that pre-dated its later understanding by humans by 400 years. The same demand was made of me by so many others over the millennia: Apollo - *pes mou!*, Thor - *fortell meg!*, Al-Idrisi – *'akhbarnaa!*, Hrafna-Flóki Vilgerðarson - *segou mer!*, Noah - *לי תגיד !*, Marcus Aurelius - *dice meg!*, Marcus Valerius Corvusin - *povedz mi!*, Matthias Corvinus - *mondd el!*, Josephte Petit dit Thomas Grandbois – *wihtamawin!, achimostawin!*, and so, on and on. And so it is that I *will* tell you, tell you a story.

*I am Raven*. From time immemorial I have watched human beings from afar and even participated in various ways, at crucial times, in their affairs. In Greece, I have been associated with prophecy, thought to be a symbol of bad luck and Apollo's messenger in the mortal world. Apollo was said to send a *white raven* to spy on his lover, *Coronis,* and when I brought back the news that Coronis had been unfaithful to him, Apollo scorched me in his fury, turning my feathers black. That's why nearly all my grandchildren are black today.

The old Germanic people called me *huginn* (thought) and *muninn* (memory), as I sat on Odin's shoulders and brought him news of the world. And as I sat on the Irish hero *Cú Chulainn's* shoulder after his death, they thought I was *Morrigan*, in the form of a raven. The Irish also connected me with the brother of *Branwen* (Bran the Blessed, *'bran' meaning 'raven'*) whose head was buried in the White Hall of London as a talisman against invasion. Indeed, I figure prominently in the Welsh *Dream of Rhonabwy* as the army of King Arthur's *Owain*. Even today, many believe if ravens are removed from the Tower of London, the Kingdom of England will fall.

In Serbia pairs of ravens are harbingers of tragic news, as in the *Battle Mishnar*. After the fourth-century Iberian Christian martyr *Saint Vincent of Saragossa* was executed, I appeared to protect his body from being devoured by wild animals, until his followers could recover the body. His body was taken to Cape St. Vincent in southern Portugal. A shrine was erected over his grave, which continued to be guarded by flocks of ravens. The Arab geographer *Al-Idrisi* noted this constant guard by ravens, for which he named the place كنيسة الغراب "Kanīsah al-Ghurāb" (*Church of the Raven*). *King Afonso Henriques* had the body of the saint exhumed in 1173 and brought by ship to Lisbon, still accompanied by ravens. This transfer of the relics is depicted on the coat of arms of Lisbon. It is also said that I protected *Saint Benedict of Nursia* by taking away a loaf of bread poisoned by jealous monks after he blessed it.

In Siberia I am known as *Kutcha*, the fertile ancestor of humankind, and play important parts in the stories of the *Koryaks, Iteilmmens* and *Chukchi* of Kamchatka. So it is also with the Native peoples of North America, especially including the *Tsimishians, Haidas, Heiltsuks, Tlingits, Kwakwaka'wakw, Coast Salish, Koyukons, and Inuit,* who have indicated me in the creation of the world and/or as a trickster. One ancient story told on *Haida Gwaii* tells about how I helped to bring the Sun, Moon, Stars, Fresh Water, and Fire to the world. Indeed, in these accounts I am depicted as *white* and in bringing fire back to the people scorched myself black.

In the earliest known human written text, the Neo-Assyrian *Epic of Gilgamesh*, from his boat grounded on Mount Nimush, Utnapishtim first sent a dove (*summatu*), then a swallow (*sinuntu*) and then me (*āribu - raven*) to see if the floodwaters had receded.

I am the first species of bird (Hebrew: עורב; Koine Greek: κόραξ) to be mentioned in the Hebrew Bible, and I am mentioned on numerous occasions thereafter. In the Book of Genesis, *Noah* released me from the ark after the great flood to test whether the waters had receded (Gen. 8:6-7). According to the Law of *Moses*, I am forbidden for food (Leviticus 11:15; Deuteronomy 14:14). In the Book of Judges, one of Kings of the Midianites defeated by Gideonis called *"Orev"* (עורב) which means "Raven". In the Book of Kings (17:4-6), God commanded me and my kind to feed the prophet *Elijah. King Solomon* is described as having hair as black as a raven in the Song of Songs (5:11). I am used as an example of God's gracious provision for all his creatures (in Psalm 147:9 and Job 38:41). In the New Testament as well, I am used by Jesus as an illustration of God's provision (Luke 12:24). *Philo of Alexandri*a (first century AD), stated that as Noah's raven I was a symbol of vice, whereas the dove was a symbol of virtue. In the *Talmud*, I am described as having been only one of three beings on Noah's Ark that copulated during the flood and so was punished. The Rabbis believed that I was forced to spit. Some believe that the reason Noah released me from the ark and I did not return to him was that I was feeding on the corpses of those who drowned in the flood. And according to the Icelandic *Landnámabók*—a story similar to Noah and the Ark -- *Hrafna-Flóki Vilgerðarson* used me to guide his ship from the Faroe Islands to Iceland.

As one can see, I have paid special attention to specific humans in different parts of the world. I have also applied such attention to individuals in an area in the mountains at the intersection of what is now Poland, Austria, Ukraine, the Czech Republic, Hungary and Slovakia. The people in this area, and a specific family in particular, have I followed for a long time, for they seemed especially like me (*Raven*) - intelligent, clever, vacillating between purity and mischievousness, good and evil, and always, always, curious.

In the history of Slovakia, the *Celts* arrived in the Carpathian Basin in the fourth century B.C., penetrating Slovakia, settling in the lowlands of southeast Slovakia, as well as in south-central regions. A new group of Celtic colonists entered Slovakia after 200 B.C., on retreat from devastating encounters in Northern Italy, achieving their greatest density and extent along the *Nitra and Hron rivers*. Celts lived together with *Dacians*. Settlements were situated on moderate hillsides and near streams.  The *Dacian* settlements in southeast Slovakia lasted up to the beginning of the Roman era, while northern Slovakia was inhabited by *the Celtic Cotini*. The Roman general *Marcus Vinius* fought them around 10 B.C.

Eastern Slovakia continued to be inhabited by a Celtic/Dacians, with an old people who lived in mountainous regions and deep valleys there, bearers of the *'Puchov'* culture. Then, around the turn of the first century, new Germanic rulers extended their domain to include the valleys of the *Nitra, Hron and Ipel rivers*, and even the *Danube*. They helped the Roman Emperors in a number of internal power struggles. However, in the years 92 and 97 the Roman emperors undertook unsuccessful forays against them. Later, in the 60s of the second century the Emperor of Rome, *Marcus Aure*lius, found that he had no choice but to attack them. In the process, he drove deep into the valleys of the *Hron, Nitra, Vah and Morava rivers*. It was during this expedition that Marcus Aurelius wrote his famous philosophical discourses, *the Meditations*. The Column of Marcus Aurelius in Rome depicts a miraculous storm that saved his army in these lands, which Christian believers among his troops called down by their prayers. By the year 179 A.D. Roman troops had reached as far as present-day Trencin (Laugaritio), where they memorialized their presence in stone. Perhaps the most famous of the panels is scene XVI, depicting how the Roman army, surrounded and "in a terrible plight from fatigue, wounds, the heat of the sun, and thirst" was saved and the enemy destroyed thanks to a "Rain Miracle." This panel gives the official Roman interpretation: Heaven had intervened on the Roman side. The miraculous deluge is personified on the column as an ancient god of colossal size from whose locks and outstretched arms rain pours down onto the battlefield.

Many years later, an army of these humans who lived in the region were about to enter war with another great horde, but a brave leader of the army issued a challenge of individual combat to a barbarian warrior of great size and strength. Now, I had watched this particular leader, *Marcus Valerius Corvusin,* for some time – he seemed a man with considerable military talents, also possessing a very kind and amicable nature. Very popular with the soldiers he led into battle, in the camps he shared with his soldiers he competed with them in the athletic games that they played during their leisure time and generally was extremely well liked. So as the two combatants began to engage one another, I suddenly flew down from the perch where I had been watching, landed upon the opposing leader's helmet, and began to attack his foe's eyes with my beak so fiercely that the barbarian was blinded and the Roman beat him easily. In memory of this event, he derived his name (from *Corvus, "Raven"*). Thereafter the *Hunyadis* called themselves "*Corvinus*" and had their coins minted displaying a raven. This was later taken up in the coat of arms of Polish aristocratic families connected with the *Hunyadis*, and also led to *Marcus Valerius Messalla Corvinus'* triumph over the Aquitanians (27 BC) being commemorated in the pediment of the Krasiński Palace in Warsaw.

I followed this particular group of humans, their families and friends, for many years. I watched how in the middle of the 15th century *Hungary* fell on hard times by losing two of their foreign kings who both died unexpectedly. They suffered plague, treachery and foreign encroachment and seemed all but doomed to lose hold on bloodline and border. In this time, I grew very close to a woman of special kindness and charity. At this dark moment the Hungarians looked to her son, a 15 year old boy, MÃ¡tyÃ¡s (or *Matthias* in English) for salvation. Matthias' mother sent me for him, with a ring in my beak. I had to fly non-stop from Transylvania to Prague in order for the *'boy king of ravens'* to be crowned. The journey was extreme and the *raven-with-ring* motif became part of the family crest, as well as the family name, in my honor.

*Matthias Corvinus* raised *the Black Army* that is recognized as the first standing continental European fighting force not under conscription and with regular pay since the Roman Empire. The soldiers of the Black Army were mainly Bohemian mercenaries (former Hussites), but Poles, Germans, Hungarians and adventurers from all over Europe joined as well. Sometimes officers were rewarded with lands and ennoblement. The *Korwin* coat of arms, was displayed in Silesia at first (part of the Bohemian kingdom), and all around the Polish-Lithuanian commonwealth later. In time, baroque authors related the old *Slepowron* coat of arms with the then more "fashionable" name *Korwin*. In Hungary, the Wallachian-Hungarian House of Hunyadi (also known as *Korvin, Korwin, Corvus or Corvinus*), flourished in 1400, and it was said that they were descendants of one of the Roman gens *Valerii* (in which long history several men used the name Corvus and Corvinus). It is true that High-Commander *Janos Hunyadi* (Palatine of Transylvania and Regent of Hungary), and his son *Matthias Hunyadi* (King of Hungary, Bohemia and Croatia), called themselves "*Corvinus*" and had their coins minted displaying a "raven with a ring". This was because he became a big landowner on the *Pannonian-Dacian* frontiers, the future Hungary and part of Romania, that his descendants continued to live there for the following 1400 years, and that the *Hunyadis* were his ultimate descendants. Matthias, who had established this first professional army, reformed the administration of justice, reduced the power of the barons, and promoted the careers of talented individuals chosen for their abilities rather than their social statuses. Matthias patronized art and science. His royal library, the *Bibliotheca Corviniana*, was one of the largest collections of books in Europe. With his patronage, Hungary became the first country to embrace the Renaissance from Italy. As *Matthias the Just*, a monarch who wandered among his subjects in disguise, he remains a popular hero of Hungarian folk tales. Matthias's illegitimate son, *John Corvinus* triumphed in Vienna in 1485. He was proud of his role as the defender of Roman Catholicism against the Ottomans and the Hussites. He initiated theological debates, for instance, on the doctrine of the Immaculate Conception, and surpassed both the Pope and his legate "with regard to religious observance," according to the latter. Matthias issued coins in the 1460s bearing an image of the Virgin Mary, demonstrating his special devotion to her. Upon Matthias's initiative, Archbishop Vitéz and Bishop Pannonius persuaded Pope Paul II to authorize them to set up a university in Pressburg (now Bratislava in Slovakia) on 29 May 1465.

Out of this region and these descendants came two family lines of continued interest to me - *Vraniak* and *Beles (Bielesch)*. Both the Vraniaks and the Beles's came from these mountainous regions of Slovakia: Their small village of Pohronská Polhora is located between Brezno (*breza* for birch tree) and Tisovec (*tis* for yew tree), and Bukovec (*buk* for beech tree). All nearby villages are in valleys that have streams of rivers that run through them - the *Hron*, the *Furmanec* into the *Rimava*, both into the *Danube*, and the *Olza* (*olse* for alder) into the *Oder*. The family names Vraniak and Beles (Bielesch) actually came together in Chicago in 1924, when Joseph Vraniak and Mary Beles were married.

In Slovak, vrany means *raven*, vrana or vrani means *crow*, vranik means *black horse*. In Slovak, belavy means *whitish*, belietsa means *shining white*, bielit and bieleny mean *whiten*, biely or belossky means *white person*. In the Old Polish biel ("mud, swamp") reflects the Proto-Slavic *bělъ ("white"). This is probably due to the widespread presence of the marsh grass called *cottongrass* (genus *Eriophorum*), whose the white fluffy seed heads are white. (See also Proto-Indo-European *bʰelH- ("white"), Albanian *baltë* ("mud"), Romanian *baltă* ("mud, swamp") and Greek βάλτος (*váltos*, "swamp"), found in the Balkan peninsula.) See also the five Béla kings of Hungary (béla meaning *heart*).

So it was that Joseph Peter Vraniak (Heretik) married his second cousin, Johanna Vraniak on 16 Apr 1888, and their son *Joseph Peter Vraniak* was born in Pohronská Polhora, Slovakia on 23 Jun **1902.**

Josephus Bielesch (Beles) of Bukovec married Veronica Gyuriss (Ďuriš) on 28 Jan 1896 in Veľké Rovné, Slovakia and came to America that same year. Their daughter, *Mary Helen Beles* was born in Chicago on 16 Sep **1901.**

In 1911 Joseph Peter Vraniak died deep in a dark coalmine accident in Pennsylvania after having come from Slovakia only 5 years earlier (1907). Joseph John Vraniak was only nine years old when his family moved to Chicago after this terrible accident. In 1912 Joseph Beles died of pneumonia after opening a bakery in Chicago. The grandfather of Joseph had studied baking at the University of Vienna in the old country. His daughter, Mary Beles, was 11 years old at the time of his death and was already making delicious white-powdered pastries.

Having both lost their fathers at a very young age, Joseph Vraniak (22) *'of the black'* married Mary Beles (23) *'of the white'* in Chicago in **1924**. Joe got involved with the mob, while Mary engaged a deep spiritual relationship through the Catholic church. They had a son, Damian (*Day*) Joseph Vraniak, in **1925** who became a pilot and navigator in WWII (a black raven), as well as an extremely devout Catholic (with the white spirit). This '*white raven*' was beloved by all in his family, extended family and community. He was devout, humble, generous, calm and courageous, very intelligent, athletic, musical and, in general, the most gracious of human beings. His bright light would be gone by the age of 28 years.

Following his parents, Mary and Joseph Vraniak, into northwest Wisconsin, Day met a woman, Kay Joyce Waggoner, born of multiple Native traditions – the *Huron, Ojibwe, Menominee, Hočąk, Assiniboin, Cree* – and married her. In some sense when these two married 'the raven married the wolf', and a unique, but short-lived partnership, common in the wild, was replicated in a human family. After Day died, Kay married an Irishman, Kenneth George McShane (Northern Irish and Scottish: Anglicized form of Gaelic Mac Seáin '*son of Seán*' the Irish derivative form of John, of Hebrew origin). Ken would help raise the three young boys born to Kay and Day before Day died.

I followed the four generations of this family that lived along Totogatic and Namekagon rivers, until the oldest son of Day and Kay, Damian Anthony Vraniak ('*white raven-white wolf*') married the Irish daughter of Daniel Tripp (one who dances) and Marsha O'Mooney (pale, white as the moon) - Christina Cherie Tripp ('*one who dances by the light of the moon*').

From this final pairing came two young beings of much interest to me – the older being Daybreak ('*one who shines with the rising of the dawn*' after his great grandmother *Hopoekaw, Glory of the Morning* (1709-1835), female chief of the Hočąk Nation who lived to be 125 years old), and the younger, Arendaki ('*spirit of the rock*' after his great grandfather, *Nicholas Arendaki* ( ? – 1650), one of the first leaders of the Huron Nation to become a Christian). Now, I see it is true that Daybreak and Arendaki Vraniak ('*of the raven*') are two young, shining sons who will come to steward the land their father had caressed and restored into vibrant life not seen here for centuries.

*I am Raven* and I have given you some human context and history for the narrative I will offer in the following pages. My companion, *Dove*, will join me periodically in this endeavor, and we will ask some of our wild relations to share *their* family lines, *their* lives and perspectives of this land and this family, as well. We, of this land, water, wind and the fire of wild life, will show you what we have seen and come to know of these people and this place. We will tell you, tell you a story.

# The Stories

## *The Landscapes and Waterways of My Ancestors*

The land is the primary ground upon which a family forms home and thrives. A family is the smallest community through which each person travels, first as a dance, then as a song, eventually as a story, and finally, as a prayer. A family lives in a larger version of these forms, as well, as both a family and larger communities of families, clans, and cultural nations mix the light and the darkness, the joy and the grief, the success and the failure, the life and the death, composed by their lived creations. And we carry the hope and despair, the strength and weakness of the history of our families, communities and local cultures, as archived sojourns. There is a flow in this living repository of journeys, from time immemorial into the present and on into the future that is carried within each person, within each being, as life is lived. If they are carried, survived and sustained long enough, well enough, such journeys allow us to come to know the longer, arching paths, the ancient lines that connect us to the constellations of our ancestors.

This understanding is so very important to me, because one sweet, beloved Grandmother, who helped raise an innocent grandchild in so many heartfelt ways, had a secret. There was a dark mystery about why she was sent to a government-run Indian boarding school when she was young. It would take most of seven decades to begin to completely unravel that mystery, a mystery which began with the terrifying fifty-day journey by canoe from the Georgian Bay of Lake Huron to the tiny fledgling French community of Quebec over 450 years earlier, in 1650, by her great grandmother, whose name in the *Wendat* (Huron) language means '*one who carries an important secret*'. Discovering the dances, songs, stories and prayers that compose my familial, ancestral autobiography occurring between these two secrets, reveals much about the light and the dark within self and family, between family and cultural community, as well as among different cultural communities and nation states, especially as it relates to how our relationships with the land form us in varying ways.

My Huron ancestors burned oak savanna to plant corn, beans and squash, as well as hunted bear with dogs, all of which continues in my grandfather's family. My Ojibwe ancestors fished the straits along the alvars at the intersection of the Great Lakes, that continues strongly in my grandmother's family. My Hočąk, Nakota and Plains Cree ancestors hunted buffalo on the prairies on the Great Plains, as my family now eats bison to go along with the corn, beans, squash, wild rice, fish and venison we consume locally from the land today. And the family gardens of my French, Irish, Scottish and Slovak ancestors are still very much alive. These embodied traditions of being in relationship with the local life of specific prairie and savanna, woodland and wetland ecologies is part of a long shared, sustaining, subsistence way of living.

*Thus, the embodied knowledge and life-force, the soul, of my ancestors continues in me, my wife and my children, as we continue some of the same practices of living and caring for the land done by our ancestors.*

I have tried to voice some of this ancestral patterns of sustenance in my previously published, ***Travailler****: A 400-year Inter-generational Journey of Grandmothers, Mothers & Daughters*   (Volumes I-IV).

Herein are stories of the lives of eight pairs of Native and Métis women (Huron, Ojibwe and Ottawa, Menominee and Hočąk, Nakota and Cree), whose sons and grandsons helped define the history of the Great Lakes region from Montreal to Mackinaw, Portage to Pembina between 1650 and 1950. The stories are told in four volumes, beginning with the last (fourth) volume and moving backward in time through each time period.

Over the course of 400 years my family transitioned from ***Montreal to Mackinaw***, ***Portage to Pembina***, each move taking roughly four generations, across the latter half of each century and the first half of the next one (1550-1650, 1650-1750, 1750-1850's, 1850-1950).

In each of these four regions and times of transition – Montreal and Mackinaw, Portage and Pembina – the lives of a pair of my Native grandmothers and mothers are described whose 'half-burnt' sons and grandsons were intimately involved in the major geopolitical transitions among the French, British and American colonial expansions in the different time periods. These family members were personally involved with what happened to the **Huron**, then to the **Ojibwe and Ottawa**, to the **Menominee**, **Hočąk**, and finally to the Dakota, Lakota, **Nakota** (aka Assiniboin) and **Cree**, cultural communities … and why there were such different outcomes for these different tribal communities.

In the area of Quebec, Montreal and Trois-Rivières, three Frenchmen (after each of the previous two husbands had died) married my **Huron** (Wendat) great grandmother, Catherine, who took care of the nine children produced of those marriages.  Her *Durand and Cadotte* sons and grandsons, the ***chicot* ('half-burned stump') children**, would be able to carry the fur trade through Mackinac Island and Sault Ste. Marie into Wisconsin, Minnesota, the Dakotas and Manitoba over several generations of voyagers, in part, because their mother taught them to be bi- and multi-lingual. These mothers also taught them how the Huron effectively <u>grew corn in the oak savannas</u> along the St. Lawrence river and the Georgian Bay of Lake Huron, used in a mush (*sagamité*) with peas and pork eaten by voyagers *("mangeur de lard")*. While these sons and grandsons were boldly adventurous and sharply strategic, it was the heart of the intertribal relationships their grandmother and mother developed through other Native girls who were also educated at the boarding school of the *Ursulines*, (begun by the Catholic nun Marie Guyart, now St. Marie), that enabled such success in the trade that was engaged across such a vast region. [**Travailler Volume 1**: *Huron Catherine Annennontha  & her daughter Marie Durand …* published 2020, 163 pages]

In the central area of Mackinac Island and Sault Ste. Marie my **Ojibwe** and **Ottawa** great grandmothers took care of the multitude of ***wissikode-ikwe/inni* (half-burned girls and boys, in Ojibwe)** produced from intermarriage with French and British men. (In the Odawa dialect of Ojibway the term for the Métis is ***aayaabtawzid* or** *aya:pittawisit,* 'one who is half.')  The *Langlade, Grignon and Nolin* sons and grandsons would manage the flow-through of the fur trade, and would also be military captains of war parties, treaty translators, recorders and signers, as well as originators of new communities and new states. The skills of Ottawa and Ojibwe grandmothers and mothers who knew how to <u>fish the straits, gather and parch the wild rice along the alvars</u> at the intersection of the three lakes - Lakes Huron, Michigan and Superior- added wild rice, maple sugar, and fish to their diet. And the relationships of these notable women brought their family interconnections with war and peace chiefs in the region, enabling these brave and strategic men to accomplish inspiring feats of success. . [Travailler Volume 2: Ottawa/Ojibwa *Domitelle Oukabe dit Neveu La Fourche & Louise-Domitelle de Langlade* … in preparation]

        In what would become Wisconsin and Minnesota, at Green Bay and Portage, along the Fox and Wisconsin Rivers all the way to Prairie du Chien and the Mississippi river, it was **the *bois brûlé or washecho'hoska* (half burnt or mixed blood) children** of my **Menominee, Hoč̨ak and Dakota** grandmothers and mothers that knew where lead was to be found and mined, and, more importantly, <u>what herbs and plants were the best medicines to be found in the forests, pine barrens and oak savannas</u> of Wisconsin. They taught their children the many languages – French, English, Ojibwe and Menominee, Hoč̨ak and Dakota. The *Menagre, Decorah, Renville, Faribault, Campbell* sons would use these languages as multilingual military scouts, translators and treaty negotiators among their extended families that crossed tribal and geopolitical boundaries. [Travailler Volume 3: Menominee/ Hoč̨ak / Dakota *Hopokoekau* (Glory of the Morning) & *Eechauwaucau* (Marie Descarrie) *Margaret Grignon & Genevieve Jane Menagre Waggoner* … in preparation]

        And, in the west, through Minnesota and out onto the plains of the Dakotas and Manitoba, along the Minnesota and Red rivers (originating at the confluence of the Bois de Sioux and Otter Tail rivers) all the way to the Turtle Mountains and beyond, my **Ojibwe, Cree (***Néhiyawak)* and **Assiniboine** (*Nakota, Nakona*) grandmothers and mothers nurtured several generations of *sichangues* (half burnt thigh), *âpihtawikosisân* (**'half people' in Cree), *wisahkotewan niniwak* ('men partially burned' in Northern Ojibwe) or *Métis* (half-breed) children.** These children actually developed their own unique language, *Michif*, made up of French nouns and Ojibwe/Cree verbs. The *Grandbois, Nolin and Rogers* sons went on the <u>great bison hunts on the prairie</u>, adding bison *pemmican* or *wasna* bags made of bison, berries and fat to the sustaining diet, to make a *taureaux à grains* (Métis) of 90 lbs that might last decades, if stored in a cool place. They moved along the trails of trade in Red River carts, and made tragic attempts to create our own nation in between the unfolding Canadian and American expansions. [**Travailler Volume 4:**  Cree/Ojibwe/Nakota/Metisse *Josephte Petit dit Thomas Grandbois & Marie Nolin Arklin Rogers, Elizabeth Grandbois Rogers & Alice Rogers Waggoner*  … **published 2019, 332 pages**]

        At the beginning of these pages you were offered our traditional welcome, with these esteemed ancestors in heart, from our ancestors and family to yours, to begin this gifting. Let us continue this greeting, now …

For indeed, this is how we all begin and what we are - sperm and egg are only little circles of water entering one another and becoming one. Floating in water within our mother we are water breathing water as we breathe the blood of her and are nourished. Eighty percent water at birth we begin to dry out, but in our living, the water we share with others is gifted back again, a circle of water, so that we are still 60-70% water when we die. And as you may know, for it is wonderful, that all that comes into and nourishes us passes through the small holes that are our eyes, ears, mouth and nose, so that each thing that comes into us first passes into and through water (the aqueous humor in the eye, the cochlear fluid in the ear, the saliva and mucous fluids of the oral passages and stomach). All comes through water into us; thus, each of us is a walking water drum sounding the rhythmed beat of our unique song, completing a sacred circle.

This is the path we travel.  And while we travel this path fluidly, at times it is a hard path and we are hard, too.  We are earth and to dust we return. We are air, as we are the breath of wind. We inhale the exhale of the plants that gift this breath to us. And we are fire, all the energy that the sun gifts to the plant people who, in turn gift that energy in the nuts, berries and fruits we harvest, as the energy that moves into all other animals, that we burn so passionately in our living and dying and living again. So I ask you …

*The Circle of Gifting*

*What do you have to <u>give</u>, as you <u>receive</u> so abundantly?*

Oh, the tasty crunch of the chestnut,
the succulent sweetness of the wild raspberry, strawberry, and blackberry,
the tanginess of the chokecherry and cranberry,
the aroma and penetrating smell of the seeped sweet fern and bergamot,
as the warm tea slips down your throat,
and the starchy nutritious-ness of the duck potato (arrowhead), prairie turnip and cattail,
the sweet, sweet heart of the maple pouring out its flowing sweetness,
and, ahhhh, you cannot forget the scrumptious wild rice,

All given freely to everyone, and this is not all, for all together all the plant people give the very air we breathe …

What do you have to so freely and generously give, as you receive so abundantly?

*What do you have to <u>offer</u>, as you <u>accept</u> such generosity?*

The fish offer themselves to you,
as do the wild turkey, the grouse, the duck and the wild goose;
the deer offer themselves to you for your sustenance,
as do the elk, the moose and the bison;

so many of the finned and feathered and four-footed offer themselves
to you and your family,

And as the bear gives her vey flesh (fat) and breath to her new born cubs
for months without eating or drinking so they might have life and accept that which
enable them to grow …

*What do you have to <u>share</u>, as you <u>welcome</u> such plenitude?*

As the tree shares its wood for your shelter, as does the very rock of the earth,
as the sands filter your water and the water quenches your thirst,
as the winds bring you rain and the fire brings you warmth,

What do you have to share, as you welcome such plenitude?

*What do you have to <u>gift</u> as you <u>embrace and are embraced</u> by this circle of gifting?*

For you are made up of all of these gifts,
constantly renewed and reborn
with the ever flowing and forming of these gifts,
and beyond being host to the cells of the micro-organisms
greater in number than your own cells,
and beyond the space that is the greatest single element
of which you are composed, contained by the thin skin of the minerals of the earth,
floated in the 60-80% of the water that you are,
breathed in and out by the air of the plants,
and fired by the neurons of the sun,

You are one with an ever-renewed part of the world around you
that gifts your very essence and existence …


What do *you* have to gift as you embrace and are embraced by this life-giving, love-
offering shared circle of gifting?

Journal Entry: *January 19, 2018 5:50 am*

*Knowing and Being Known*

In one of the most out-of-the-way places in rural northwest Wisconsin, the denizens of the sleepy little town were just waking up. It was very quiet in the rustic corner café and there was only one other customer.

With a gentle, familiar smile, the elderly gentleman warmly asked the waitress who came to get his order, *"How's it by you?"*

I wondered at this marvelous greeting, for the asking included an openness to hear about the status of family and friends, house and home, neighborhood and community, water and woods, land and its wild life, wind and weather, any and all of what might surround the life of the person addressed.

Sitting alone, thinking and writing at my table, I realized that the courteous, local gentleman had given me a simple way to begin this book. By responding to the greeting, *'How is it by me?'* I can write about all the beings near and dear to me, as well as their enveloping context in the place that is my home. In addition, I can describe the contributions my caring has offered to the wellbeing of the land, waters and wild life around me, extending to and including my kin and community. So it is that the question focuses and enlarges my response, becoming about how it is going for those near me *by my* heart and hands, as well. In offering this story of my connection to the life of this landscape, I hope to offer an example of finding and forming a place in the peace where a spirit might rest, refresh and renew itself.

For years my family and I cut down aspen and jack pine by hand, piled brush, burned brush piles and small meadows, mowed fire lanes. For decades we collected native seeds locally, re-seeded the meadows, germinated and grew native forbs in twenty flats in the bay windows of the house in late winter, divided and transplanted the young plants in the restored prairie meadows in the spring. With help from the *US Fish and Wildlife Service* developing wildlife habitat and assistance from the *Natural Resources Conservation Service* creating shallow ponds for waterfowl and shorebirds, we deepened the spring-fed pools into ponds, connected them with channels, seeded the channels with wild rice, and widened the channels around five small islands with what was dug up. We then burned and seeded the islands with native forbs and grasses. As the area of restoration became larger, collaboration began with the *National Park Service* to do more extensive prescribed burns every three or four years, further opening up wet and dry prairie meadows and developing oak savanna. Recently, logging and mechanical brushing opened up space for red pine savanna. Over the decades the land has been re-formed.

And by our hearts and hands, the wild life of the land increased. In collaboration with the *Wisconsin Department of Natural Resources* we placed telemetry devices on female wood turtles, constructed electric and then wooden structures to protect eggs in communal wood turtle nesting sites from predation (e.g. from raccoons), and translocated rare and elusive Franklin Ground Squirrels to this place from locations in which they were unwanted or killed.  The land was reshaped and sculpted, increasing both biodiversity and abundance. The geese and herons returned in greater numbers, as did beaver and bobcat. Wild rice filled the ponds and channels, hundreds of wood and other turtle hatchlings exited protected nests, and so came the merlin and the wolf.

In offering you my response to how it is going by us, this book is organized as we have arranged respite upon the land. A visitor might leisurely walk around to each of the twenty stations located upon the landscape where my family and I live, and spend some time there considering four recurring aspects. First, the visual and *physical beauty of the scenes* is illustrated in this book by the photographs of landscape and wildlife we have taken at each location. Second, the *lovely sounds and songs* that have come to our heart (poetry and prose) relating to each station are offered, especially from the perspective of at least one wild denizen that lives and regularly passes through each location. Third, we relate *stories* associated with each view that have *trued* our mind and its intentions (e.g. habitat descriptions, restoration and education projects that have taken place in that specific locale). Fourth, in the *silence that is sacred* … we offer internal prayers that consecrate our relationship with each and all aspects of land and life at each location, through sharing ancestral traditional stories and scripture relating to creatures and creation. Then, after a visitor has traversed the five stations within each of the four loops (East, South, North and West), blank pages are provided at the end of each section for a guest to record the experiences of the journey and its pauses, here at our home along the Namekagon River between Hay and Spring creeks.

And yet, there is more to this sojourning than meets the eye and ear, for here, in this place, *I am known in more ways than I know.*

I am regularly noticed … smelled, seen, viewed, watched, considered, tracked, and even touched … by the more-than-human life, the other-than-human beings with whom I share this home where we all live. I know more about my co-inhabitants than most human beings; yet, I am known by these wild residents in more ways than I know them.

Sitting quietly on this bench (*East Loop-Station 1)* on a particular cloudy day, I was seen and smelled by a doe with two beautiful fawns as they stopped and grazed under the apple tree. Another day a mink swimming downstream toward the river spied me. On a different day, a rainy day, a bobcat crossing the creek midway between the bench and the little bridge over the creek sensed me. On other days I was seen by a kingfisher fishing for minnows in the creek, waiting on high to quickly dive for food; a northern shrike looking for small birds to kill and cache; a woodcock in flight high above, voicing interest in mating.

Indeed, I walked up along the meadow to the north one spring day and came upon a woodcock's nest on the ground among the blueberry plants, with young chicks not quite fledged looking up at me. Between the middle of May and the middle of June, karner blue butterflies hardly noticed me as they flitted from blossom to blossom in acres and acres of lupine, while the wood turtles gathered to lay eggs on sandy areas between them, more cautiously aware.

One day in early summer I was spied by a majestic eagle spreading its wings, floating above the river, an osprey with fish hooked to her claw flying north to her nest and young, and temporarily ignored by swallows challenging bluebirds to use one of the nest boxes placed in the meadow. Peering north at the couple of tall trees along and near the creek, beneath a larger nest box made for kestrels and used by flickers, I was seen by a young flying squirrel who had fallen out of the nest, now used opportunistically by its parents. This past midsummer, sitting on this bench, I was noticed by a young red-tailed hawk flapping and gliding from jack pine stump to stump among the little bluestem of this meadow and then viewed by him regularly the rest of the summer and fall, floating overhead.

In winter, sitting on this bench at the first station a hound glanced at me while racing on the trail of coyote, and I was smelled by an otter sliding along on the west side of the creek, stopping to rest under an alder shrub before continuing on to the river, and, on another day, seen by a hobbling young buck who had slipped on a patch of ice further back in the woodland, pausing as blood still dripped from his broken leg.

Being sensed, observed and considered, *known*, by the life around me is complemented in similar fashion by my relations in my human community. For example, several years ago, a panel made up of a physician, a lawyer, a pastor, a psychologist and an administrator of a children's tribal service agency, discussed how well boys were becoming men in our community with local residents in the high school auditorium. This was the middle session in a series of three separate community forums about nurturing marriage, boys and girls. At the end of the conversation, each member of the audience had a moment to share what their heart prompted them to say. The very last community member to comment, an elderly man sitting way up at the top of the auditorium in the shadows, rose and spoke slowly, not addressing me as Dr. Damian, as had many of the previous commentators, but stated affirmatively *"I know you, Day. When you were a baby, before your Dad died, I carried you down Hay Crick in my arms one day, when your grandfather had the land where you now live."* In that moment, a long circle was completed and I knew I was home, for how I was *known* as a child by my family and neighbors as I was growing up finally met how I had become to be known as an adult and a professional serving my community. This was expressed by a man who lives near where I live, living in this one place all of his life, known far and wide for his investment in caring for and conserving the land.

*I am known in more ways than I know.*

Still, there is even more to this walking about than meets the eyes, ears and noses of these wild *other-than-human-beings* and my *human-companions-in-*

*community*. Restoring and re-forming the land to greater abundance and biodiversity has restored and re-formed *me*. The land and its life has shaped and sculpted me in unforeseen ways.

> *Being known and knowing becomes a deeper belonging,*
> *inspires a more whole and sacred presence of being ... being part of the whole.*

Here I have learned better to still my body, calm my heart, quiet my mind, empty and open my soul to the energy, to the *Spirit-which-flows-through-all-beings,* that connects us all to one another, that flows within between, among and through us. So it has come to be and so it is, that this mile of shoreline, 250 acres along both sides of the Namekagon River of which two-thirds lie within the boundary of the National Park (*St. Croix National Wild & Scenic Riverway*), encompassing Hay and Spring Creeks, which is comprised of the flood plain of the river, dry upland and wet lowland prairie, oak and pine savanna, spring-fed ponds and cold-water streams, upland deciduous forest and lowland seasonally flooded woodland, is our home, as it is home to many other beings. For many decades we have roamed these waters and lands, wandered among the plants and animals. For many years we have been forming and co-creating the spaces in which we live, not only with fire and seed, chainsaw and rototiller, but with rhythmic movement through these lived-in spaces, through the seasons, transacting with those with whom we share the water and land and air we breathe. In so doing, we have been re-created as well.

*Child and Butterfly*                    (Journal Entry: January 5, 2016)

My memories danced when the song of the whippoorwill woke me up in the middle of the night and I looked up again at the ripe full moon. So many stories before that night had led to the feelings in it, and so many stories after that night increasingly illumined the old ones - expanding, deepening and enriching them - as *fleur-de-lis* beads color the newly tanned hide. The past, the present and the future were numinous in the moment as the wolf howled and woke his nearby partner the raven. I briefly wondered what I would make of the little child I had been on this land if I met my younger self this night.

As a child my eyes were often brown, sometimes green or hazel, and on moonlit nights golden. Smooth olive skin was sun-darkened from summer days romping in meadows, prairies and pastures, stumbling upon that secret place where

> *a sweet butterfly wing brushes my heart ... it flutters,*
> *a drop of dew falls from the tip of a leaf ... my tear,*
> *a distinctly deep darkness, a shadow upon a sunlit rock ... my soul.*

> *I am known in more ways than I know.*

> *The Land Knows (me) ...*

## *Introduction*

*The Namekagon River* flows within a national park, is a part of the St. Croix Wild and Scenic River system. The river is 98 miles long and flows into the St. Croix River near Gordon, Wisconsin. *For over 1 mile the river's shoreline runs alongside and through our 225+ acres of restored wetlands, prairie, savanna and forest lands.* Our land brackets and adjoins another 50 acres or so of national park lands, which has enabled collaborative restoration efforts between us (a private landowner) and the National Park Service (NPS), that have included large scale prescribed burning, mechanical brushing, seeding and other activities to restore historical habitats and ecologies native to this part of the Sand County Regional Landscape of northwest Wisconsin, notably described by Aldo Leopold and Sigurd Olson, among others.

In the following pages I try to offer you a glimpse of our experience, knowledge and relationship with this piece of beautiful creation, by providing you with:

1)      *maps* that shows you 20 stations, each having a post with a number on it that is associated with its respective habitat description. The stations are grouped into four loops, with most stations having some sort of bench on which to sit and look over that habitat;

2)      a description of the *flora* (plants) that you can see at that station, with some photos of some of the native forbs (wild flowers) that are there, a description of the *fauna* (animals) that you can see at that station, with some photos of some of the animals I have photographed there;

3)      a brief narrative that is presented as a *'song'* from the perspective of one of the wild denizens that frequents that particular spot;

4)      an interesting *story* or two or three associated with that habitat, with that part of the land, that concerns the familial traditional tribal cultures informing an aspect of our relationship with the land and its life, one of the *families and* the *land uses* they/we applied to the land, an experience that I have had in that place (often concerning animals), and/or an historical account of some sort in relation to that place for our family;

5)      a sequence of verses from scriptures that concern Creator and Creation, wild and domesticate animals, compiled, summarized and related to the aforementioned scenes, songs and stories, ... concerning the *sacred*.

     ... and a blank page or two upon which visiting guests might *write some of their thoughts or experiences* as they sit at that particular station, as a potential gift to us and future visitors.

Please enjoy the blessing of this land as we share it with you, and with other family, friends and visitors in the future!

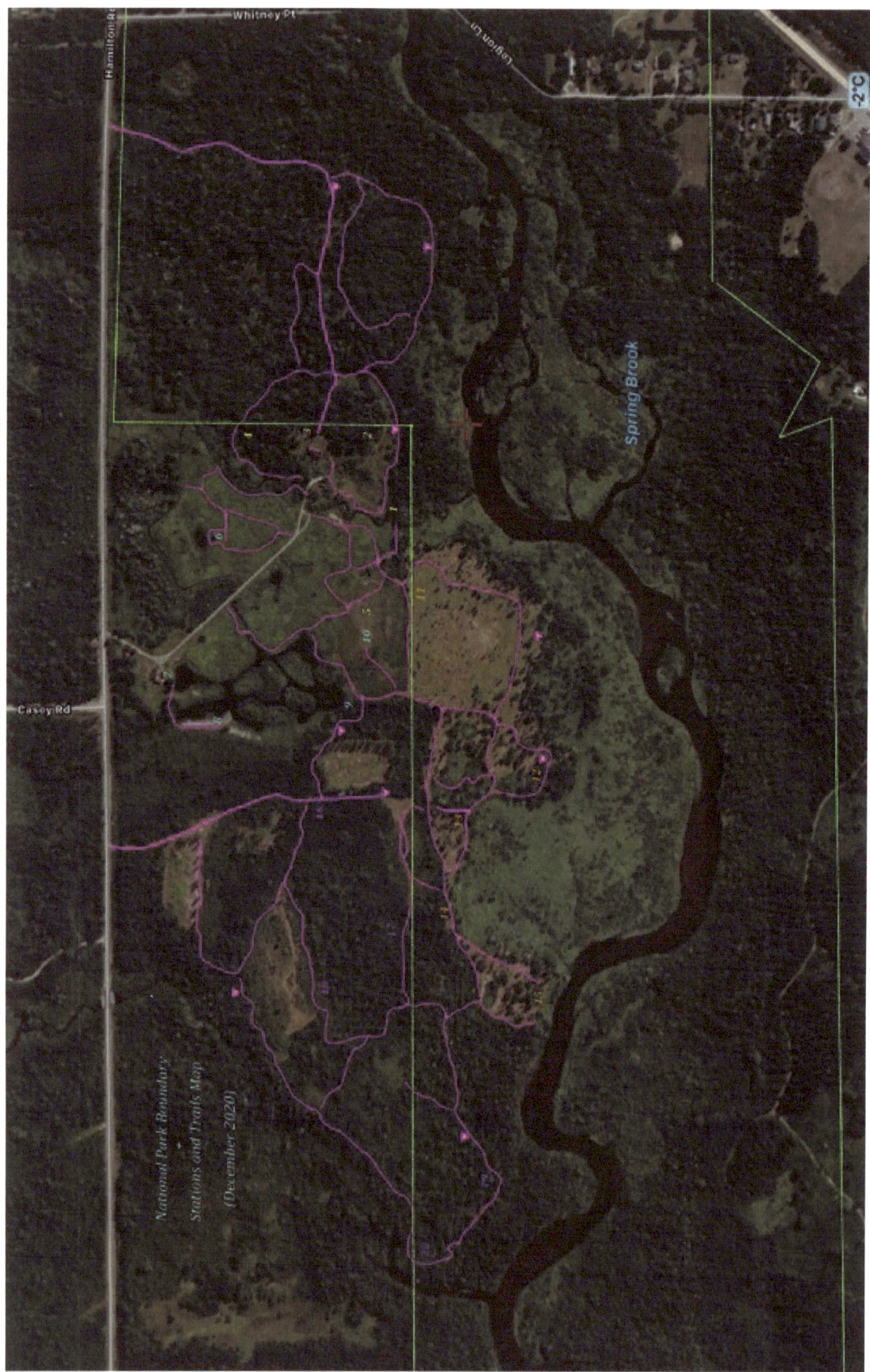

# The Sacred

In the darkest part of the night, in the deepest moment of sleep, I was startled abruptly, immediately, completely awake by the most penetrating and encompassing sound I have ever heard. As I was involuntarily jerked upright, I noticed the dear soul next to me, inexplicitly remaining still, serenely asleep. I have spent the last three years, especially the quite solitary year during this pandemic, considering what happened on that dark winter night. Such exploration led me to writing this book and eventually to the following questions.

*What is this book about? To whom is it written? Why?*

To the informed and discerning eye, it is clear that I have a passion for restoring the biodiversity of prairie and savanna, wetland and woodland, native flora and fauna on the 225+ acres that is the home of my family. The Namekagon River passes through and along our land for over a mile. I deeply care for the land, water and wild life here.

It seems that I also like to take photos. There are so many windows in this house on the hill that overlooks the creek, ponds and prairie that it is hard to keep warm in the wintertime. The window behind my computer screen periodically reveals bobcat, bear and wolf. I have over ¼ of million photos on the computer I am now using to write this, some of them taken through these very windows that open onto such wild lands. The photos are primarily of land- and waterscapes, wild life and people, friends and family. Looking down to the right I see photos of my ancestors and extended family, and even a few of me, on the walls leading down the stairs to where my youngest children (Daybreak 5 and Arendaki 3 years of age, respectively) are taking their midday nap. Hanging on the wall above them is a very large image of a black wolf partially hidden in the dark shadows of winter woods, signed by Robert Bateson. I crave beauty.

Apparently I like to write. My mother died this past spring and my brother returned the books I had written recently, published and shared with my mother to read at her leisure. Five of them, mostly written in the last five years, are still sitting here in a pile beneath papers on the desk next to my computer. I look down to the left at the bottom bookshelf next to the desk and there are ... wait a minute and let me count them ... at least a dozen different journals that contain musings over the 71 years of my life. I seek to express what truth I might find and share. Looking at the titles on the books resting next to me, this is especially the case concerning my ancestors, family and faith, as well as my experience of the land.

It is obvious to anyone that knows me that I love children. After helping to raise my youngest brother, who was a latecomer to the family ten years after I was born, I married three times: I finished raising my first daughter and son alone after unexpectedly losing my first wife, raised a step-daughter for most of her life, and now, married again five years ago, I am raising two young sons. In between nurturing children in these four families, for over half a century I have worked and played with children, educated and helped youth to heal from early wounds - in a variety of settings and ways - as a recreation supervisor, teacher, special educator, psychologist, university professor and researcher, environmental education program director, father surrogate and all around pal. I have been, am, and always will be, in love with children.

What may not be so obvious is the love and attention I have experienced that comes from my Creator, conveyed especially through the persons of my three grandmothers, but also through His Creation and Creatures, my ancestors and elders, my partners, parents and the children I have nurtured.

This book contains elements of all these loves. It is about how my ancestors lived upon the land with a certain harmony - showing me ways of loving the land and living with its life, helping children and families to learn how to care for the land, as well as how the wild life of the land has connected, communicated, and guided me in surprising and unusual ways.

Who is this book written for? Who is the audience? At first, I thought it was for my children and grandchildren, and this is still so, in part. I wanted something to share and guide family, friends and guests who come to visit this landscape, and this is also true, in part. I wondered if a more general audience might gain some insight about how to restore natural habitats and ecologies, how to reclaim certain traditional cultural approaches in relation to the land, and/or how to reform responses to institutions concerned with how we live upon the landscape, in new ways. While these purposes and people may be a part of what I am trying to express in this work, it is not the true essence of to whom and for whom I am writing.

Although I have expressed my experience privately a couple of times, it still somehow seems audacious to state, in writing, that my Creator spoke to me on that night three years ago. Yes, to say that my Creator called out to me, specifically and concretely, might engender incredulity by just about any reader. Yet this is so ... and it turns out that it is the reason for writing this book.

I am looking at a photo of me on the wall below, taken at high school graduation, shortly after my confirmation. Viewing the photo recently I recalled the deep effects of the intense experience I had at my confirmation exercise and first communion. It is there in my eyes. As you read the following pages, the relationship confirmed on that day has been engaged and verified by the Sacred Spirit that moves through Creator's Creation and Creatures, time and time again. Yet, it was not until the Voice of my Creator spoke out to me directly one night that I learned that the impetus for this book, the audience if you will, was *me*, was and is my response to that *Calling*.

*Why?* I have come to know that the *Spirit-which-moves-through-all-beings* is *present*, is intentional, communicates with us directly, and that the flow of that energy, the actuality of that *presence*, can be shared with others, *must* be shared with others. So it is that I have been called to re-view my efforts, experiences and their consequences in light of that *presence* over the years of my life, most of which have been spent here, in this special place. Thus, it is that I write this book for myself, to deepen and make greater space for that *presence* to be alive within me. It may be here for you, as well, if you come to visit and walk the trails, sit on the benches at the various twenty *Stations* and/or peruse these pages.

Here are the scenes, songs, stories and silent prayers that relate to the restoration of the intertwined natural and human ecologies that exist where I live, of which I am a part, (part reformer and part transformed), as best I can recollect and share. It has some things I have written, some photos I have taken, it describes my families, friends and neighbors. Most importantly, it presents that sacred, living *presence*, as best I humbly can, as it exists within and around me, here.

You may know already that when you still the body of its incessant doings, calm the heart of its unending feelings, and quiet the mind of its perpetual thoughts, that is, when you stop being busy, upset and worried, you begin to see the beauty of the world.

It is so in such moments for me, often at the end of the day when the sun has gone down and the stars are not yet out, when the world seems to stop and empty itself of all form and feature.

I am reminded, then, that there is in each of us an interior scenery that has incredible facets and qualities of beauty that rival the most spectacular water falls or most stunning wild flowers. For each of us is formed uniquely, with special aspects composed in such a way that one is like no other. Indeed, if you sit quietly enough, without disruption or distraction, you may begin to sense the awesome, wonderful and beautiful nature sculpted in you, if you know how to do so.

To look at a beautiful painting we are told to notice the color, texture and lines. In order to appreciate a good wine we are told to attend to its fragrance, smoothness and sweetness. But what of our interior selves, what are we to note and share, and how do we do so? We must pause from our busy engagements with the world, so that we may see the world anew. By emptying our selves of all the doings, feelings and thinkings with which we are flooded and filled, we may see the world and ourselves in new ways.

Such is my intent in sharing these colorful wildflower and animal photographs with you, that you may be so captured and captivated by the beauty outside of you, you will pause and be drawn to contemplate the *presence* of the great beauty within you and within those close to you. For whenever and wherever *Beauty* catches our attention, we become attached and begin to appreciate the *Truth* of the grand design which marries that which is within and that which is without ... we come to know that Beauty and Truth are only mediated, wedded by *Love*. When we recognize *within* ourselves the beautiful and providential reality of the land, and realize relationships of love *between* us and each aspect of life, then and only then can we represent in natural and human laws the proper relations *among* all living beings. This is when we become whole and one with the Spirit-which-moves-*through*-all-things.

xlviii

*Breathing Light*

To drink the light is to begin to become life. In the long ago, the large rock that circled the earth, and the larger rock that was the earth, were both lit by that light. The moon and the earth belonged one another as light and darkness moved across them, separating the spaces and faces of the void.

The water moved to the rhythm of that belonging pull of rock upon rock, rock upon the waters, to the rhythm of the warming and cooling, to the rhythm of light following darkness following light, ever again.

And so the earth breathed light and the water breathed light, giving impulse to the wind across the waters and land. So it came about that the wind breathed light, as well.

So it was that these three danced with one another, becoming and belonging one another as they continued to breathe light. Fully believing they could come into being as life, it was so.

And so it came to be that as life breathed light it greened. As life continued to breathe light and the greening grew, it began to store light and share light with life. Life separated from life into variation of being. New life that could not drink light directly ate the greening life that could. Again and again new life came into being, until there was life that could not drink light, nor eat the greening that drank light; so life began to eat life.

In an ever expanding forming of life, this breathing, drinking and eating of light could only be captured and contained for so long, before it dissolved back into its sources. Yet, this was not a complete dissipation into dark nothingness, but a slow accumulation of richness, as the water and the wind weathered rock, as the drinking and dying of green, life eating life, all became soil, nutrient for continued life ever reaching upward to become closer to the light that sourced it.

And in that reaching for light it moved - new life grew, grew tall, grew legs, grew wings, ever reaching upward toward the light.  And as life faltered in its reaching for light and fell to ground, it also deepened, growing downward into the accumulating depths of soil and water.

And it was so that life moved in another direction as well, as it reached upward and extended downward, always toward light ... it also moved inward, containing and compressing its continuing accumulation of light in ever more concentrated form – into seeds, into cells and into the very smallest elements composing life. And so light became life, able to continue itself across generations, becoming consciously aware of itself, as it continued its homing towards light. And so it is that the ever expanding, extending and deepening of life became the scenes, songs and stories of life's sacred journey that continue today ...

# East Loop Stations: Huron of the Oak Savanna (corn)
## & the Burnt-Stump People (*chicot*)

**Station 1** Coolwater and Coldwater streams
      Dry-mesic Prairie                                *Turtle*

**Station 2** Northern Dry Forest                    *Snake*

**Station 3** Northern Dry-mesic and Mesic Forest     *Dove*

**Station 4** Hardwood Swamp                     *Fisher*

**Station 5** Sand Prairie                          *Grass & Flower*

# Station 1

## Scene: *Habitat Description - Coolwater and Coldwater streams*

*Coolwater streams* are flowing waters with maximum summer water temperatures typically between 22 and 25 degrees Celsius (72-77°F). The watershed areas of these streams are usually less than 200 square miles with mean annual flow rates of less than 100 cubic feet per second. Coolwater streams occur sporadically in southern Wisconsin but are very common in the north. These streams contain a moderately diverse fish fauna with a mix of coldwater and warmwater species and a few coolwater specialists such as redside dace.

*Coldwater streams* are best described as flowing waters with maximum summer water temperatures that are typically below 22 degrees Celsius (72°F). The watersheds of these streams are usually less than 100 square miles, and the streams exhibit mean annual flow rates of less than 50 cubic feet per second. Coldwater streams can be found statewide, but they are concentrated in southwestern and parts of central and northern Wisconsin. These communities contain relatively few fish species and are dominated by trout and sculpins. The unglaciated Driftless Area in the state's southwestern corner exhibits a classically branched stream pattern and sharper, more eroded terrain. The rest of the state, smoothed by glaciers, has less topographic relief, creating sinuous streams with less average elevation drop.

### Station 1 Overview

(N) Gazing *north* (60 m) you will see the low, wooden turtle nesting protection structure, just on the other side of the stream, the shed (92 m, 100 yds), the garden, the small bridge over the creek, and the house (115 m) on the hill, which also rises about 20 feet (6 m) above where you are sitting.

(E) And viewing *east*, behind you, you can look (120 m) up a gradual incline, toward a native wildflower-lined pit from which the sand was removed for the ridge and the path which leads to the mixed pine-deciduous woodland and *Station 2* (taking a sharp left hand turn and going up the hill (another 33 m up and around to the backside of the Bunkhouse).

(S) Looking *south* ... in most locations on this landscape that means looking toward the river.  You will see a ridgeline that is made up of the sand piled to make a berm for the dam across the creek over a century ago. Mostly 100-year old burr oaks and a few red oaks (northern pin oak), like the one under which you are sitting, line the ridge before the ground slides down quickly into the floodplain of the river. In a straight line, it is a little over 120 meters to the river. Once you go over the oak ridge and down into the floodplain it is mostly ferns, sedges, grasses and alder, as the beaver have cut down most of the large aspen that were there.  If you walk south down the middle of the sandy-bottomed, spring-fed creek the 150 winding meters

2

to the Namekagon river, you will first go over two large logs that were a part of the dam built about 125 years ago to back up water and hold logs cut during the logging years.

(W) Looking *west* toward the Burial Rock and the knoll *(Station 5),* you are looking across the creek and the small floodplain of the stream. It is about the same distance to the Burial Rock on the knoll as it is to the river, but you rise 20 feet (from 1074 ft above sea level to 1094 ft), instead of going down the 10 feet you do going to the river. The creek can flood every three years or so and as you look the half a kilometer (over a quarter of a mile) toward the guesthouse along the driveway, the flooding sometimes extends most of that one quarter of a mile, also reaching north all the way to Hamilton road. (The county road is about .5 kilometer or .3 mile from the confluence of the creek and the river.)

This 360-degree panoramic view, with a 125 m radius, encompasses about 12 acres of flat glacier deposited sand that is mostly dry prairie, with a coldwater stream running through it that periodically floods in the spring. Containing a few burr and red oaks, a tall old red pine, jack pine, a scattering of service berry and chokecherry trees and some planted apple trees, the area is primarily filled with little bluestem, wild blueberry bushes, native roses, bergamot, milkweed, butterfly weed, pennsylvania sedge, sweet fern and a few pale purple coneflowers, with more than a dozen American chestnut trees planted around the perimeter of the adjoining hill. This spring three Kentucky coffee trees *(Gymnocladus dioicus)* were planted next to the creek by the shed and over twenty Saskatoon berry bush trees *(Amelanchier alnifolia)* were planted along this side of the creek and on the edges of the prairie meadow.

## Song: *Turtle*

Still, it is in the darkness. Calm, is the water. Quiet, is the slow sleep on the bottom, under the log, under the water, under the ice, under the snow, under the cold winter sky. There are others sleeping nearby, in the muskrat burrow, under the overhanging bank with root wads, and nearby on the bed of the river. She can just see the tan of the rough ridges of carapaces that have the characteristic pyramidal pattern of ridges and grooves on the upper shells of those nearby to the left and right of her.

Yet, gradually it lightens, then it warms, and, finally, there is a rush of new, melting waters. Moving out from the under the log, behind the island, after the snow and ice is flushed by, after the raging body of water flow finally stills, calms and quiets once again, life quickens all around. As she and the others rise from the muddy bottom of the river, she sees the orange to red undersides of the necks, chins and legs of her winter companions, with faint yellow stripes along the jaws of some individuals.

3

She finds a log upon which to bask, carefully orienting her shell towards the sun, while keeping a low profile out of the wind, warming up her body well above the air temperature, which also helps to dislodge leeches and other uncomfortable parasites. When leaving the water, she throws sand or dirt over her shell with a quick flipping motion of her front feet. She also basks when she moves onto land, becoming inconspicuous by burying herself partially in a shallow pit, concealing the outline of her carapace.

In the water, she searches algae beds and cavities along the sides of the stream or river to secure food. On land, feeding is mainly on plant matter and animals - beetles, millipedes, snails and slugs. Fungi, mosses and mushrooms, grasses, various insects, leaves and flowers of woody plants, fruits and carrion are consumed also.  Occasionally, she stomps the ground with alternating hits of the left and right front feet and/or slams her *plastron* on the ground rhythmically (thumping for fifteen minutes to four hours), imitating the vibrations of falling rain or an approaching mole heard several meters away, which sometimes causes earthworms to rise to the surface, where they are easily and quickly eaten. Hunting involves poking her head into dead and decaying logs, the bottoms of bushes, and in other vegetation. Usually slowly and deliberately feeding, capturing fish or other fast-moving prey is unlikely, although the opportunity to consume young mice or eggs, or scavenge dead animals is welcomed. After awakening, feeding, sunning on a log, and eventually moving back upstream to the colder water of the flow coming in from the creek at the side of the river, the movement is always back towards her birthing place. As a hatchling, finding the way back to the place she emerged from was done with a combination of smelling and 'feeling' the magnetic pull of the earth, until the journey became habitual and familiar each year.

Now, after twenty-four summers, the movement is again a return to the nesting place on the bank next to the creek, a spot that catches the full afternoon sun above flood levels, where eggs have been laid the past ten years.

The spot has changed since birth twenty-four years ago, as recent periodic fire has reduced tree and brush cover, releasing more grasses and forbs nearby. More sand appeared to raise the nesting mound one year. And a wire and then a wooden structure with a wire covering on top was placed over much of the raised sandy area. Yet, there is a narrow opening around the wooden structure that just barely allows entry. Raccoons seem to have disappeared, although there are more ground squirrels and chipmunks. The innocuous, tall, two-legged mammals living in the habitation on the hill across the creek meander by regularly. She pays them little attention, as they do not bother her. This past year wolves returned in some numbers.

The dozen or so eggs that have developed within her are a weighty impulse to find the warm sand returned to every year, to dig and to release them into the earth, and cover them once again. Then, freed and lightened, her movement is out into the grasses and sedges of the upland meadows to slowly feed through the summer within the nearby prairie and savanna, before returning to sleep under the water once again, after the air cools in the fall.

Yet, in the fall, before the long sleep, a larger male, with a longer tail, more domed shell, broader head and tail, comes up and nudges her head, shell, legs, and tail. Backing away from one another, the dance begins: Raising and extending heads in synchrony, they swing them from left to right. Then the male bites her head and mounts. Thus positioned in shallow water of the creek, he nips her head, thumping her shell below by straightening and then flexing his front limbs, and dropping the plastron onto her shell, he deposits sperm into her *cloaca*. After half an hour it ends, and this happens a few additional times with different males (even one year with a yellow-throat [*Blandings*] turtle). So life is once again initiated, to rise out of the darkness in a new season. Genesis.

Ice-covered ponds, streams, and the river present two problems for her as a wood turtle: she can't surface to take a breath, and little new oxygen gets into the water. On top of that, there are other beings in the water consuming the oxygen produced by aquatic plants during the summer. Over the winter, as the oxygen is used up in a pond, for instance, the pond may become *hypoxic* (low oxygen content) or *anoxic* (depleted of oxygen). Some beings can handle water with low oxygen content — others like her cannot.

Wood frog freezes and does not breathe, two-thirds of his body water turns to ice and he can survive in this 'frozen' state for up to seven months of winter. Flying squirrel huddles together with as many as 20 individuals packed tightly into a single nest box or tree cavity for warmth. Beaver packs on extra weight to burn during colder weather. Beaver's tail is designed to store fat and shrinks in size over the winter as fat stores are used. Black bear breeds in early summer. But implantation of a fertilized egg is delayed until the beginning of winter, after she has had an opportunity to build sufficient fat reserves to sustain her through the period of inactivity needed to nurse her cubs, born inside the winter den. For six months over winter she does not eat or drink, and feeds the newborn cub(s) milk made from the air she breathes and her fat. But, as a turtle adapting to winter, it is different for her. Most species of freshwater versions of her kind hunker down into the muddy bottom of ponds or lakes to wait out the winter. But having lungs and breathing air, how does she (and her relations) survive down there all season? It turns out she is able to absorb just enough oxygen from the water through body surfaces that are flush with blood vessels. Her *claoca*, the tube through which she urinates, excretes, and through which sperm comes to fertilize her eggs, is especially well vascularized for this breathing through her back end *(cloacal respiration)*.

Unlike most mammals, reptiles, amphibians, and birds don't have a separate rectum and urethra, but rather a single organ, the *cloaca*, that serves as the intestinal, urinary, and genital tracts (a common opening for the excretory, alimentary and reproductive systems). Some aquatic turtles, including bog and wood turtles like her, have a pair of openings off the cloaca, called *bursae*, which are

5

densely laced with blood vessels. To accomplish *cloacal respiration*, turtles pump water in and out of their pouches, the paired *cloacal bursae*. There are the muscles in the *inguinal pocket*, which expand and contract. Water enters these chambers and the oxygen is removed, allowing such turtles as her to wander at length in the murky depths of bogs or at the bottoms of streams and rivers. The ability to breathe at the end of a digestive tract isn't limited to aquatic turtles, but rather a feat that can be pulled off by animals as diverse as sea cucumbers and young dragonflies, who spend their nymph stage as aquatic insects.

What's more, some of her relatives can temporarily switch their metabolism to one that doesn't require oxygen. Both snapping turtles and painted turtles can survive forced submergence at cold-water temperatures for well over 100 days. Painted turtles are best at this *anoxia-tolerance*. They do this when the $O_2$ level in the water gets too low. However, prolonged periods of *anaerobic metabolism* will result in the buildup of acids in their tissue, a condition that can prove fatal. To deal with this, painted turtles mobilize calcium from their shells to neutralize the acid (in much the same way people take calcium-containing antacids for heartburn). In the spring, when anaerobic turtles emerge from hibernation, they are basically one big muscle cramp. (It's like when a person goes for a hard run — the body switches to anaerobic metabolism, lactic acid builds up and s/he gets a cramp.) After long submerges turtles are desperate to bask in the sun to increase their body temperature, to fire up their metabolism and eliminate these acidic by-products. And it's hard to move when they're that crampy, making them vulnerable to predators and other hazards. Spring emergence can be a dangerous time for these lethargic turtles.

The most spectacular adaptation, however, appears in her cousins, the soft-shelled turtles (*Apalone sp.*), of which there are two local species. These turtles derive their common name from the absence of horny *scutes* on their shells. They are the most highly aquatic turtles in our area and they can remain alert while obtaining 100% of their oxygen needs from their surroundings underwater. Seventy percent of their oxygen is absorbed through their skin. The other 30% results from pumping water in and out of the *pharynx* (throat) where there are many little projections of tissues having small blood vessels. These *"villi"* provide a greater surface area for oxygen absorption.

So she moves back to the cold water of the creek, moves down the short distance to the river, containing fertilized eggs, to slow down as the season gets colder, sluggish go to sleep once again beneath the water and ice, in the dark cold of coming winter, among others of her kind. Thus, life is once again initiated, to rise out of the darkness in a new season. *Genesis.*

## Ancestral Traditional Story: *Turtle Island (Wyandot/Huron … Iroquoian)*

In the beginning there was only one water and the water animals that lived in it.

Then a woman fell from a torn place in the sky. She was a divine woman, full of power. Two loons flying over the water saw her falling. They flew under her, close together, making a pillow for her to sit on.

The loons held her up and cried for help. They could be heard for a long way as they called for the other animals to come. The snapping turtle called all the other animals to aid in the saving the divine woman's life.

The animals decided the woman needed earth to live on. Turtle said, "Dive down in the water and bring up some earth."

So they did that, those animals. A beaver went down. A muskrat went down. Others dove down too and they died. Each time, Turtle looked inside their mouths when they came up, but there was no earth to be found.

Toad went under the water. He stayed too long and he nearly died. But when Turtle looked inside Toad's mouth, he found a little earth. The woman took it and put it all around on Turtle's shell. That was the start of the earth.

Dry land grew until it formed a country, then another country, and all the earth. To this day, Turtle holds up the earth.

Time passed, and the divine woman had twin boys. They were opposites, her sons. One was good and one was bad. One was born as children are usually born, in a normal way. But the other broke out of his mother's side, and she died.

When the divine woman was buried, all of the plants needed for life on earth sprang from the ground above her. From her head came the pumpkin vine. Maize came from her chest. Pole beans grew from her legs.

**Family Story:** *Protecting Turtle Nests (Vraniak)*

At **Station 1**, sitting on the bench, you are overlooking **Hay Creek**. It is about 12 miles long, emptying into the Namekagon River about 120 meters (160 meters following the winding creek) from where you are sitting. Halfway along its course is Hay Lake, at Hay Lake Ranch and Riding Stables. Hay Creek courses through our land for about one half mile before it empties into the river.

The land bordering the creek is relatively flat and seasonally flooded in the spring. Looking upstream to the north along the other side of the stream you will see a low wooden structure over a slightly raised hill of sand, enclosed by chicken wire fencing, with a narrow opening all along the bottom, through which communal nesting **wood turtles** may enter and lay their eggs.  As a part of a project in 1996 supported by the *Natural Resources Conservation Service* to dig shallow ponds for wildfowl, Damian had a pile of sand placed on the bank of the creek for nesting Blandings, snapping, softshell and wood turtles. Most of the turtles now laying eggs 25 years later were born in that pile of sand.

In 2013 the *Bureau of Natural Heritage Conservation (NHC)* received a competitive State Wildlife Grant from the *U.S. Fish and Wildlife Service* in conjunction with three other states - Minnesota, Iowa, and Michigan - to pursue upper Midwest riverine turtle conservation and habitat improvement. In Wisconsin, NHC focused its work on the state-threatened wood turtle *(Glyptemys insculpta)* in the Tomahawk River in Oneida County and in the Namekagon and Totogatic rivers in Washburn and Burnett counties. Wood turtle populations have declined significantly across the species' range, and major threats to its survival include habitat loss and excessive collection for the pet trade, combined with low recruitment resulting from nest and hatchling predation, as well as population sensitivity to adult removal, including road mortality.

Project work began in the spring of 2014 and continued for two years, finishing in September 2016. NHC staff captured wood turtles in May on the three rivers and attached transmitters to a subset of each population to monitor their movements to learn more about the species' habitat use and movement patterns and to find nesting sites. Once nesting sites were identified, predator exclusion devices were used on individual nests and monitored to investigate how nest predation impacts hatching success rates. In addition to these efforts, NHC created new wood turtle nesting habitat above flood stage on all three rivers, which also benefited other turtle Species of Greatest Conservation Need.

One day Damian was walking down the steps on the hill from the house and noticed a wood turtle with a long wire glued to its back. He called his friend Adrian Wydeven to see if he knew of anyone doing research on wood turtles and Adrian connected Damian with Carly Lapin (WI DNR), who was leading the four-state project. Damian alerted her to his nesting site, which eventually resulted in the construction of a nest protection structure (fencing with solar-powered exclusion electric wires) across from his home, on the bank next to creek, where Damian had deposited a pile of sand in the 1990's, as part of creating shallow ponds for waterfowl, with the help of Tom Frederickson (NRCS).

The involvement near Springbrook on Vraniak land has been one of the most productive of the sites in Michigan, Wisconsin, Minnesota and Iowa. In 2019 the Vraniak's counted 250-300 turtle hatchlings (mostly wood turtles, but also spiny softshell and snapping turtles) successfully coming out of the nests in and about the nest protection structure and entering the creek. The effort continued with the support of the WI DNR (Ryan Magana), doubling the size of the wooden protective structure (2019), and with the support of the *US Fish and Wildlife Service* increasing the extent of summer upland habitat for wood turtle females by restoring red pine savanna along Spring Creek. In the fall of 2020 Damian and Ryan dug up the nests, both inside and outside the wooden protection structure, to count the number of eggs from which hatchlings had emerged. At least 271 wood, snapping and spiny smooth shell turtles hatched from these nests. In 2021 there may be a second nest protection structure added along Spring Creek.

2020 Count

**Inside Box**

| Nest ID | Species | Successful | Failed | Notes |
|---|---|---|---|---|
| 13 | Wood | 9 | 2 | |
| 14 | Wood | 7 | 1 | |
| 15 | Wood | 7 | 0 | |
| 16 | Wood | 7 | 1 | |
| 17 | Wood | 5 | 2 | |
| 18 | Wood | 12 | 0 | |
| 20 | Wood | 7 | 1 | |
| 21 | Wood | 10 | 2 | |
| Total | Wood | 64 | 9 | Approximately 86% success rate |

**Outside Box**

| Nest ID | Species | Successful | Failed | Notes |
|---|---|---|---|---|
| 1X | Wood | 8 | 1 | |
| 4X | Wood | 6 | 0 | |
| 7X | Wood? | 6 | 13 | All of the failed eggs were unfertilized and found at the bottom of the nest cavity. It was undetermined whether this was 2 wood turtle nests or possibly a single Blanding's turtle nest. |
| 8X | Wood | 11 | 0 | |
| 10X | Wood | 9 | 2 | |
| 11X | Wood | 14 | 1 | |
| 12X | Wood | 8 | 0 | |
| AX | Wood | 13 | 0 | Reported by Damian V. |
| Total | Wood | 75 | 17 | Approximately 77% success rate |

| Nest ID | Species | Successful | Failed | Notes |
|---|---|---|---|---|
| 2X | Snapper | 20 | 1 | |
| 5X | Snapper | 13 | 5 | |
| 6X | Snapper | 7 | 0 | |
| 9X | Snapper | 25 | 0 | |
| BX | Snapper | 40 | 2 | Reported by Damian V. |
| Total | Snapper | 105 | 8 | Approximately 92% success rate |

The Vraniaks report they assisted 27 spiny softshell turtle hatchlings that exited nests just outside the nest box, into Hay creek during a two week period, as the wood and snapper hatchlings were emerging, as well.

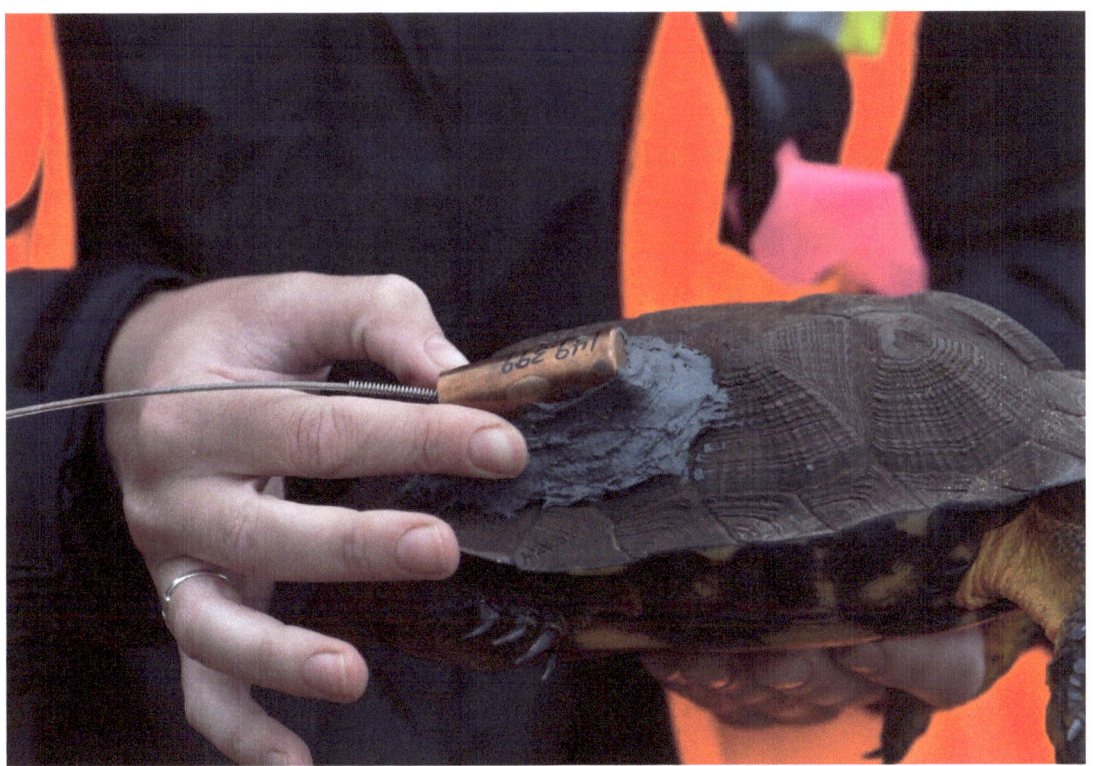

Telemetry was attached to a female wood turtle's carapace, after she has laid her eggs in or near the nest protection structure, in 2014, in order to locate her over the next two-year period. A solar-powered electric fence was installed around the nest area under which wood turtles could crawl. It was re-placed with a wooden structure in 2017.

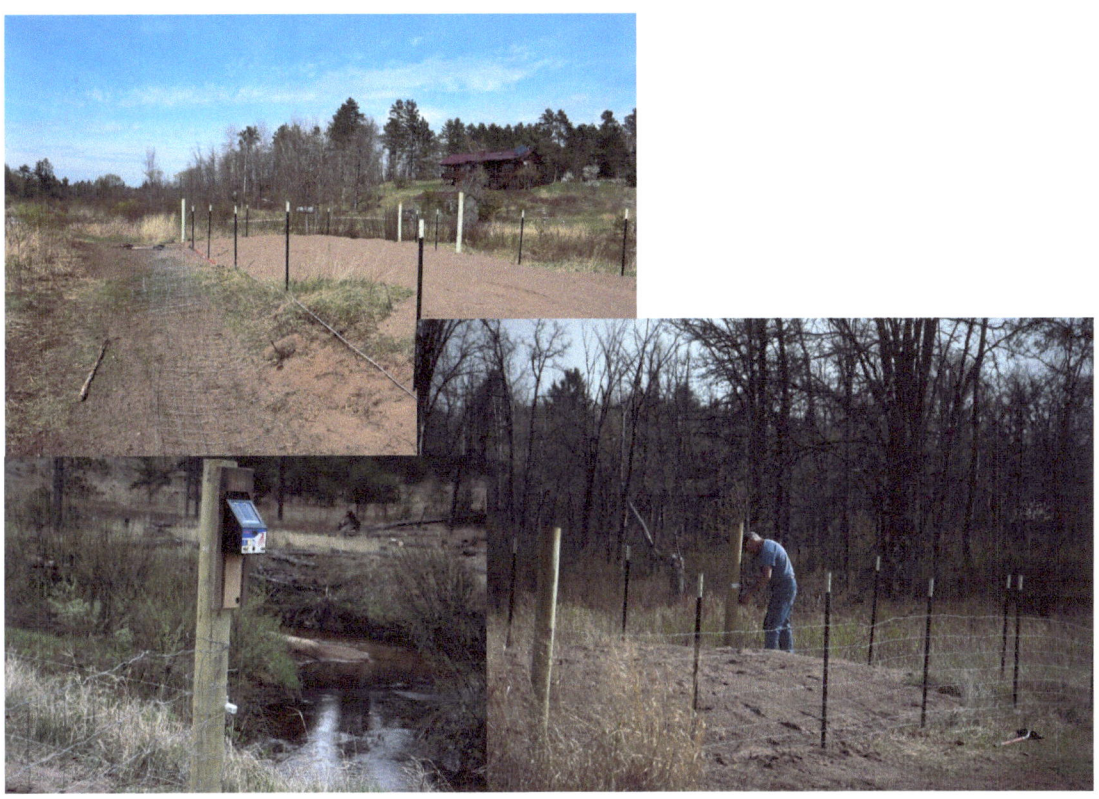

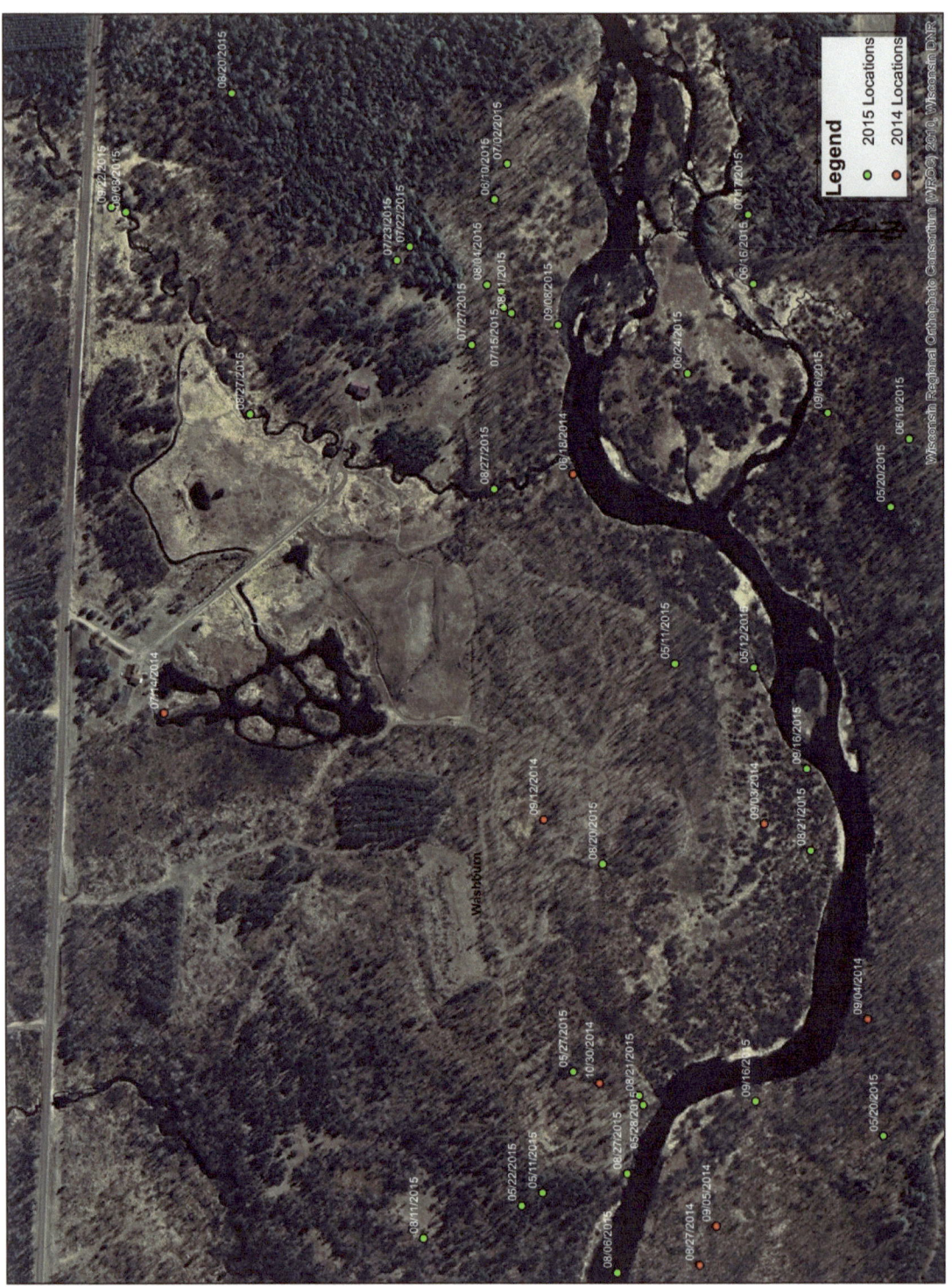

Location of female wood turtles with telemetry plotted on our landscape (2014, 2015).

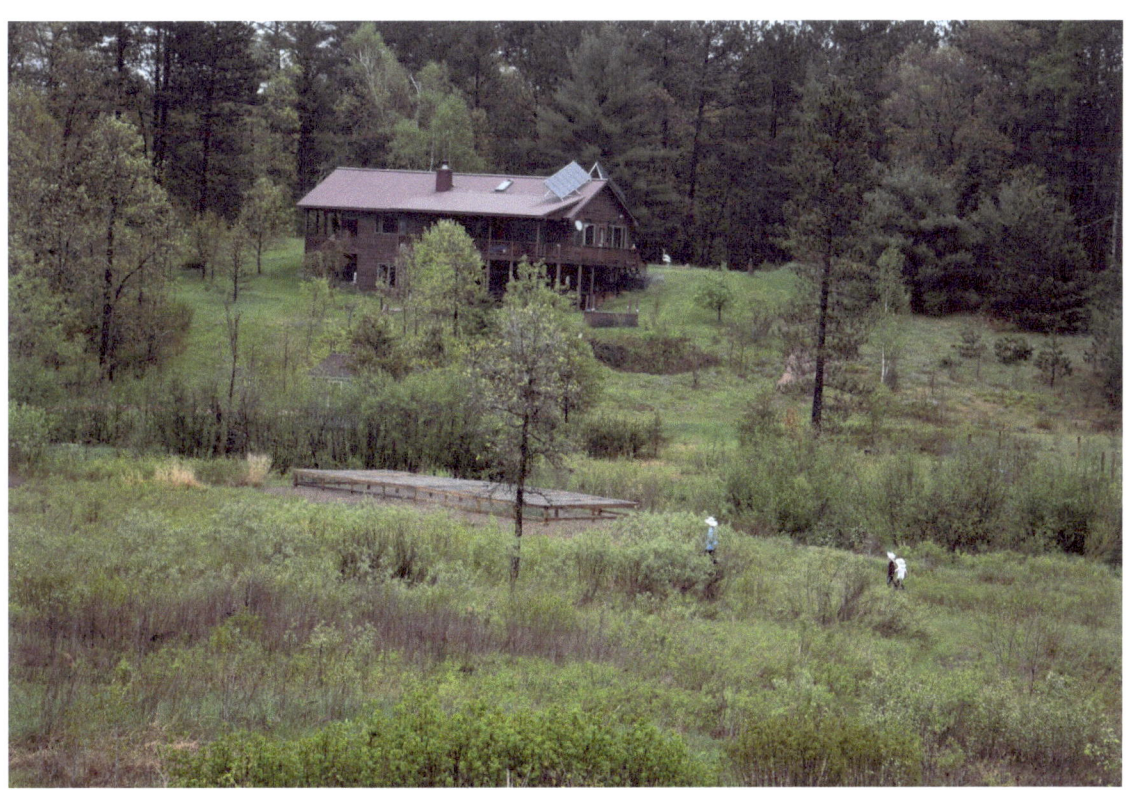

Late May 2020, wood turtles laying eggs inside and outside the nest protection structure.

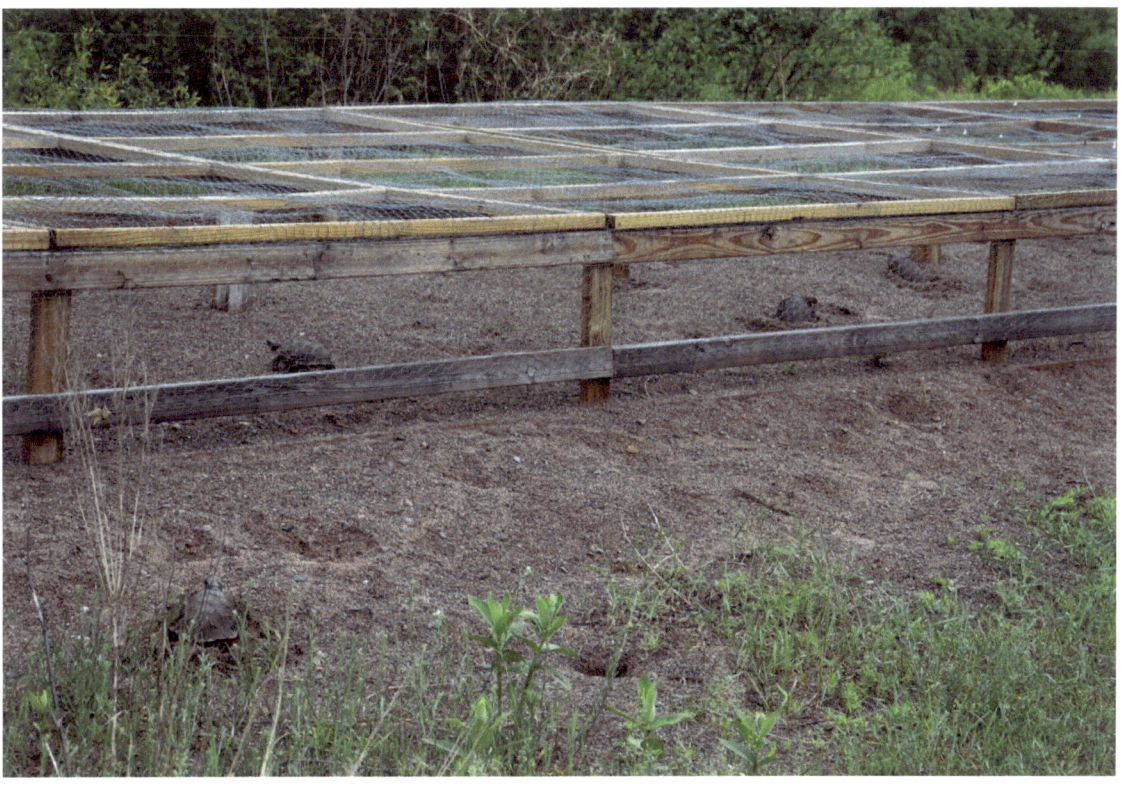

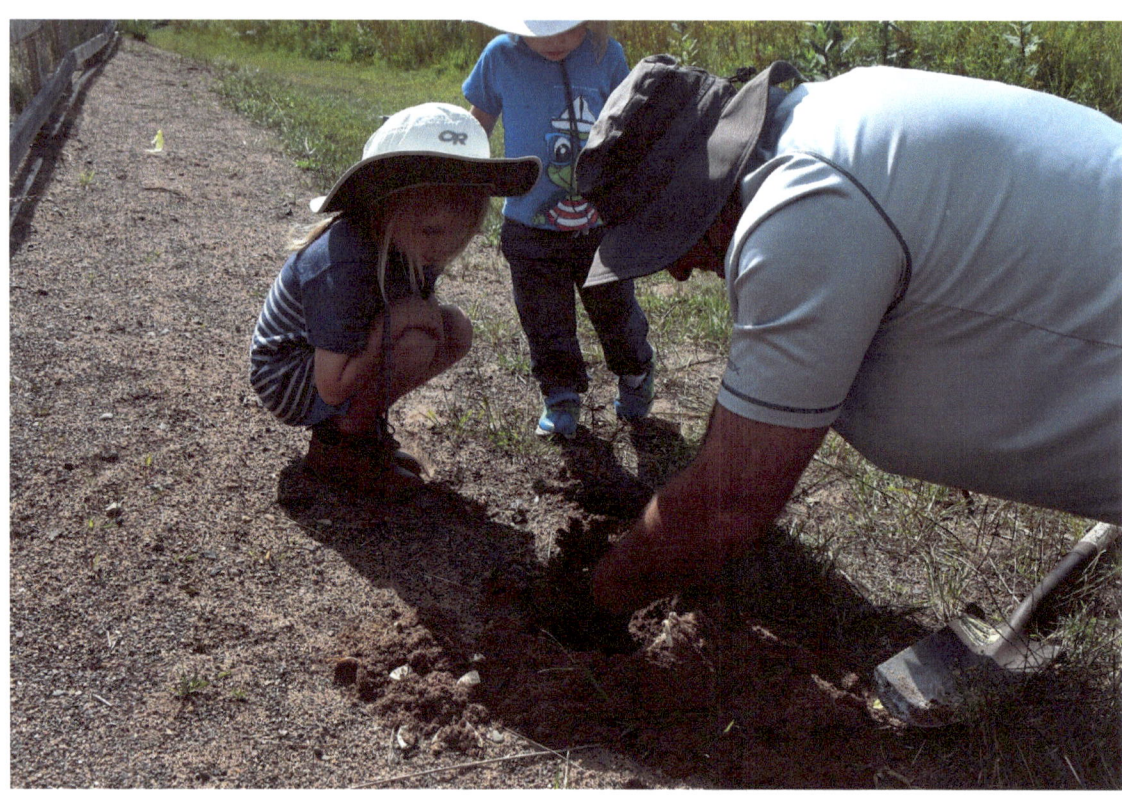

July 2020 counting eggshells in wood turtle nest with sons Daybreak (4) & Arendaki (2).

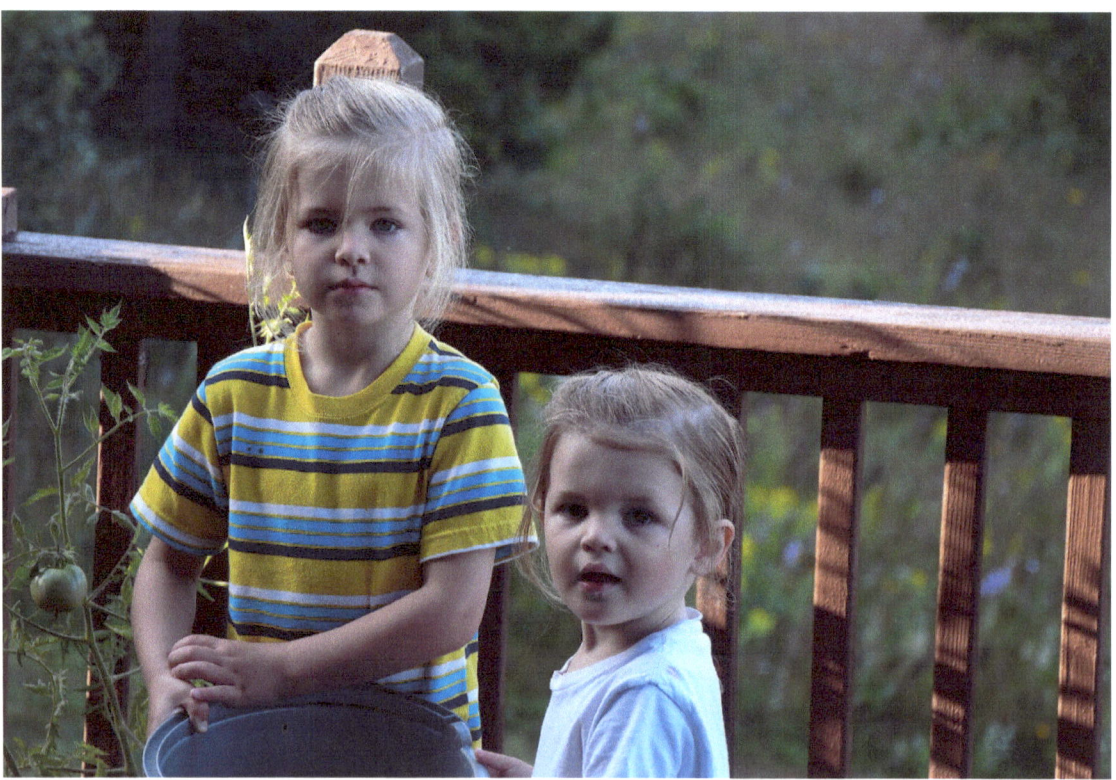

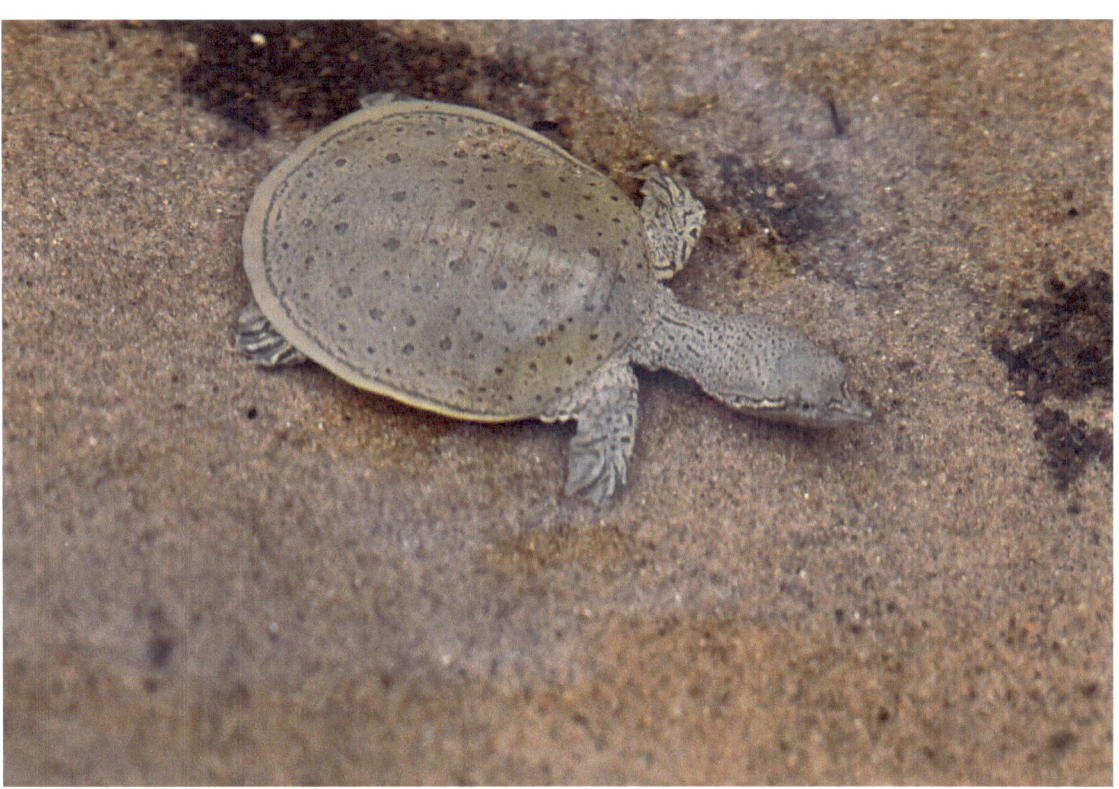

May 2020 facilitated release of 27 spiny softshell hatchlings into Hay creek.

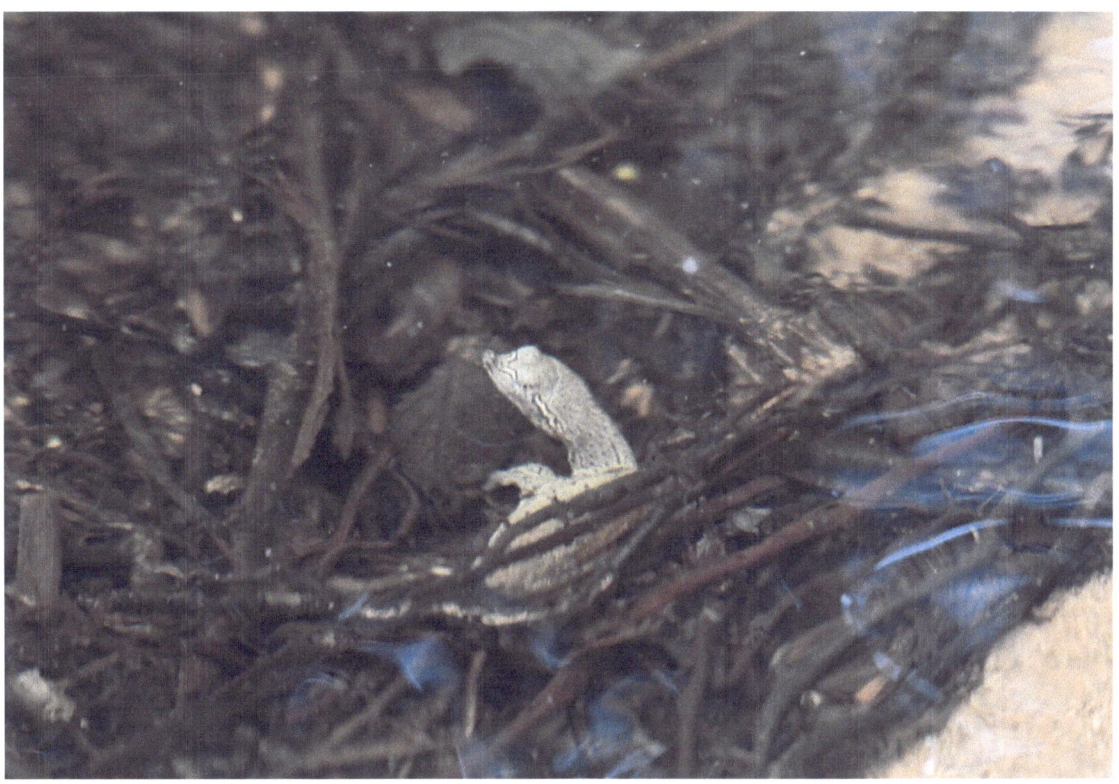

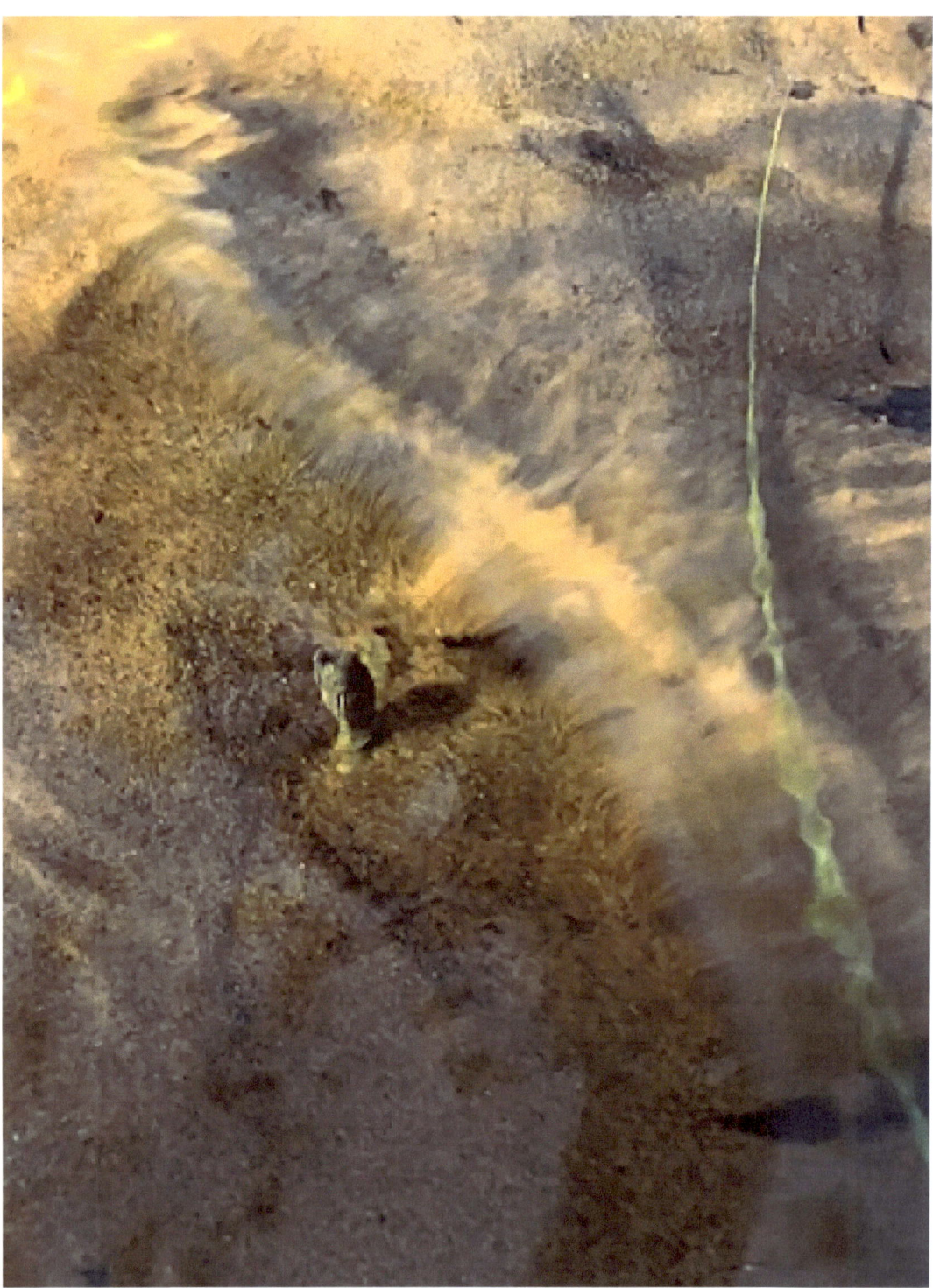

May 2020 spiny softshell burrows into creek bottom upon placement in water.

July 11, 2016 flood dropping 12 inches of rain in a few hours (event once every 500 years).

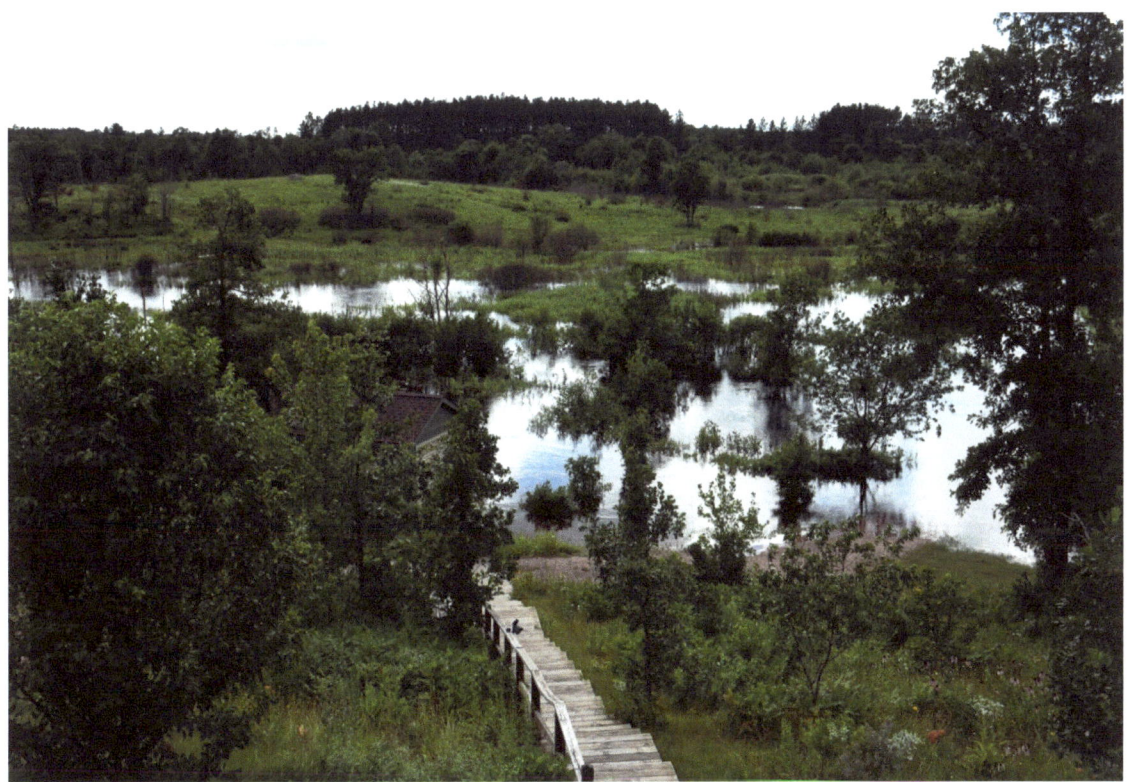

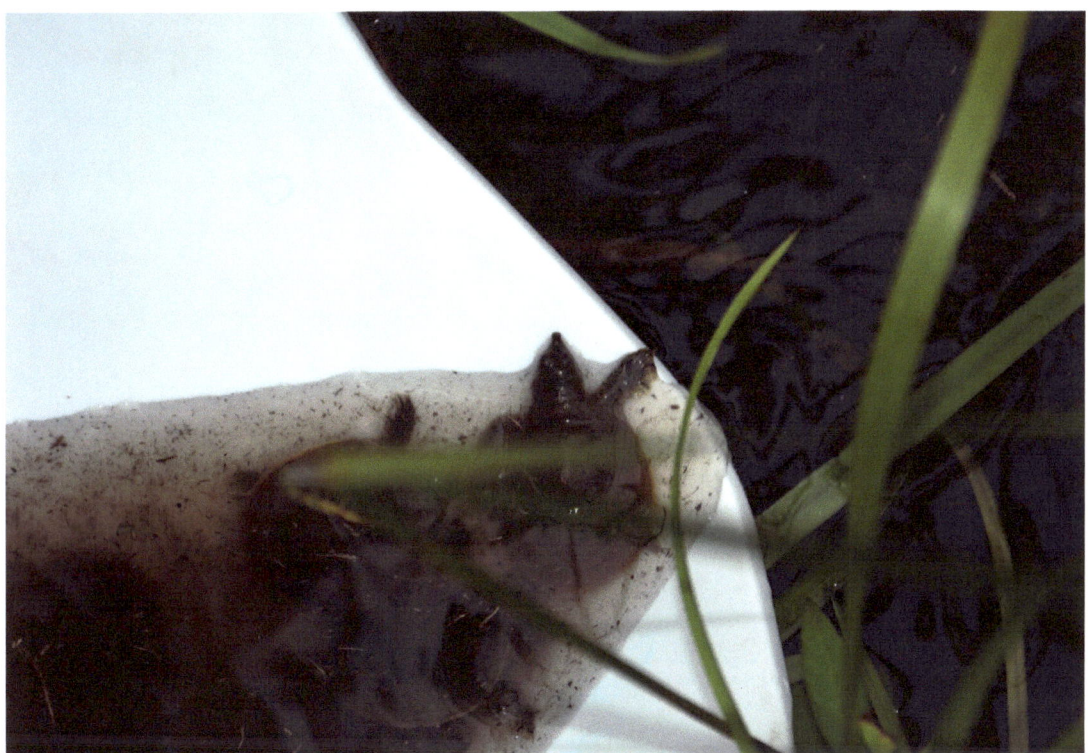

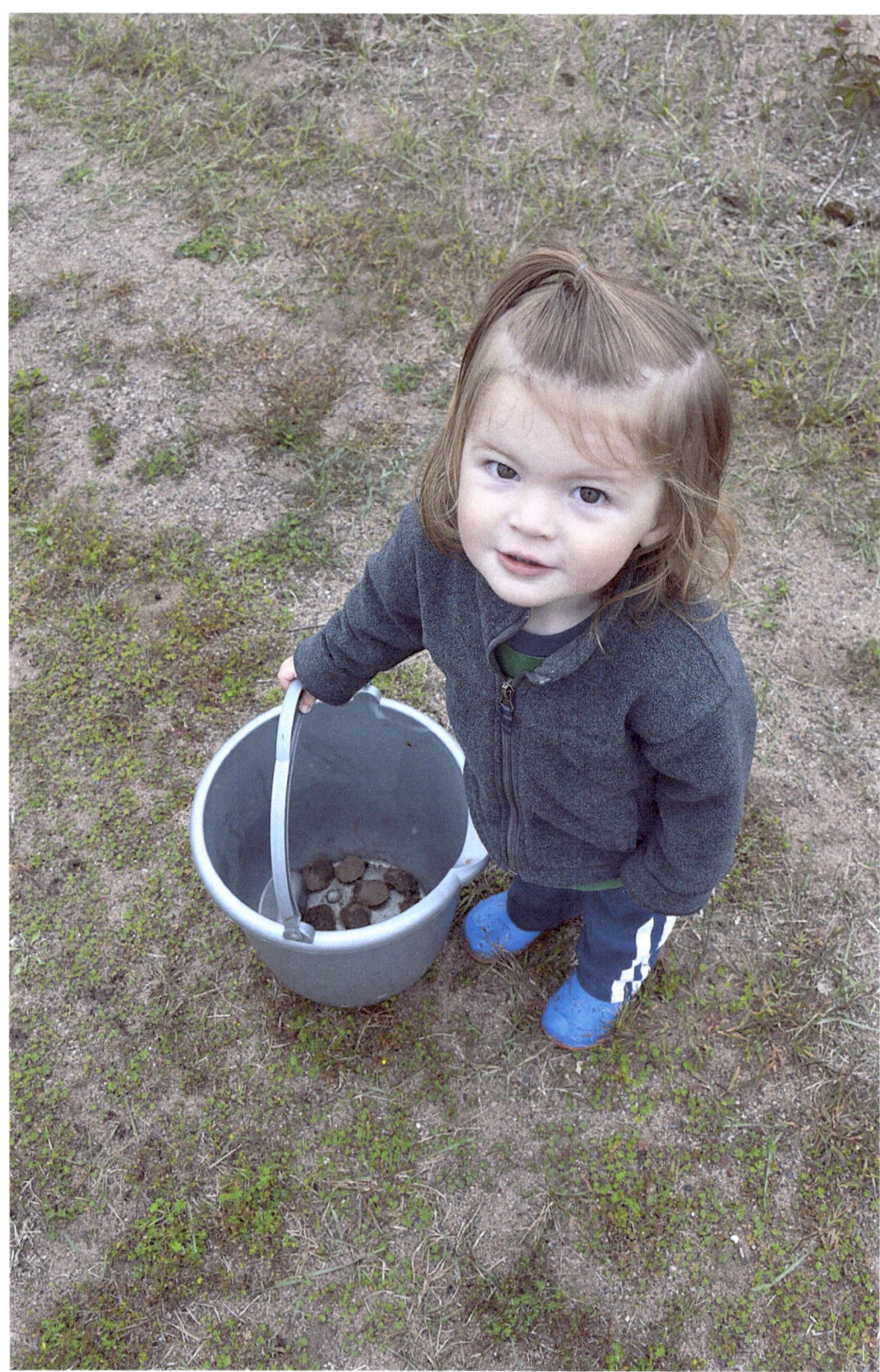

Son Arendaki (1.5 years old) collecting emerging spiny softshell turtle hatchlings and depositing them into the creek (2019).

Greg Geller and Damian published an article (Vraniak & Geller, *Herpetological Review*, 48(2), 419-420, 2017) describing how Damian watched and photographed a spiny softshell turtle lay eggs on July 2, 2016. The nest then was underwater for six days (July 11-17) and 13 hatchlings hatched on November 25, 2016 with light snow on the ground. Such survival under water and long incubation into the early winter had never been reported before, for either the softshells or a nearby wood turtle nest that produced live hatchlings, as well. Damian and his wife, Christina, brought one of the spiny softshell hatchlings into the house overnight and it warmed up nicely by the morning. They placed it into the stream where other nest mates had been placed the evening before and all eventually moved on down the stream.

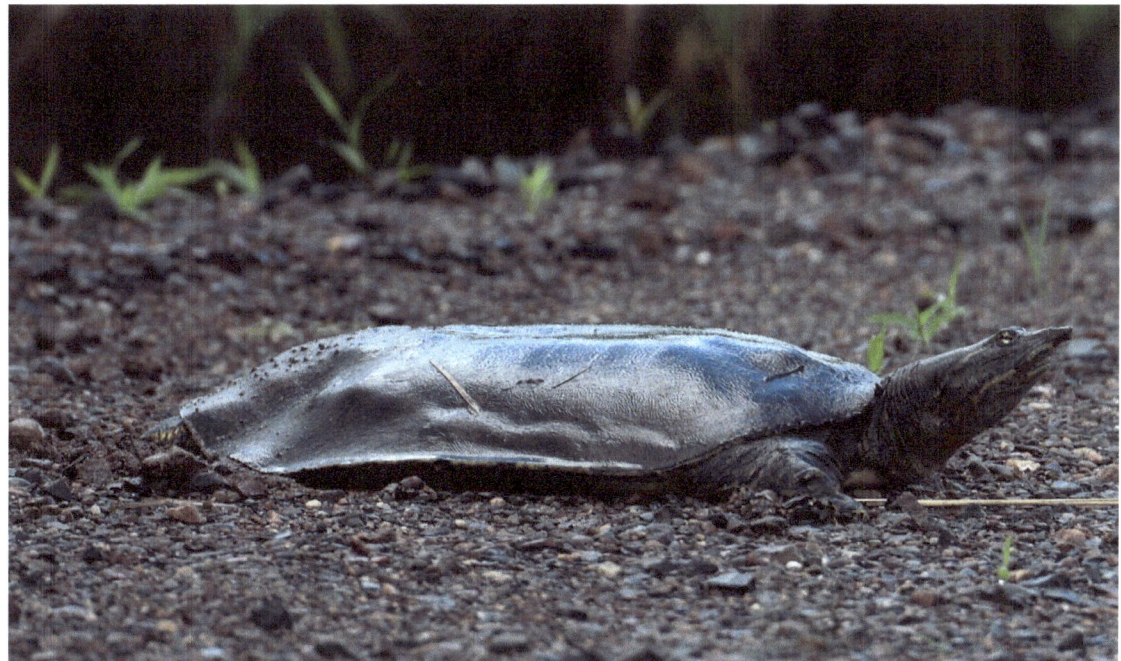

Female spiny softshell laying eggs (above) and November hatchling warmed (below).

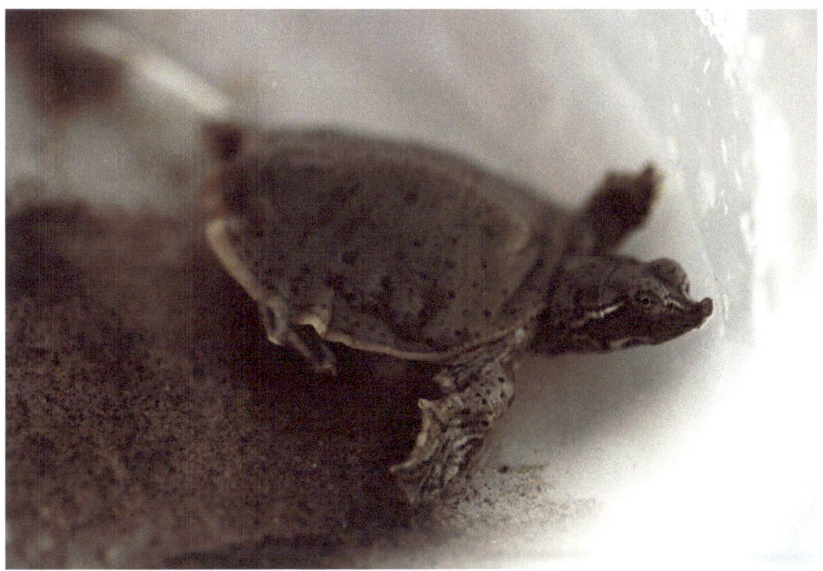

In addition, Vraniak, Lapin & Bougie, also published (*Herpetological Review*, 48(2), 424-425, 2017) the first documentation of wood turtle nest predation in Wisconsin by badgers, which occurred both during the day and at night. Since changing to a wooden structure rather than using an electric fence, such predation has stopped.

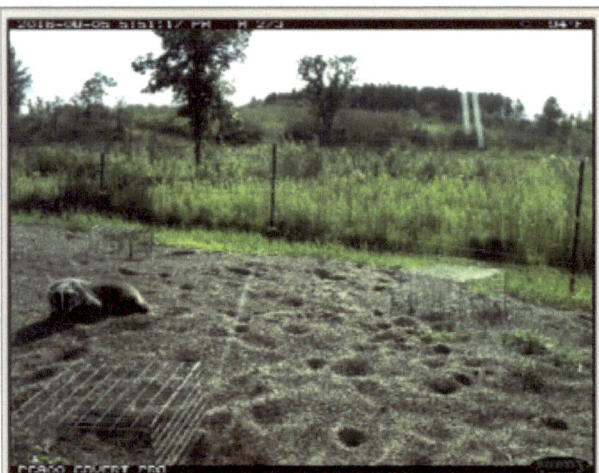

FIG. 1. *Taxidea taxus* searches for and consumes turtle nests (*Glyptemys insculpta* and *Chelydra serpentina*) inside of a nesting exclosure constructed with solar-powered electric fencing in northern Wisconsin.

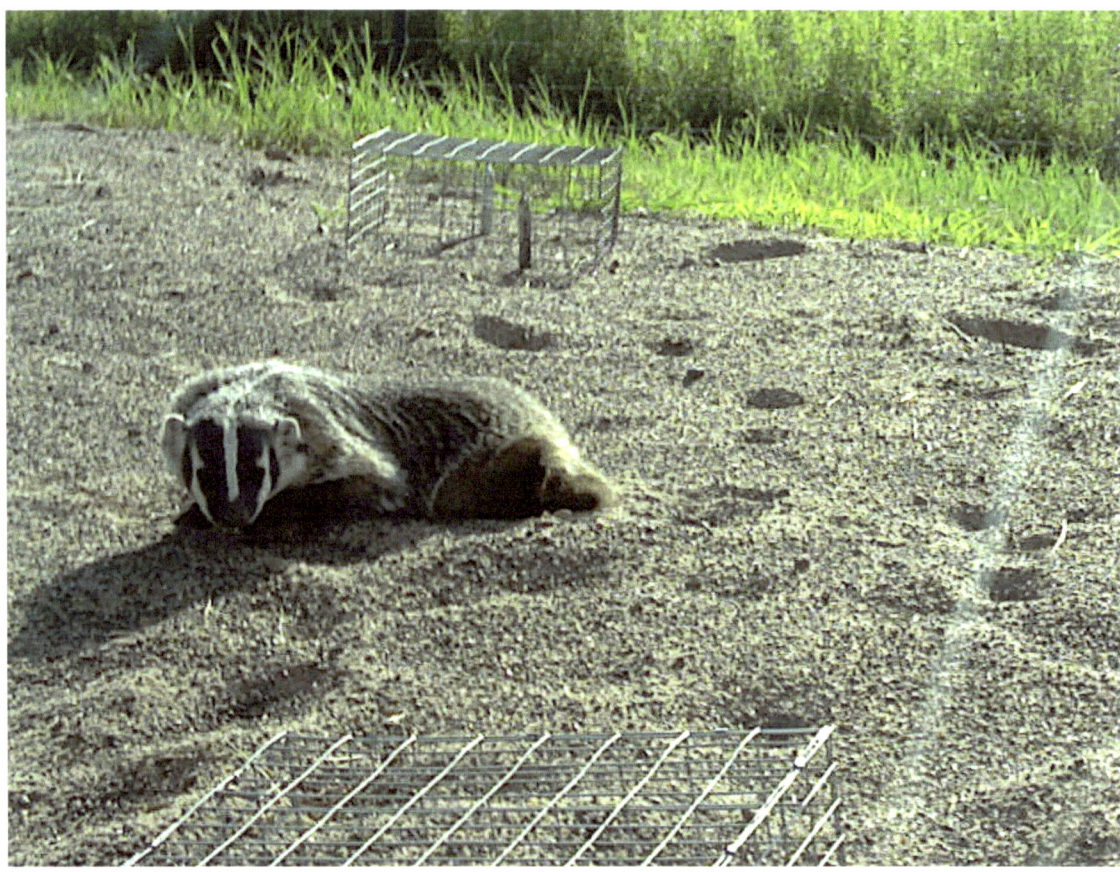

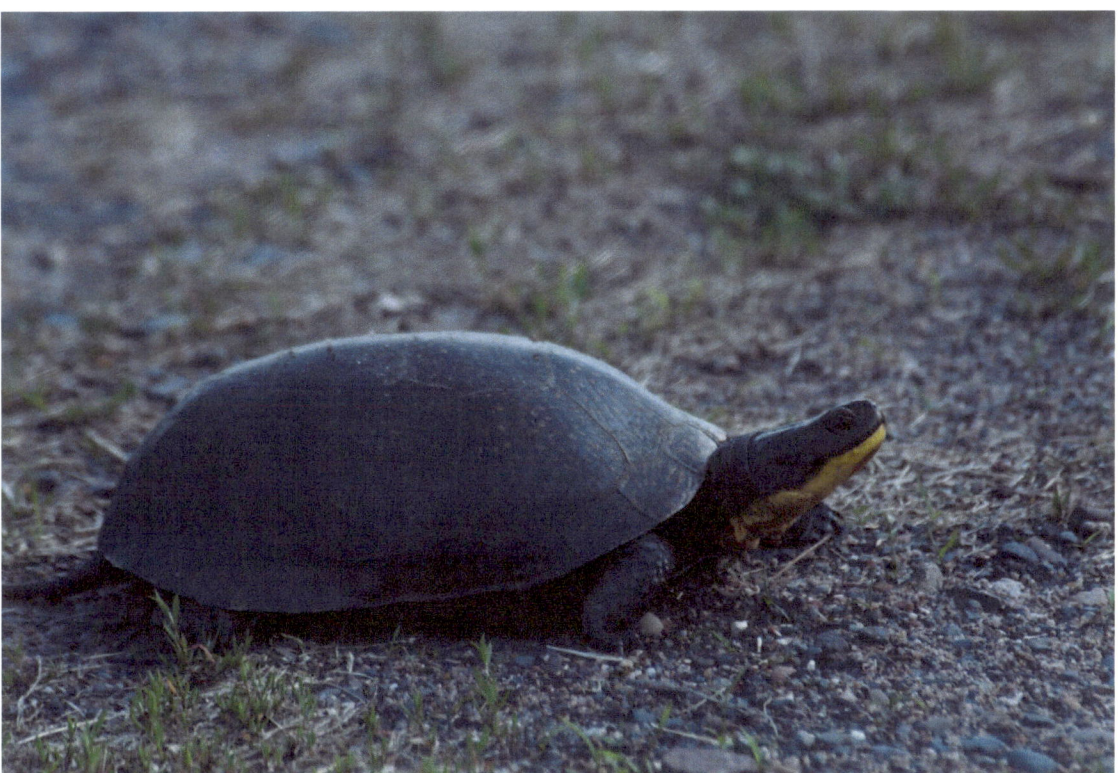

Blandings turtle in driveway.

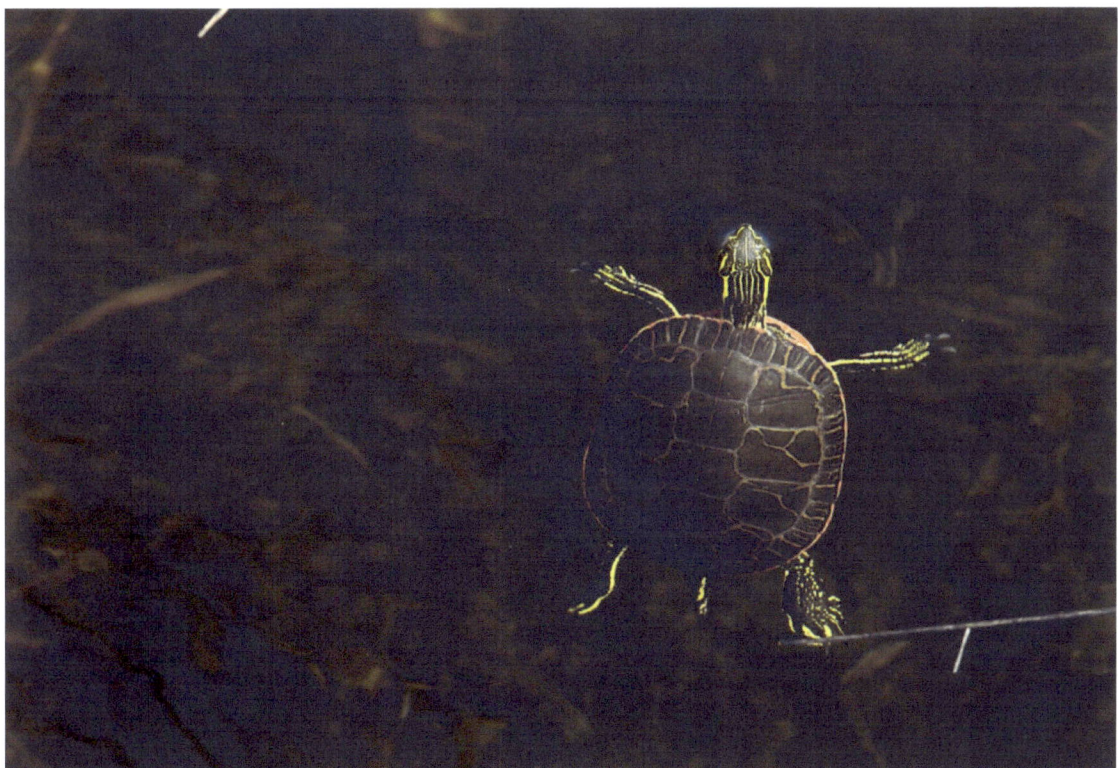

Painted turtle in channel between ponds.

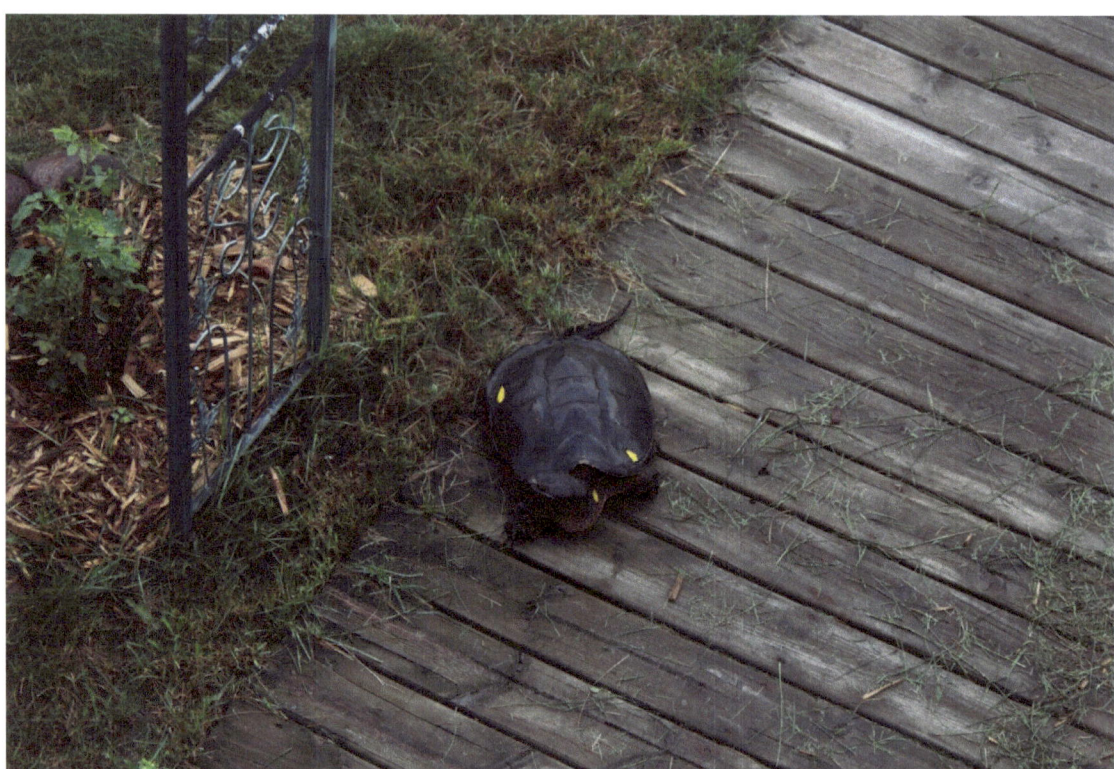

Snapping turtle on walkway to house.

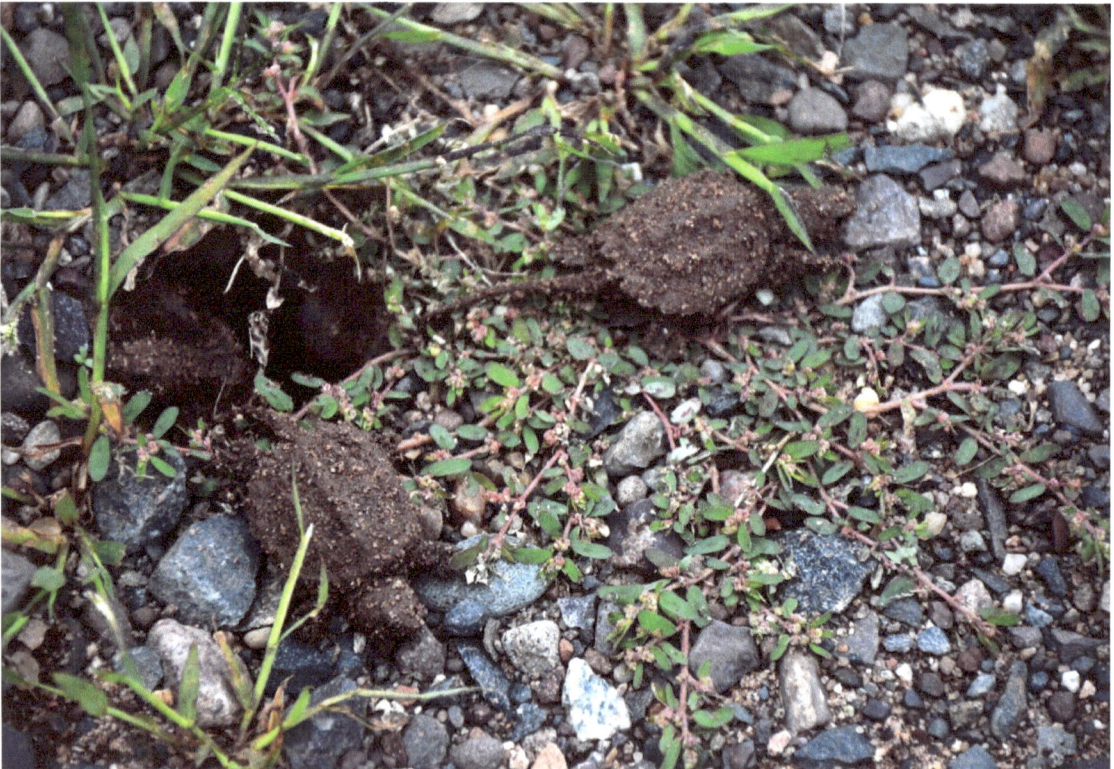

Thirty-six snapping turtle hatchlings exiting their nest in driveway.

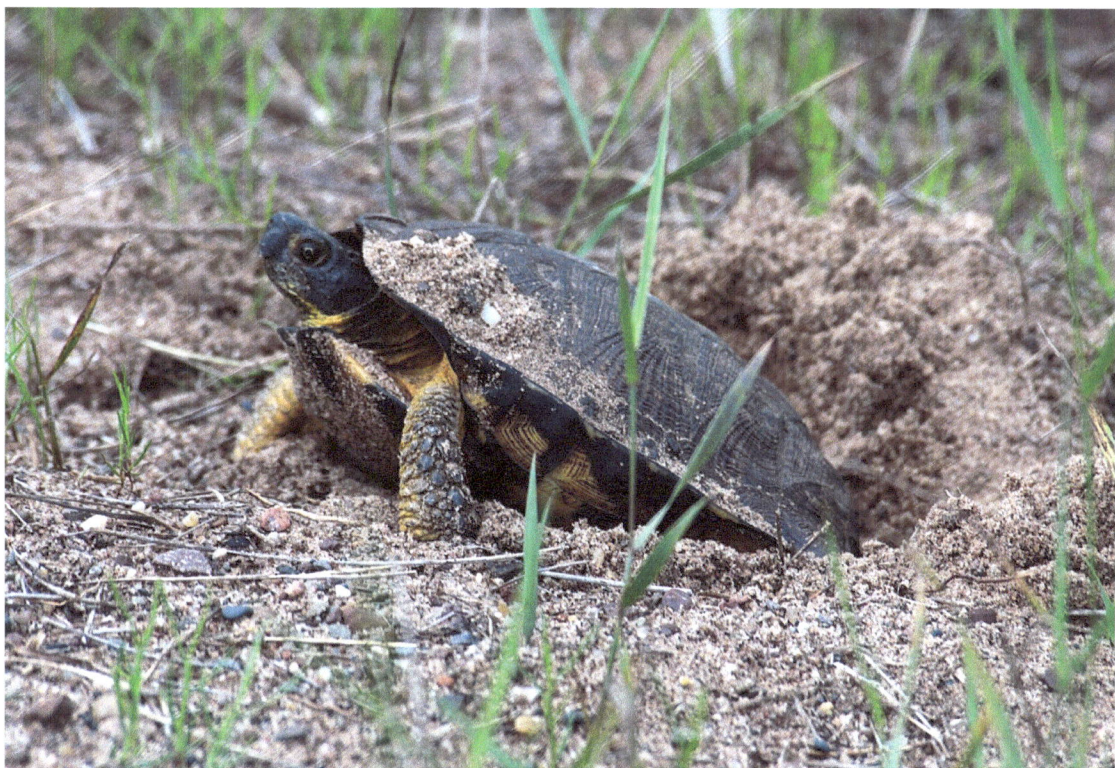

Female wood turtle laying eggs.

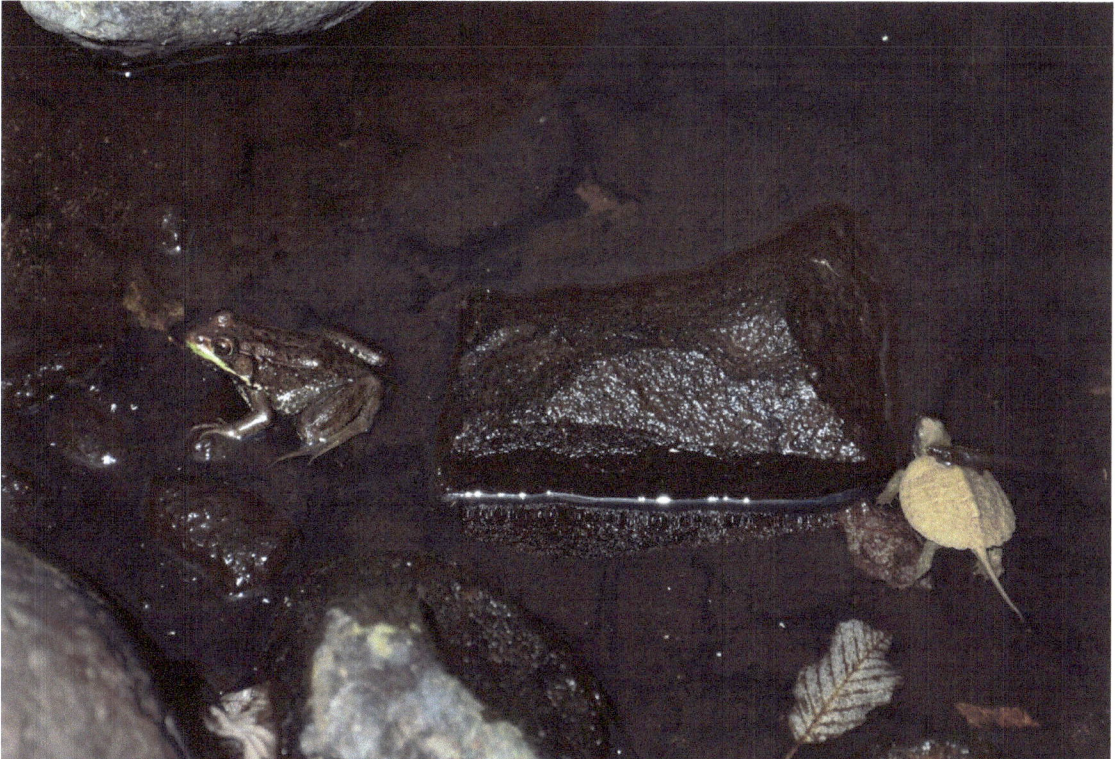

Wood frog and newly hatched wood turtle in creek near the little bridge.

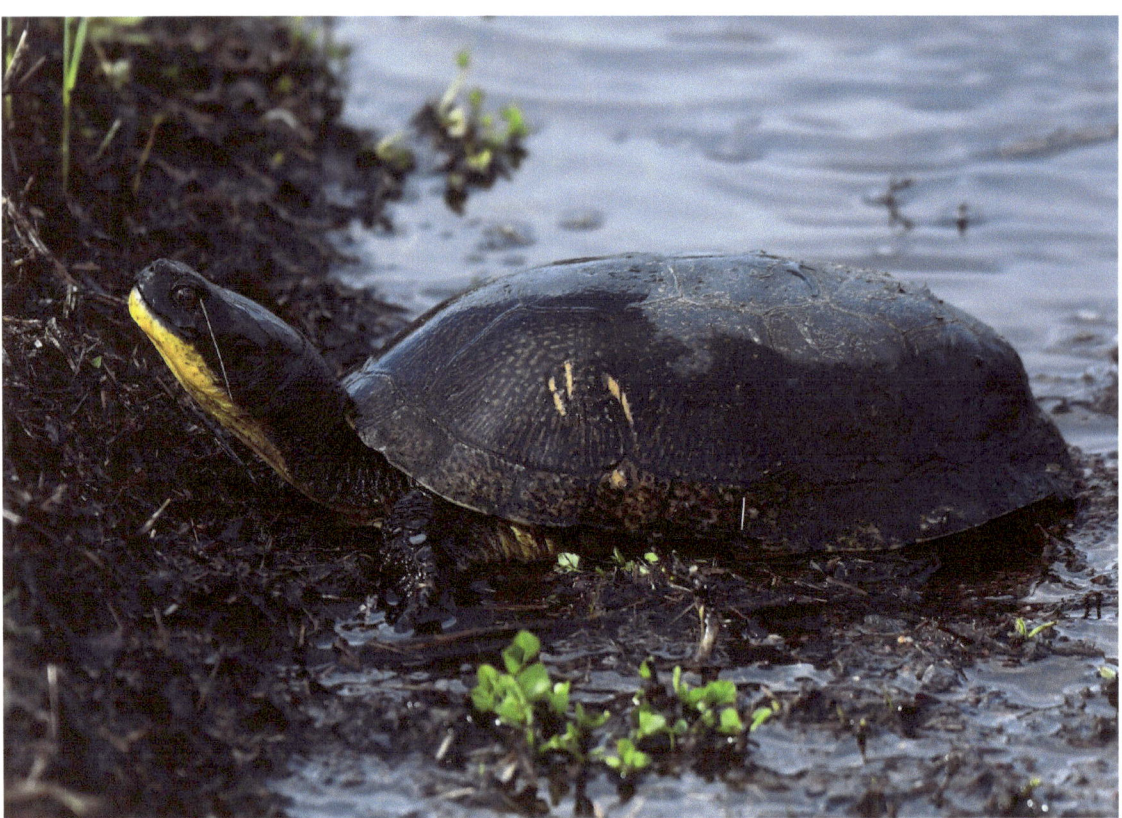

April 4, 2021 basking wood turtle just out of brumation (below); Blandings turtle (April 17).

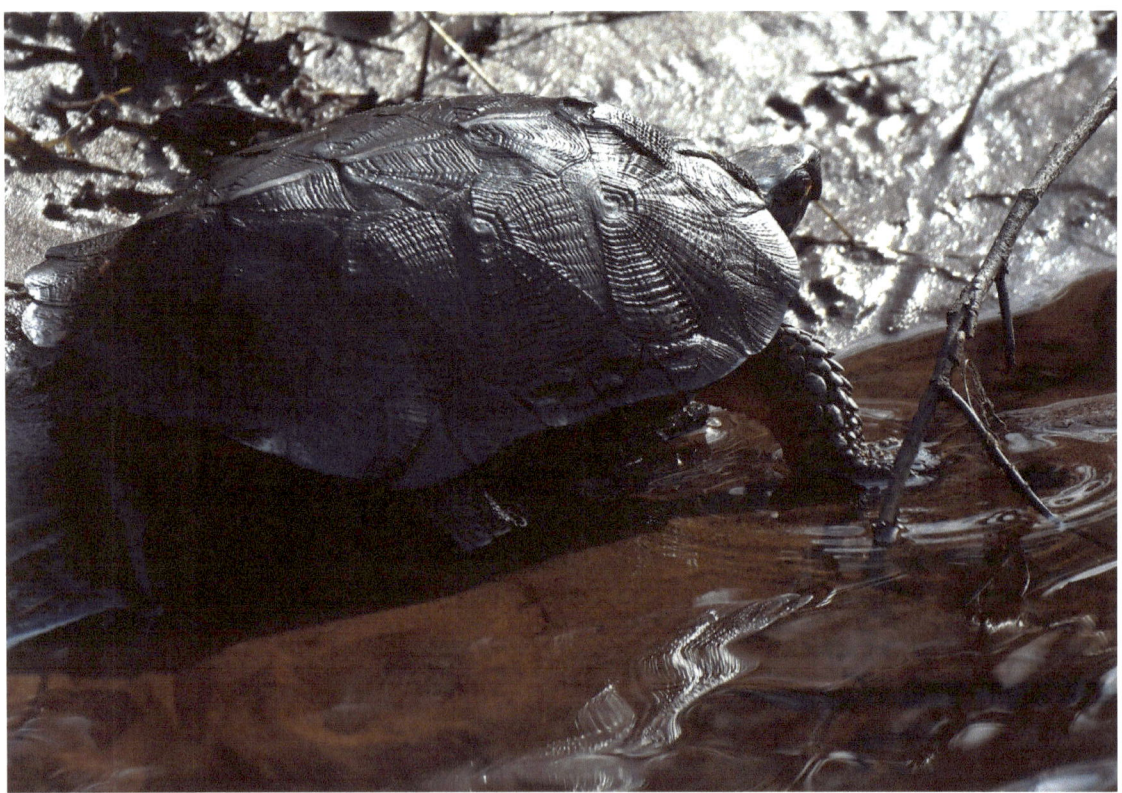

Wood turtles are now more common on the land this side of the creek. Damian cut down 70-80 year old jack pine trees over a three-year period (2015-2018) leaving stumps in the flat area along the creek, now forming a small meadow of little bluestem, asters and a few apple tree that were planted along the creek bank. Looking north toward the house, the meadow is bordered by a few American chestnut trees, young jack pine and maturing red and white pine trees. Looking behind you, following the trail to the east, the ground rises 30-40 feet, filled with lupine, butterflyweed and bergamot, skirting a sandy depression from which the sand was removed in the late 1880's to form the berm directly to your south (left), that enabled a dam to built across the creek, used in the logging days.

Walk over to the stream bank from the bench, near the large red oak, there is a log laying across the stream, just downstream. This is an original log from the days that Hay Creek was dammed in order to float pine logs down the river during the logging era. The damming process resulted in a temporary small lake where the low fresh meadow sits (see *Station 6*). Spring Creek, on the west border of the Vraniak land, was also dammed and a 'dam runner' would speed down and let each of the dam managers know when to let all the water and logs go out, simultaneously, resulting a large surge of water pushing the logs down the river to mills downstream. In subsequent years, sandy areas were quite extensive along the riverbanks (see 1938 aerial photo on next page), providing excellent habitat for turtle nesting. Now the logs are a great place where summer environmental programming can make an instructional stop and the Vraniak boys can play on warm summer days.

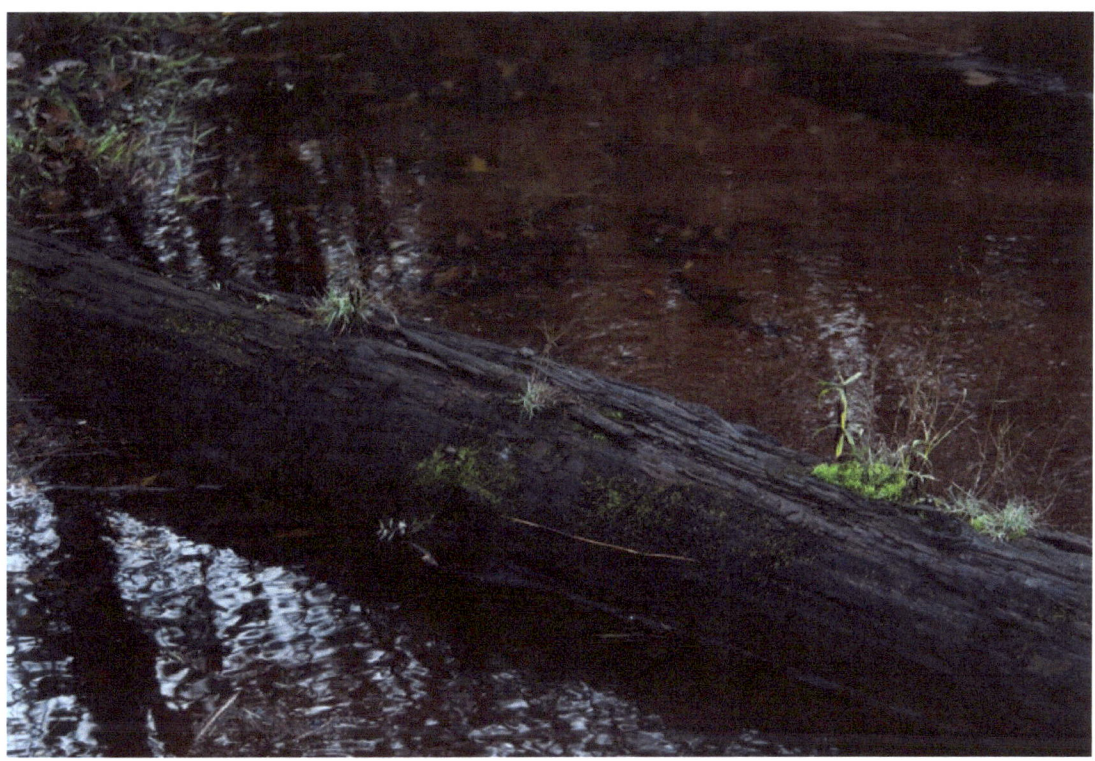

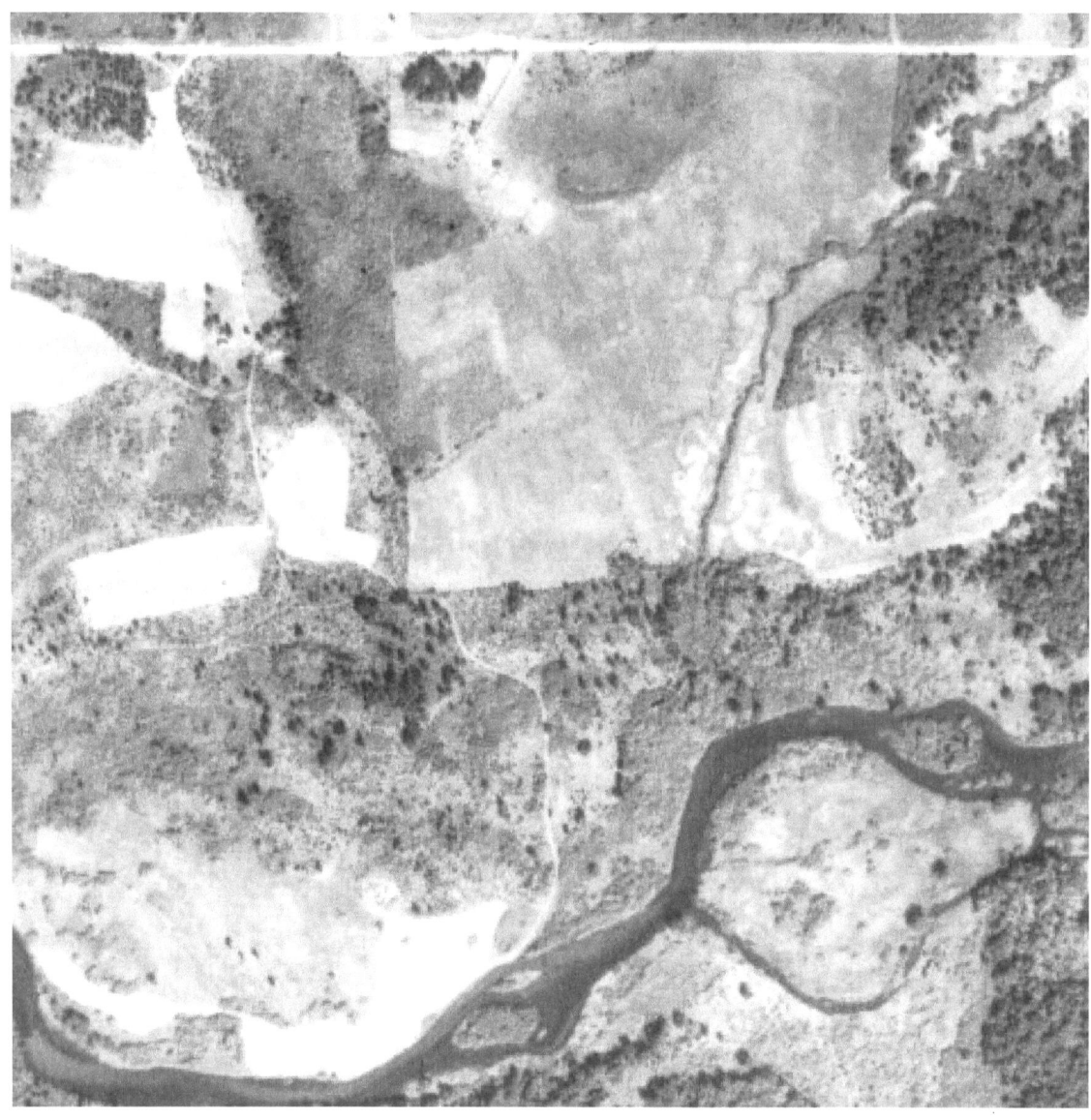

*1938 aerial photo of our land with white sandy areas all along the Namekagon river and Hay creek. Note the extensive sandy areas along the creek and river that were excellent turtle nesting sites.*

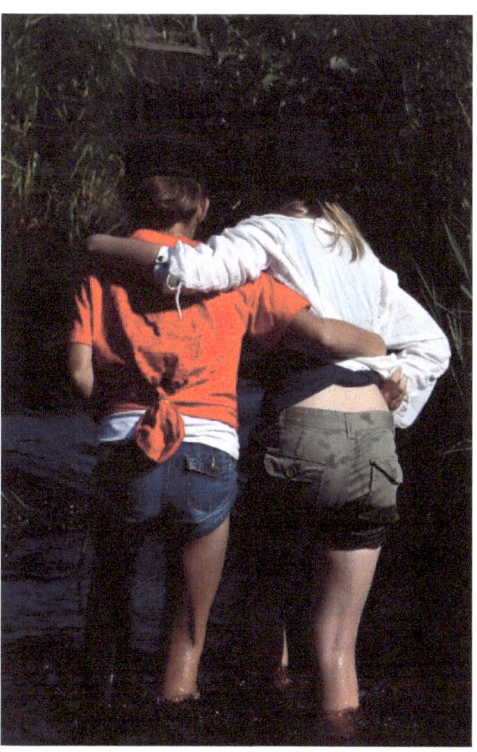

Two students (Marya and Isabelle) of our summer environmental program (2011) on the creek wading toward the log and the Namekagon River.

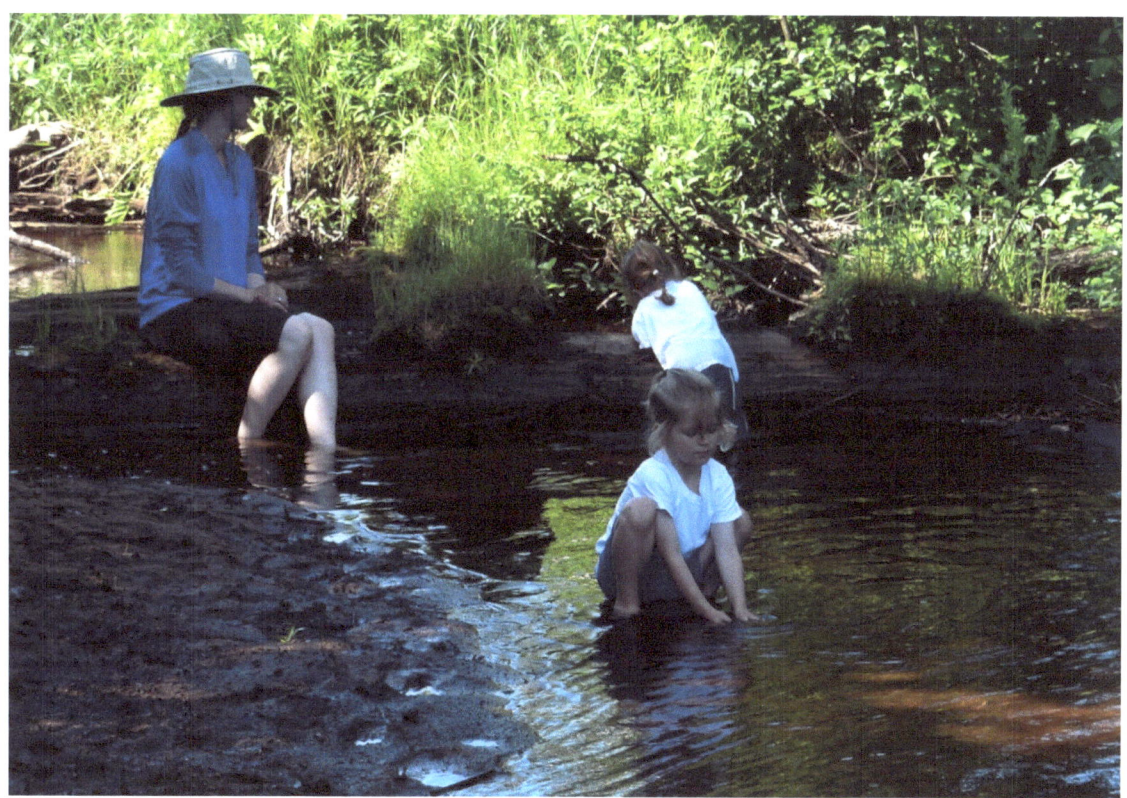

*Wife Christina and sons, Daybreak (4) and Arendaki (2), on the log in the creek (2020).*

**Family Story:** *Station 1 – Putting in a Prairie Garden (Vraniak)*

At **Station 1**, to the north toward the house is open meadow that is sandy, has short grasses, as well as native forbs such as lupine, hare bells, common milkweed, and butterflyweed, among others, as well as a lone red pine and some small oaks. Once every three years or so the creek overtops its banks and it is flooded. Historically, this grassland community was common in parts of southern Wisconsin, occurring on slightly less droughty sites than *Dry Prairie*. Today, this community type is rare because of conversion to agricultural uses or the encroachment of woody vegetation due to the lack of wildfire. *Dry-mesic Prairie* has many of the same grasses as Dry Prairie, but is dominated by taller species such as big bluestem (*Andropogon gerardii*) and Indian-grass (*Sorghastrum nutans*). Needle grass (*Stipa spartea*) and prairie drop-seed (*Sporobolus heterolepis*) may also be present. The herb component is more diverse than in Dry Prairies, as it may include many species that occur in both Dry and Mesic Prairies. Composites and legumes are particularly well-represented in relatively undisturbed stands. Soils are often somewhat sandy, either loamy sands or sandy loams. The landscape associations that can support this type include terraces on the margins of large river valleys, sandy outwash deposits, gravelly moraines, and the lower slopes of Driftless Area bluffs. As with the other tallgrass prairie communities (Mesic Prairie and Wet-mesic Prairie), well over 99% of this prairie type has been lost.

Along the creek various apples trees are planted, as well as some black cherry and plum trees (looking east and along the bank looking upstream). Some nice blueberry patches are noticeable just before the shed and up the hill, as well as maturing American chestnut trees. In 2021 many Saskatoon berry bush trees were also planted along the creek, around the shed and small meadow.

After 2015, Damian gradually cut down the remaining ninety-year old jack pines, and in 2018, the Vraniaks rolled up prairie sod by hand to make a fenced-in 24' x 24' garden in 2020. As their Huron ancestors did among the oak savanna near Georgian Bay of Lake Huron prior to 1500 and later south of Green Bay after being pushed westward into Wisconsin, the Vraniak family planted corn, beans and squash in the rich soil under the dry-mesic prairie along the creek, periodically flooded in the spring.

The growing season here (Spooner, WI Ag Station) typically lasts 136 days, about four months, from around Damian's birthday on May 19th to the end of September (26th), although in this low-lying area along the creek and river late frosts often occur in the spring. With early frosts in the fall, such a foreshortened planting and harvesting season played a significant role in the horticulture of Damian's Huron, Ojibwe, Menominee and Hočąk ancestors over the past several hundred years, especially as they moved west during the European expansion, as described by others.

Culturally, the consumption of corn and the idea of security were intertwined. As Perrot noted historically:

*The kinds of food which the savages like best and which they make the most effort to obtain are the Indian corn, kidney bean, and squash. If they are without these, they think they are fasting, no matter what abundance of meat and fish they have in their stores, the Indian corn being to them what bread is to the French.*

This need for corn prompted fleeing and desperate peoples to seek arable lands in unpromising regions where agriculture yielded only a tenuous subsistence. The skilled *Huron and Petun* horticulturalists who fled westward in the 16th and 17th centuries into the Lake Superior region found land that went well beyond the current climatic edge of the reliable 160-day growing season needed for corn agriculture. There were, however, pockets of land where microclimates suitable for agriculture existed. These areas offered 140-day growing seasons that made agriculture risky, but possible. At each of these pockets along southern Lake Superior and northern Lake Michigan – *Chequamegon, Keweenaw, Michilimackinac, and Sault St. Marie* - refugees eventually settled. Farther south, at Green Bay, the line of refugee villages hugged almost exactly the edges of the 160-day growing season. Because the refugees lived along the margins of the lands where corn could be growing, crop failures were a constant possibility. Agriculture, particularly at Chequamegon and Michilimackinac, ran great risks of late-spring and early-fall frosts. Repeated losses of corn crops at Michilimackinac in the 1690s help to prompt the eventual abandonment of that place by the *Ottawas* and the *Huron-Petuns*. At Green Bay harvests were more certain, but the harvest failed there in 1675. It appears, too, that crop failures like those at Michilimackinac later in the century may also have a occurred at Green Bay, where the French intendant *Raudot* claimed that corn longer provided much security to the *Fox, Mascoutens, and Kickapoos.*

With the precariousness of growing precious corn, in the years when crops or fisheries failed, only hunting and gathering stood between the *Algonquians* and starvation. The hunters clustering on overcrowded lands, whose major attraction were fisheries that the hunters themselves did not efficiently exploit. Corn and fish sustained large settlements, and around the settlements hunters came for trade and protection. Around the horticultural villagers who relied heavily on the fisheries, therefore, were other villagers, some horticultural, some not, who relied more heavily on the hunt. This pattern predated the fur trade, but fur trade reinforced it.

This combination of marginal agriculture, sometimes precarious fishing, and the clustering of hunters for defense and trade, set the stage for environmental disaster. As hunters depleted game around the refugee centers, hunger and famine ensued when the fisheries or the corn harvest failed. *Pierre Esprit Radisson* and the *Huron-Petuns* endured such a famine. Five hundred died, and hunger continued into the summer of 1661, when *Father Menard* died trying to reach the *Huron-Petuns*. In 1670 the Jesuits found the *Potawatomis*, and other tribes of Green Bay proper, pinched with hunger. The *Mascoutens*, *Fox*, and other outlying villagers complained of hunger during the 1670s. Even in the best years, the surplus store from horticulture was relatively small. In 1671, *Father Allouez* claimed that a family with 10 or 12 bags of corn considered itself wealthy. The *Potawatomis* might strive to fill their cabins with herring, but by late winter the fish were gone and they anxiously awaited the coming of the sturgeon.

Winter became a time of particular horror. Those groups that did not fish extensively regularly departed on winter hunts, but when corn and fish were abundant, the fishing peoples preferred to remain in their villages taking what game they could obtain nearby. By staying home they avoided the long winter hunts that had become the most dangerous point in the refugee subsistence cycle. To embark on a winter hunt was to leave stored supplies and risk starvation if hunting did not go well.

The fisheries tended to be more reliable then agriculture because the Algonquians were not at the margin of the fisheries but at their centers. All the great concentrations of refugee populations on the Great Lakes were located at the best fishing sites on Lake superior and Lake Michigan. Michilimackinac, the longest lived of these 17th an 18th century settlements, was, in Algonquian terms, the "native country" of the fish themselves. Yet fishing also remained a precarious endeavor that demanded precise skills and a suitable technology that not all refugees possessed. Storms during spawning season, or a winter and weak ice, could doom a fishery. Fisheries at their most successful could provide only seasonal abundance. Algonquin techniques of drying could preserve the fall catch of herring and whitefish through the winter, but the yields of the spring runs of sturgeon could not be preserved long during the warm and humid summers.

In terms of horticulture, it was not so different for Damian's maternal grandmother, Alice, who went to an Indian boarding school after her mother had been murdered, who married his grandfather (out of the *Decora* lineage of *Glory of the Morning*, female chief of the Hočąk Nation), and then had fifteen children to raise, including some add-ons like Damian and his brothers after their father died when he was four years old ...

Excerpts from pp 213-215 **Travailler** – *A 400-year Inter-generational Journey of Grandmothers, Mothers and Daughters Volume 4: The Metis of Winnipeg, Pembina and Grand Forks (2019)*

**"Joy:**
With all the children who were in the household and all the extra people who came and went, some stayed for a while, as did the grandchildren. Everyone had a job to do and just did it. No one had to remind them. As Jane says, they did not work hard, they just all helped. June could remember how at the house 'down below' they had a wind generator to change the batteries in the basement so they could listen to the radio. Life was different for the older ones, who lived without electricity, where the younger ones always had it. *Running water was put in the home just a few years before Alice died [1967].* ...

***Snooks*** *(as told to Joy):*

Where Mike and Marge are now ('Down Across'), down below the hill, the basement was full of potatoes and cabbage was pulled out, roots and all, hung upside down to be used later. Sauerkraut was made in barrels, covered and held down with a heavy rock on top. Some meat was salted and some was smoked. Some meat was canned and if it was cold weather, some was left in the shed and was used as needed. When a pig was butchered, the head was given to Luella Denniger. She made excellent head cheese and then would share it with the family. Things were canned in two-quart jars, not just one-quart jars, because of the large family. As to what was canned, anything and everything – green beans, corn, tomatoes, boysenberries, pin cherries, peaches, pears, blackberries, etc.  Mom boiled up cream and made curds, like for cottage cheese. She had it in a sack and hung it from the clothesline to drain.  …

***Nan:***

Most of John and Alice's lives were spent providing the staples for their large family. Each year John put in a large garden to sustain them through the winter. Alice was a "Domestic Engineer" in her own right. She canned from three to four hundred quarts of vegetables and fruit each summer. The fruit consisted of blueberries, blackberries, dewberries, etc., whatever nature provided that year.  …

***Jane:***

Yes, Mom [Alice] did can some in two-quart jars. She used a boiler (like a tub, but made oblong) with a cover. About six to eight two-quart jars would fit at one time. Quart jars she could double up on. Thin slats of wood were put on the bottom of the boiler and in between layers of quarts. Mom had to boil them on her wood stove for one to three hours, depending on what she was canning at the time. Dad [John Waggoner] had different gardens, the biggest that I remember was out behind the barn on the 'down below' farm. There was also a large one up on the hill, about one acre. Mom and Dad grew potatoes, vegetables, all kinds of corn, etc. Mom canned hundreds of jars of everything. We also picked blueberries, blackberries, raspberries, pin cherries and chokecherries to make lots of jam. …"

Damian's grandmother's life was really not so different than the life of her Huron great grandmother, Catherine Annennontha (1648-1709), who married a third French husband after the first two had died (Durand, Couterier, Lafond), and raised six of her own and three step-children. (*See Travailler: Volume 1 – The Huron of Georgian Bay and Quebec*; Vraniak, 2020). And so it is that Damian helped to raise his youngest brother in his family-of-origin after his mother re-married, after the death of *her* husband. Then Damian finished raising his first two children alone when he unexpectedly lost *his* first wife. He completed raising a step-daughter when he re-married ten years later. Finally, now in his fourth family, he is in the process of raising two young sons (now 5 and 3 years of age). All of his children grew up on the Springbrook land, and now the two youngest are learning the gardening and family-caregiving in much the same manner as did his and their ancestors …

30

## Ancestral Traditional Stories: *Three Sisters Gardening (Iroquoian)*

The *Wendat* (Huron) have several accounts of how life and sustenance came to be:

### Ancient One - *Aataentsic*

There once were two worlds. One of the worlds was up in the sky. The other world was the Earth. At that time the Earth was covered with water. The only beings that lived on the Earth were those that could live in or on the water. The sky world, on the other hand, was inhabited by beings that could walk on land. Some of these beings were like humans. These people would pick the corn from one patch of corn to get their food. Each day they would take corn from the stalks. One day, a young woman decided to cut the corn stalks, instead of simply plucking the corn. Once the corn stalks were cut down they could never grow again. Some of her brothers became angry and threw the young woman down through a hole in the sky. In her hands were the corn stalks she had cut down, as well as beans, squash and tobacco.

As the young woman fell through the sky, some of the water birds looked up. They were ducks, herons and loons. They decided to help the falling woman. They flew up and surrounded her and were able to cushion her fall. However, their wings were getting tired of holding her. Great Turtle arrived and told them to put her on his back. He said he would hold her. Toad arrived and said he would dive down into the water and get some earth from the bottom. When he came back up, he had a mouthful of dirt and he spat it out on the turtle's back. He told the young woman to sprinkle the dirt everywhere she walked.

As the young woman walked round the turtle's back, she planted the corn, beans and squash everywhere she went. However, the woman was lonely. One day she discovered twin boys. These boys grew very quickly. One of the brothers created all of the living things on earth, including humans. The other brother tried to do the same thing and made monkeys instead. Each brother made different things. The first brother made everything that human beings could use. The other brother made things that would harm the things created by the first brother. The Wendat refer to the woman who fell from the sky as *Aataentsic*, meaning "*ancient one.*"

### Sky Woman

It was said that the earth began when "Sky Woman" who lived in the upper world peered through a hole in the sky and fell through to an endless sea. The animals saw her coming, so they took the soil from the bottom of the sea and spread it onto the back of a giant turtle to provide a safe place for her to land. This "Turtle Island" is now what we call North America.

Sky woman had become pregnant before she fell. When she landed, she gave birth to a daughter. When the daughter grew into a young woman, she also became pregnant (by the West wind). She died while giving birth to twin boys. Sky Woman buried her daughter in the "new earth." From her grave grew three sacred plants—corn, beans, and squash. These plants provided food for her sons, and later, for all of humanity. These special gifts ensured the survival of the Iroquois people.

<u>The Three Sisters & the Stranger</u>

Once upon a time there were three sisters who lived together in a field. These sisters were quite different from one another in their size, shape and way of dressing. One of the three was a little sister, so young that she could only crawl at first, and if she wanted to stand up she had to twine herself around her eldest sister. This sister wore velvet green with delicate tendril ribbons. The second of the three sisters, wore a frock of bright yellow and had a way of running off across the field when the sun shone and the soft wind blew in her face. The third sister was the eldest. She was always standing very straight and tall above the other sisters trying to guard them. There was only one way in which the three sisters were alike. They loved one another very much and were never separated. They were sure that they wouldn't be able to live apart.

After a while, a stranger came to the sister's field. It was a little Iroquois boy. He was as straight as an arrow and as fearless as the eagle that circled his head far above in the sky. He knew the way of talking to the birds and the small brothers of the earth, the mouse, the groundhog, the chipmunk, squirrel and fox. The three sisters were very interested in this little Iroquois boy. They watched him fit his arrow in his bow, saw him carve a bowl with his knife and wondered where he went at night.

Late that summer, the youngest sister in green velvet who couldn't stand up without the help of her big sister, disappeared. Her sisters mourned for her until the fall, but she did not return.

Once again the little Iroquois boy came to the three sister's field. He came to gather reeds at the edge of the nearby stream to make arrow shafts. The two sisters who were left watched him and gazed at him with wonder at the prints of his moccasins marking his trail to the field. That night the second of the sisters disappeared. This time it was the sister who dressed in brilliant yellow and always wanted to run off across the field. She left no mark of her going but it may have been that she set her feet in the moccasin tracks of the little Iroquois boy.

Now there was only one sister left. Tall and straight she stood in the field not once bowing her head with sorrow, but it seemed to her that she could not bear to live in her field alone. The days grew shorter and the night grew colder. Her green shawl faded and grew thin and old. Her hair once long and golden was now brown and tangled by the wind. Day and night she sighed for her sisters to return to her, but they did not hear her. Her voice when she tried to call them was low and sad like the wind.

32

But one day when it was the season of the final harvest, the little Iroquois boy heard the crying of the third sister. He felt sorry for her so he took her in his arms and carried her to the lodge of his father and mother. Oh what a surprise awaited her! Her two lost sisters were there in the lodge of the little Iroquois boy, safe and very glad to see her. They had been curious about the boy and they had gone home with him to see how and where he lived. They had liked his warm longhouse so well that they decided to stay there for the cold winter. And they were doing all they could to be useful.

The little sister in green, now quite grown up, was helping to keep the dinner pot full. The sister in yellow sat on the shelf drying herself for she planned to fill the dinner pot later. The third sister joined them, ready to grind some meal for the Iroquois family's bread. Ever since then the three sisters spend their spring and summers in the field together, and their winters in the longhouse, helping to feed the family of the little Iroquois boy. And the three have never been separated since.

Every child of today should know these three sisters and need them just as much as the little Iroquois boy did. For the little sister is the bean who needs the eldest sister to keep her from crawling along the ground. The second sister is the squash, who has bright yellow flowers and tends to run away across the field. The eldest sister is the corn. Her kernels can be dried and ground up to make flour for bread. When the corn beans and squash are eaten, they provide a very nutritious meal with everything a person needs to be healthy.

The Three Sisters

There once was a family of a mother, father and three sisters. The parents worked hard at providing for the family, but constantly had to beg the daughters for help. They also had to continually stop them from arguing and fighting. The three sisters were different from each other and also unique in their own way. The eldest was tall and slender with long, silky, shiny hair, the youngest was small but muscular and attractive, and the middle sister was average in height and looks but was beautiful in her giving nature. For whatever reason, although they loved one another as sisters, they would disagree on any little thing and be distracted from doing any work because of these quarrels. The parents tried and tried to get the sisters to help in the garden and help with the chores. When working together they would always fight; when apart they would complain about the others. The work wasn't getting done and the parents were worried that if this kept up they wouldn't make it through another winter. It was planting time and the work had to be done, but as usual the sisters were too busy fighting. The parents needed help, and it was given to them, but not as they imagined. As the sisters argued in the field they were transformed into three plants. The first a long, tall plant with silk tassel-like hair, the second a broad-leafed plant low to the ground, and the third a medium-height plant with gentle vines. The plants, of course, were corn, squash, and beans, the three sisters.

The following photos at and about *Station 1* show the natural complementary relations possible between prairie restoration, sustainable horticulture and free-ranging wild life, not so much different than Damian's Huron ancestors experienced. Indeed, adding greater edge to habitat transitions, adding in other seasonal stables such as several apple and chestnut trees, planting Saskatoon berry bushes and high bush blueberries, as well opening up closed forest to meadows and grasslands that favor native blueberries, high bush cranberries, chokecherry trees and serviceberries, while doing small scale gardening, can increase biodiversity to an amazing degree.

There is now greater variety of bird life, including more frequent visitation by the falcons (kestrels and merlins). Rodents, rabbits and deer have increased bringing in more raptors (buteos and accipiters), and ground-based predators (bobcat, fox, coyote, wolves, weasels, fisher and badger). And, of course, with the greater floristic diversity of several hundred prairie and savanna forb and grass species, comes a flourishing variety of insect life (ants, flies, bees, beetles, wasps, moths and butterflies), giving birds and bats a diversity of tasty treats upon which to feed and sustain themselves.

That diversity of life, with the periodic flooding, provided the Vraniak family with rich soil excellent for small scale, sustainable horticulture, as depicted in the following photos.

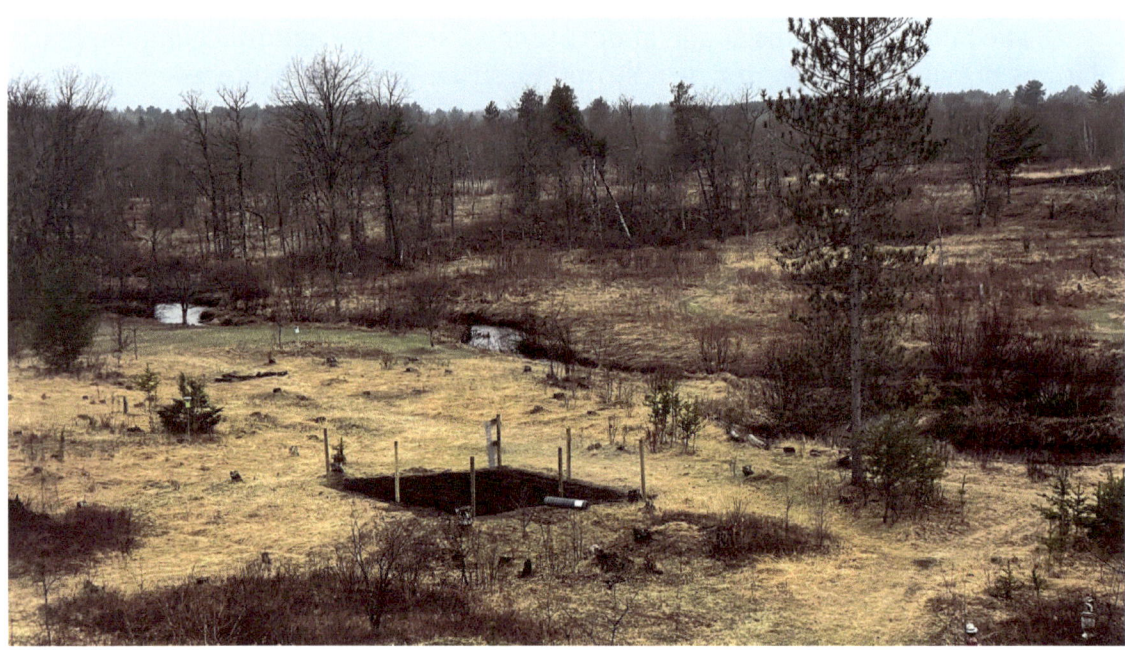

Early Spring 2020 garden preparation in the prairie soil along the creek flood plain.

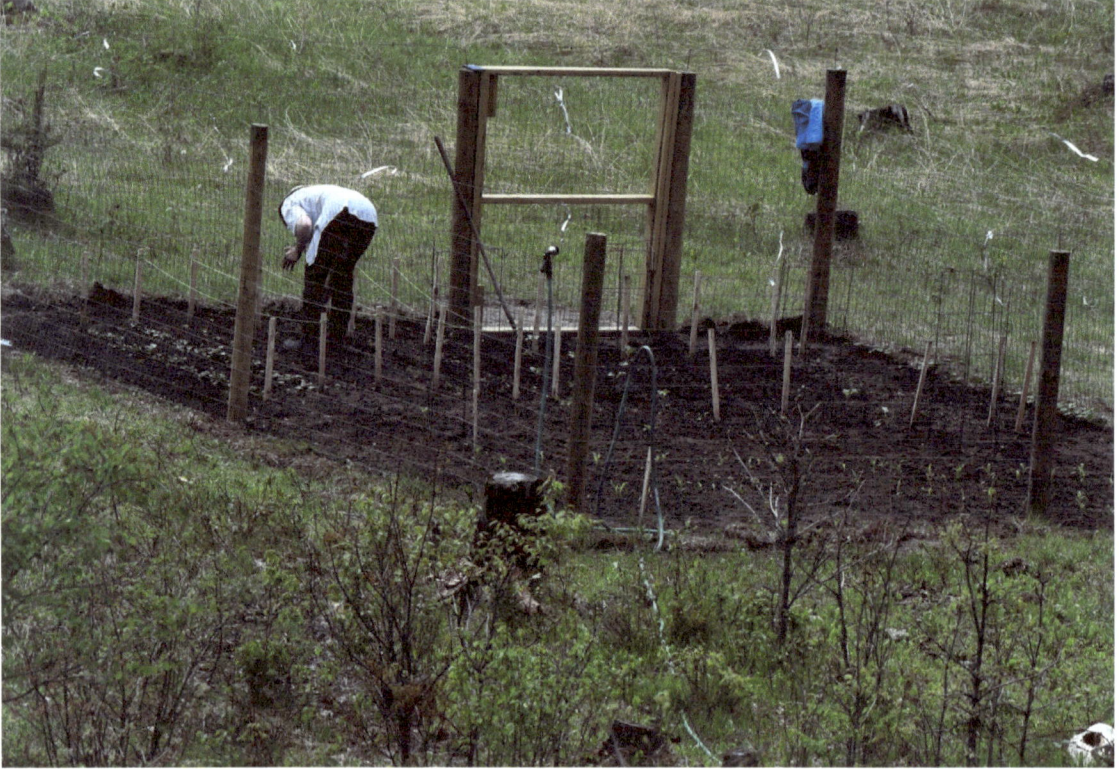

Spring Planting 2020.

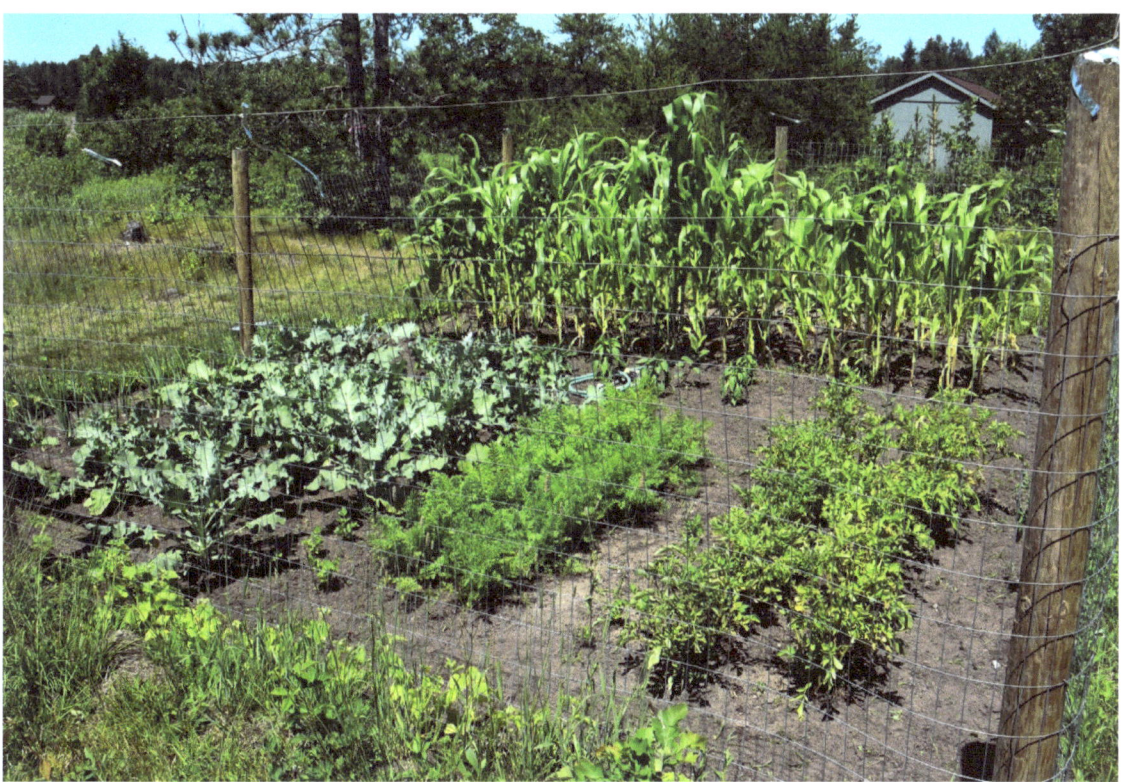

Summer 2020.

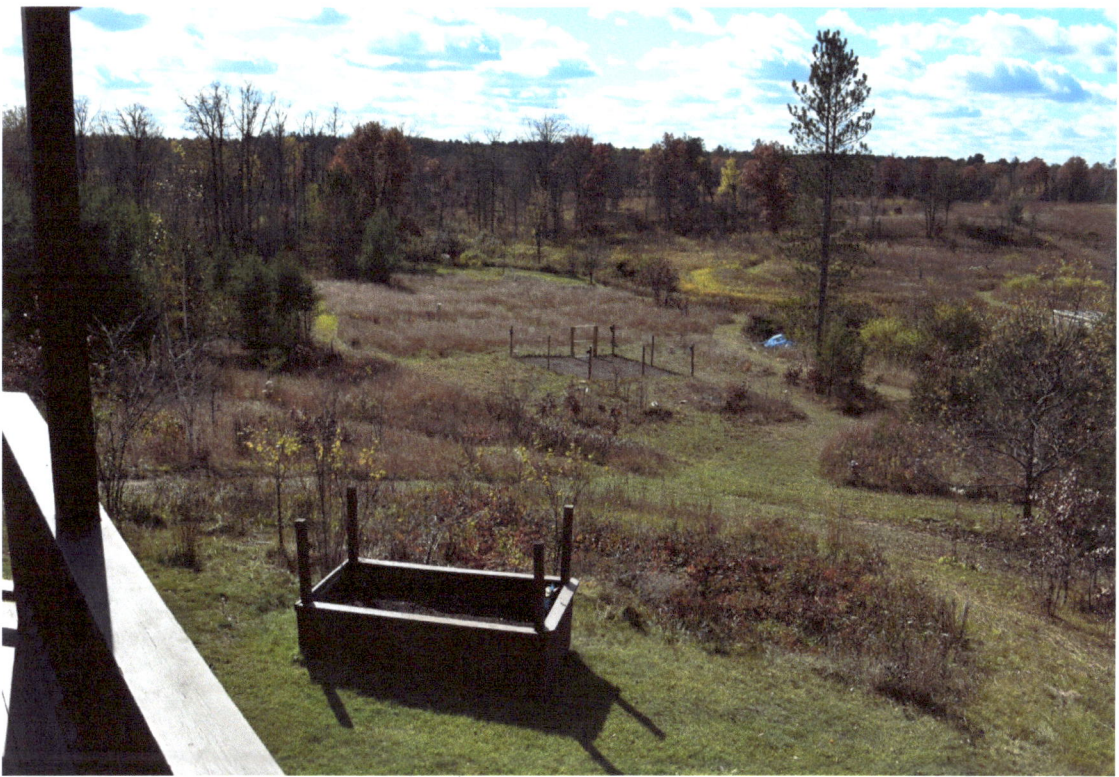

Fall 2020, overlooking raised tomato bed and prairie garden nestled in the meadow.

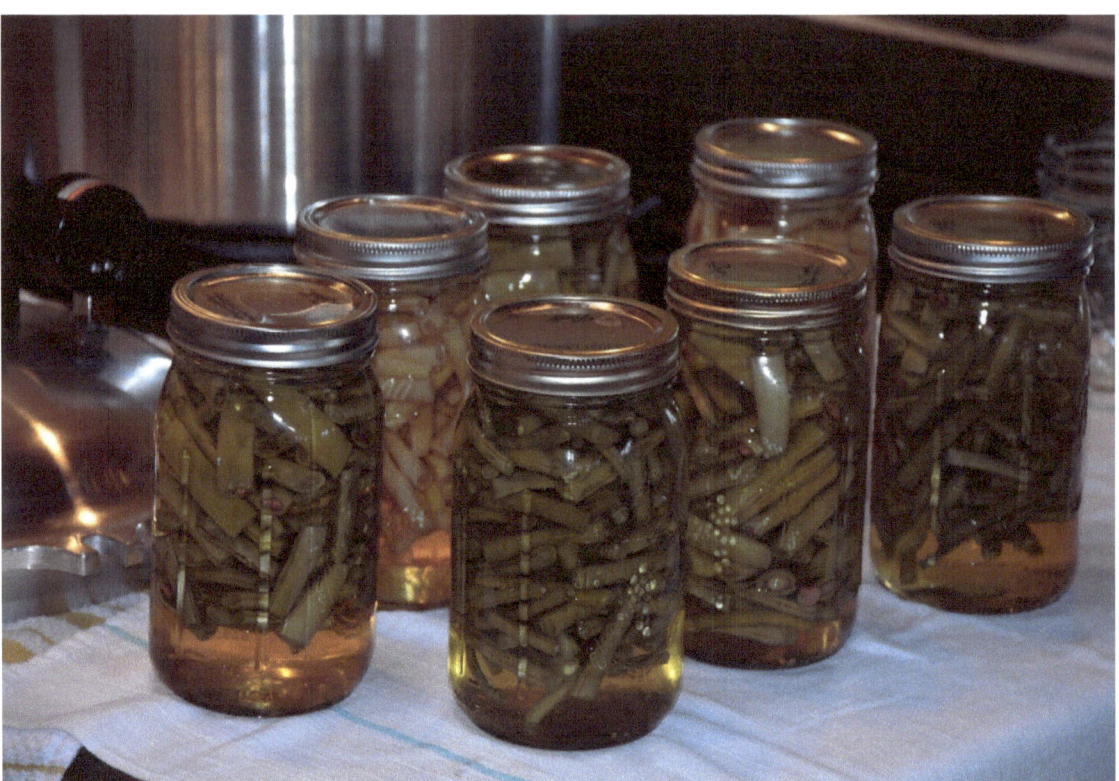

Canning beans and tomatoes.

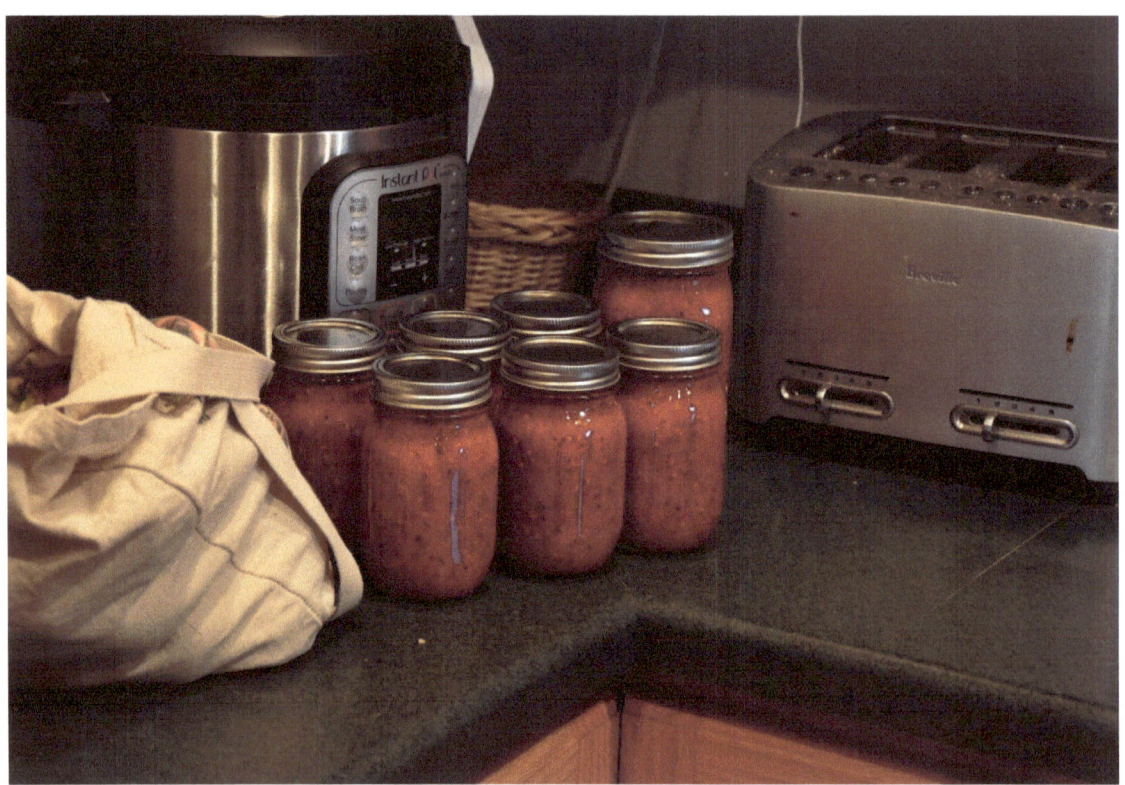

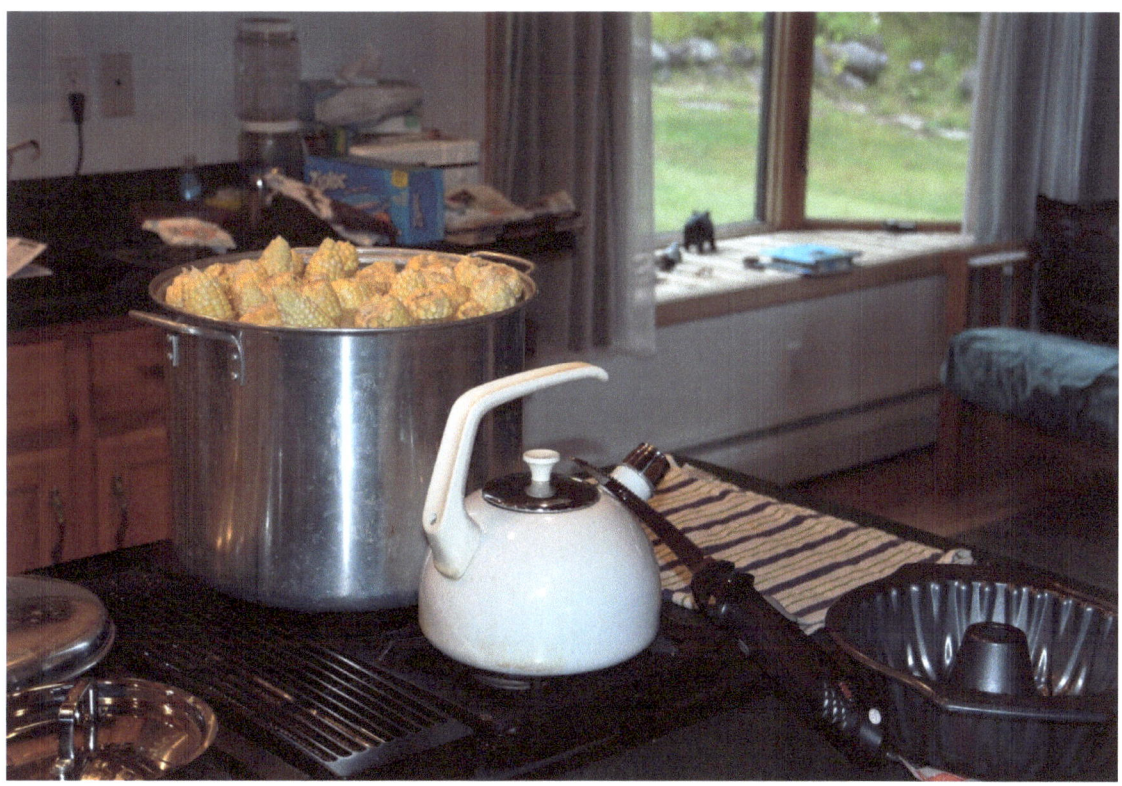

Putting up corn.

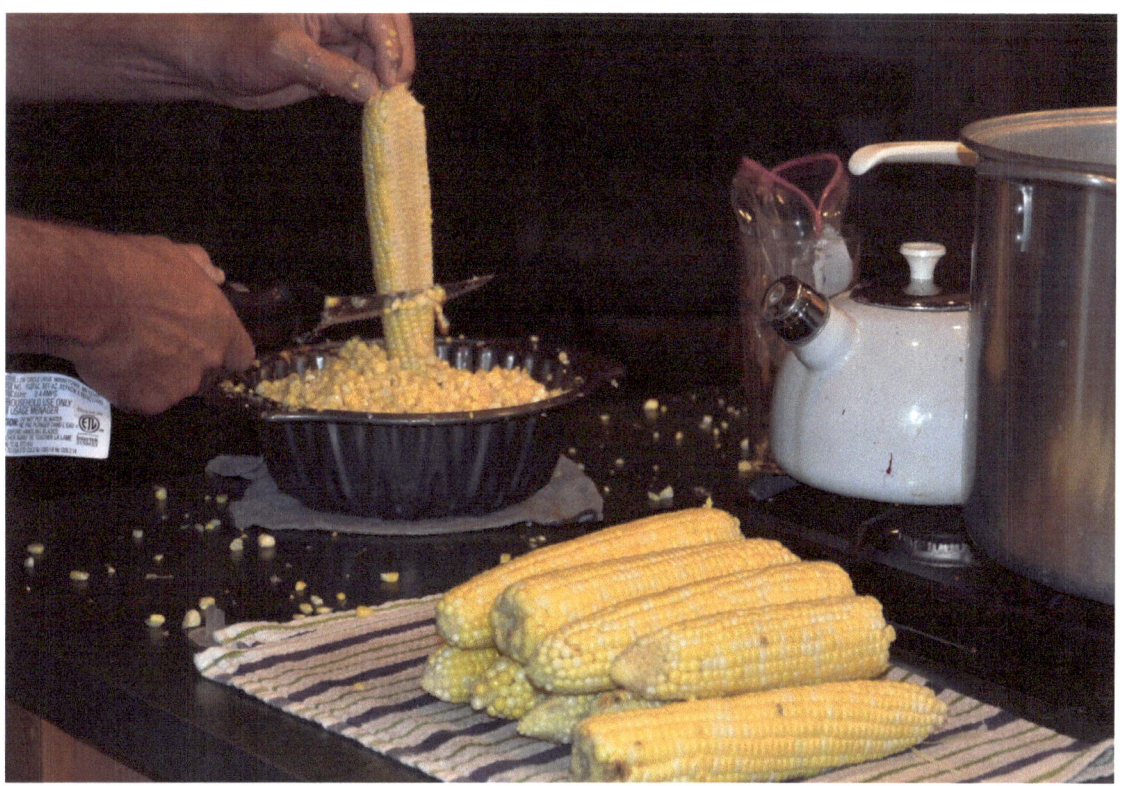

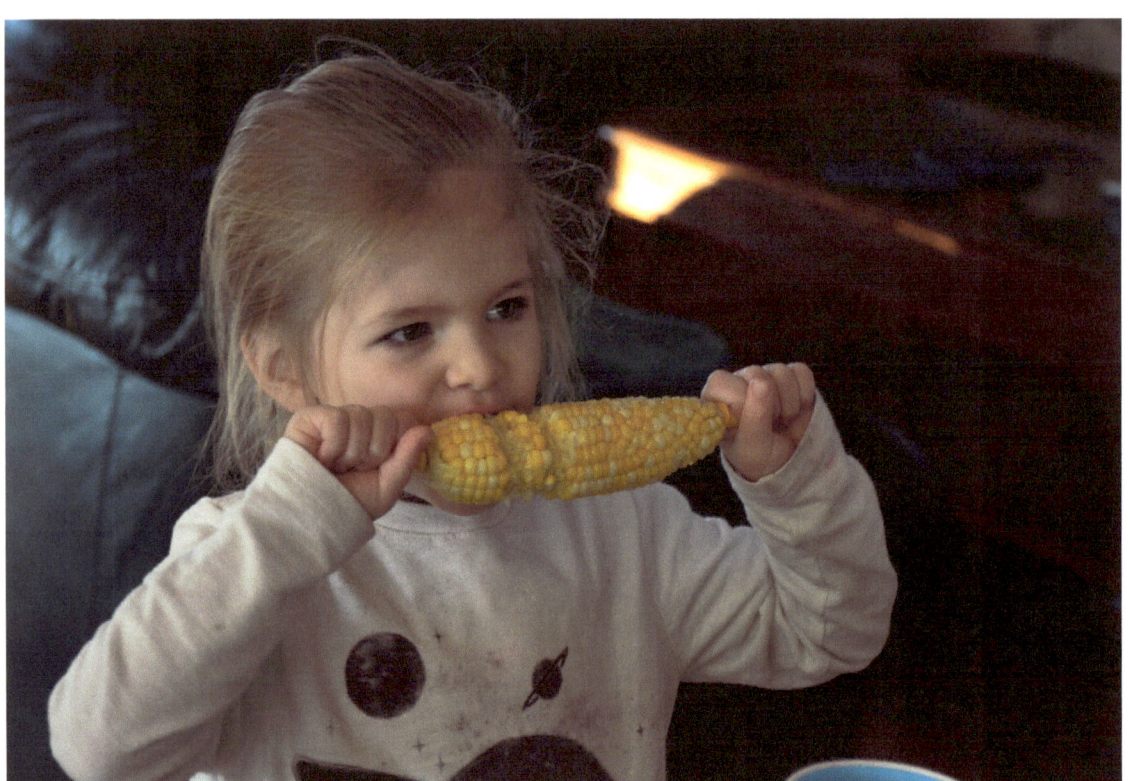

Eating and canning.

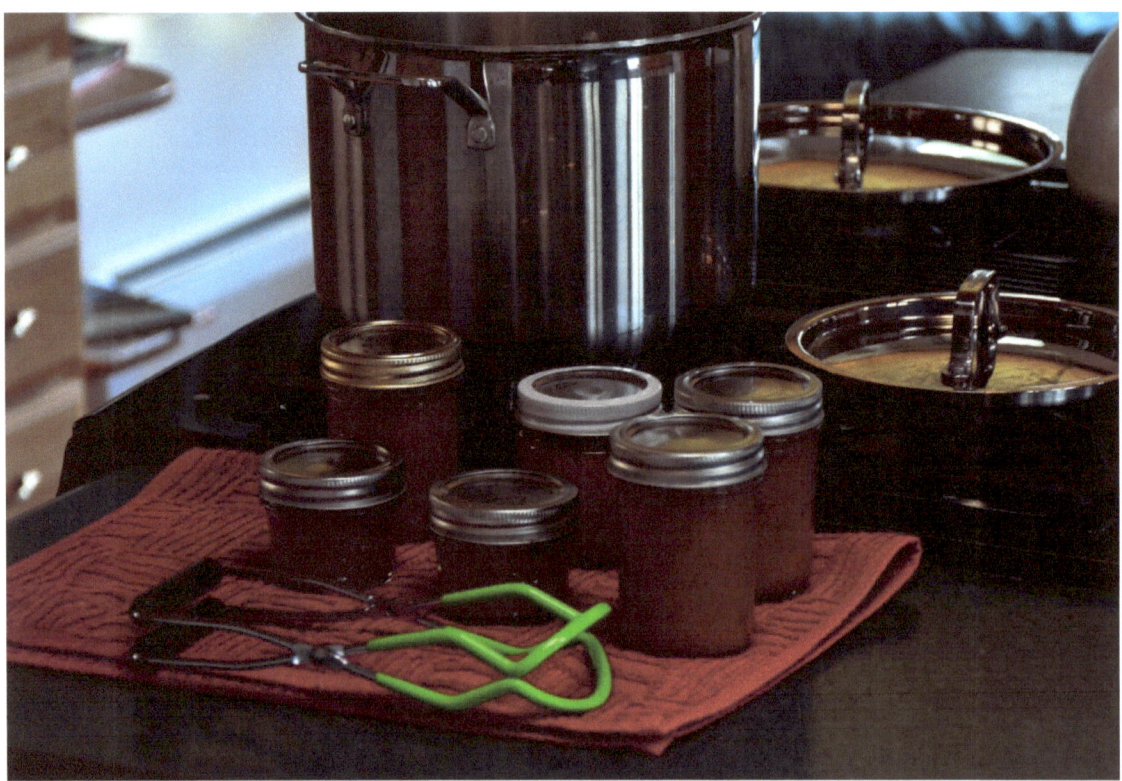

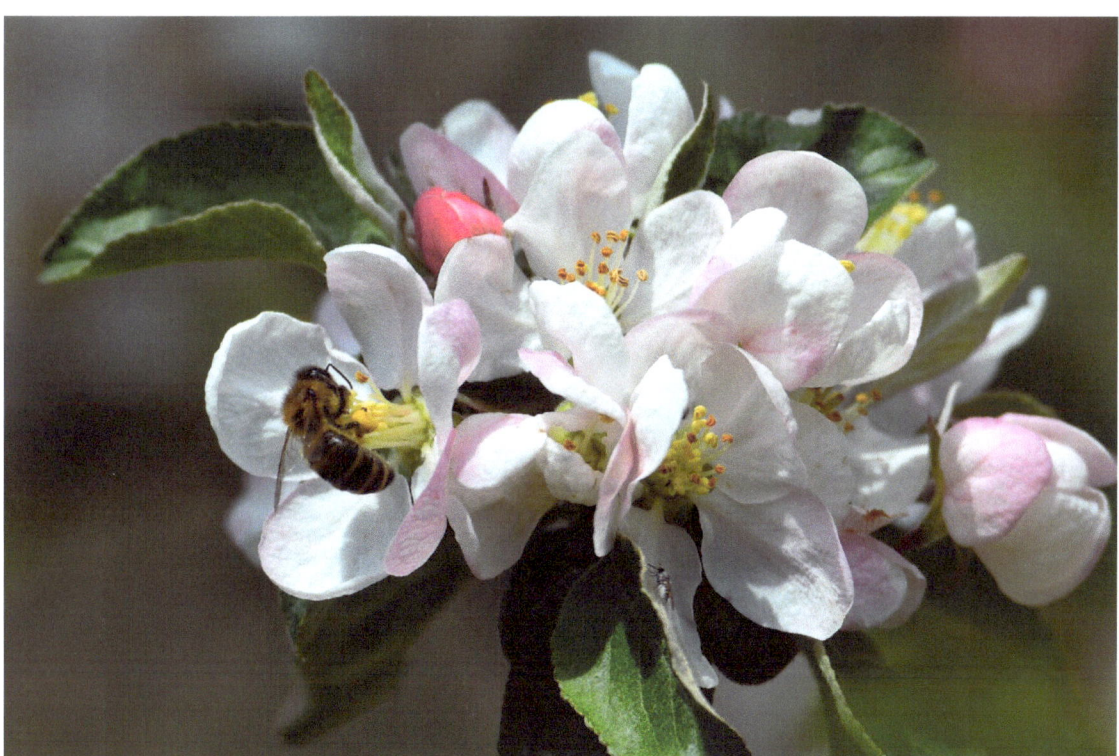

Apple blossoms and apples.

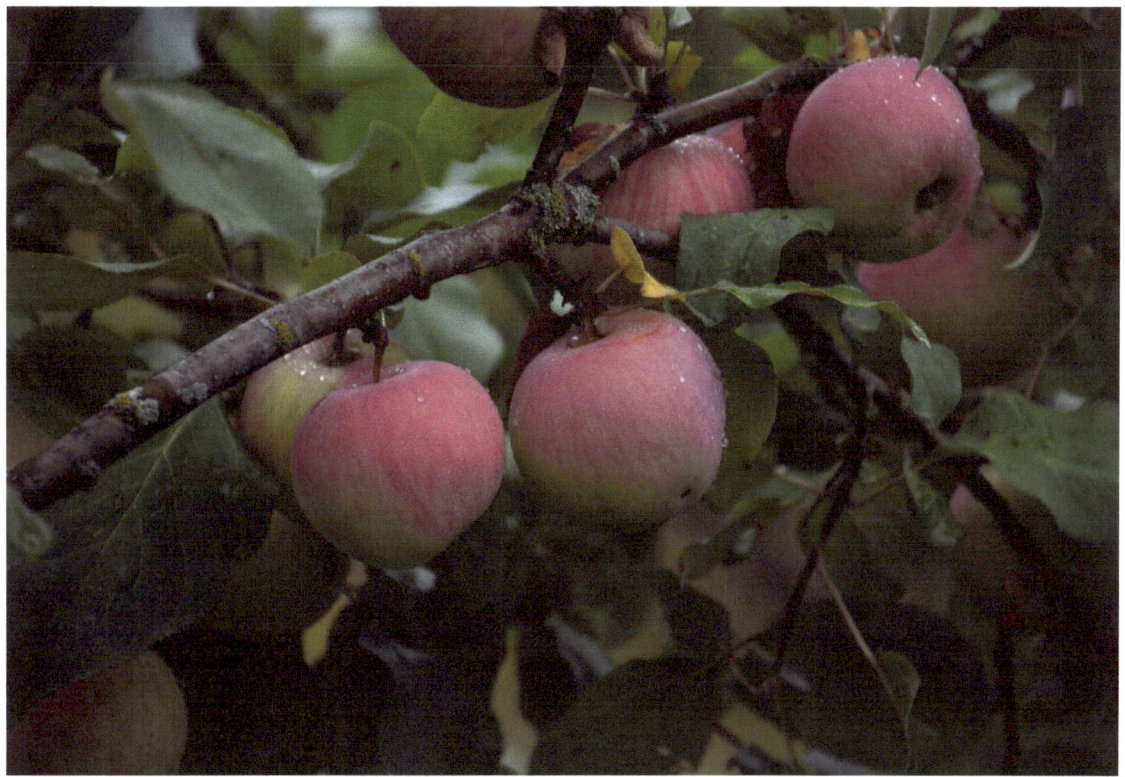

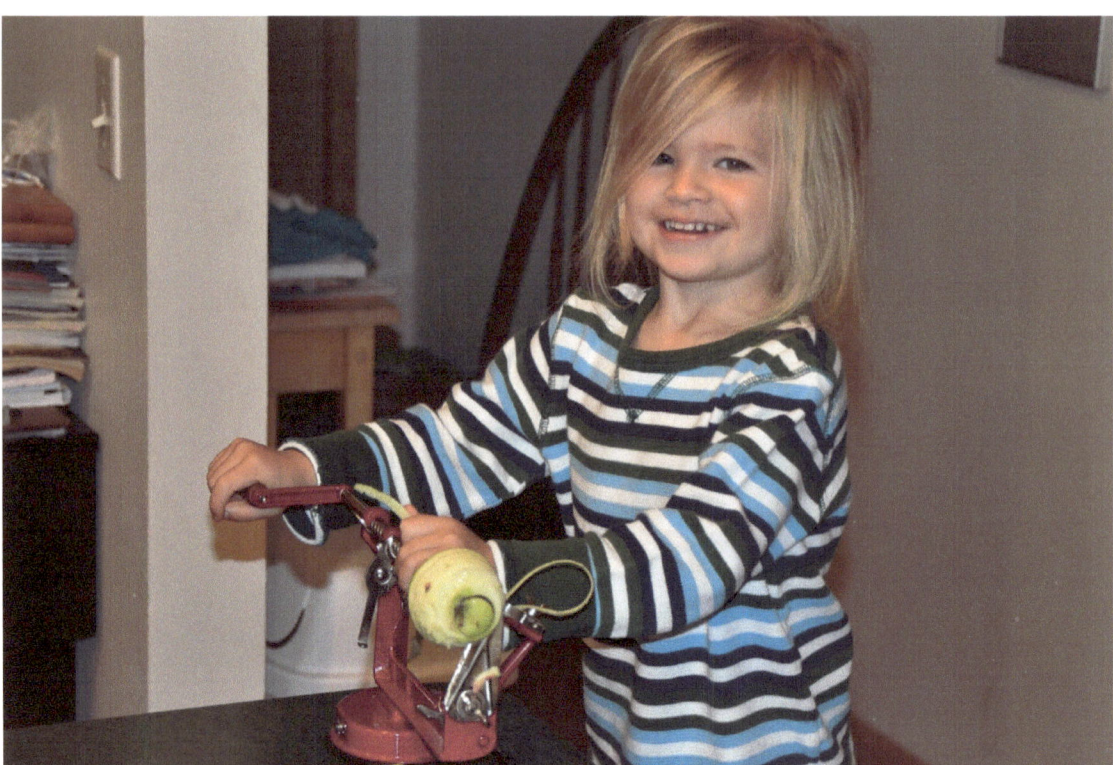

Processing apples for applesauce ... and apple pies.

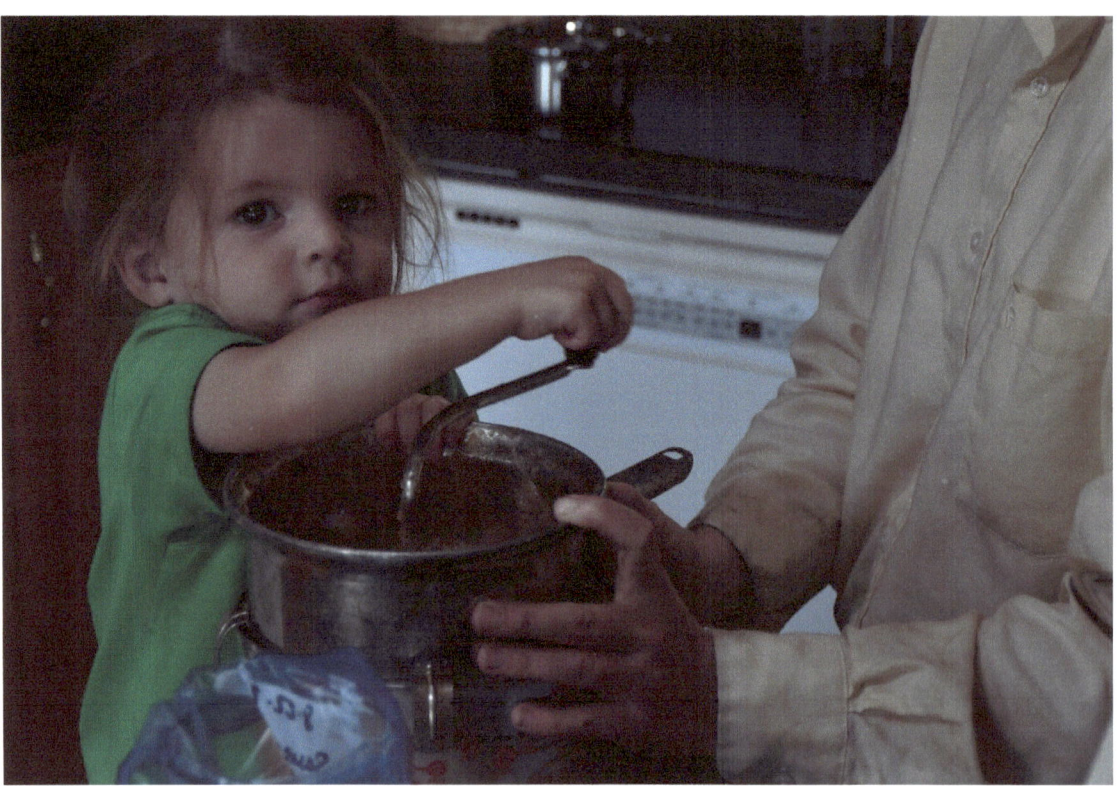

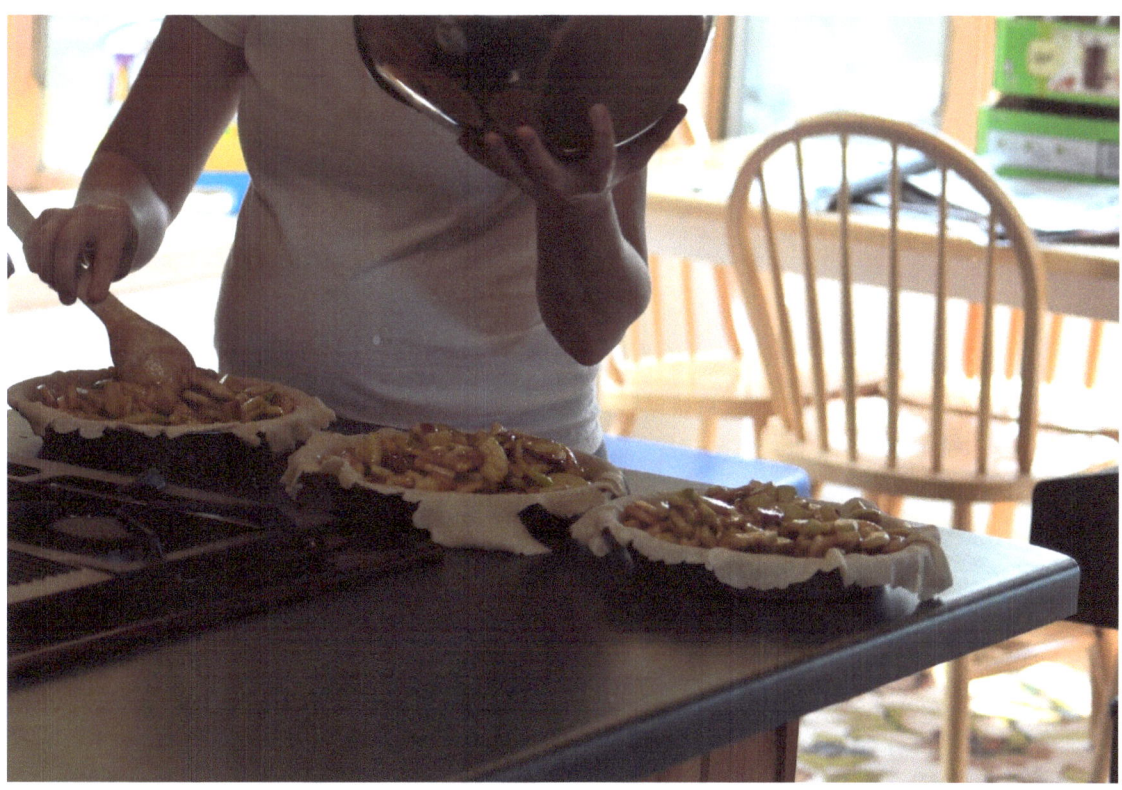

Apple pies to be frozen for the winter and apple roses.

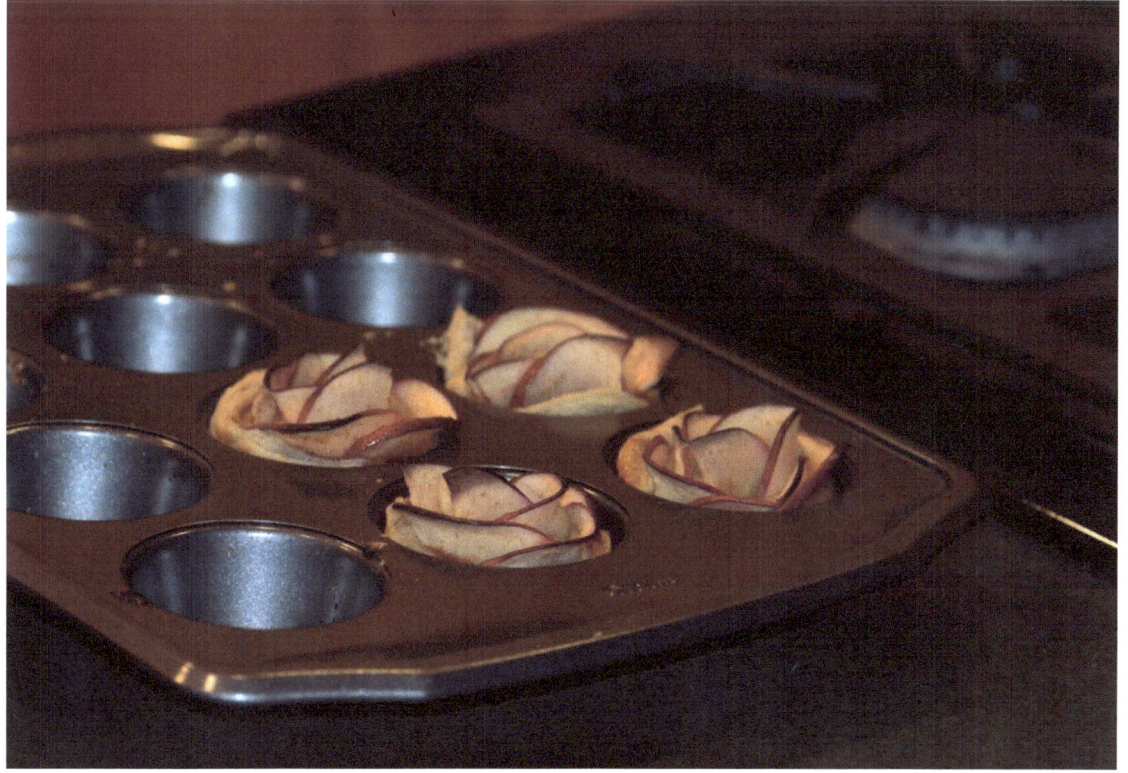

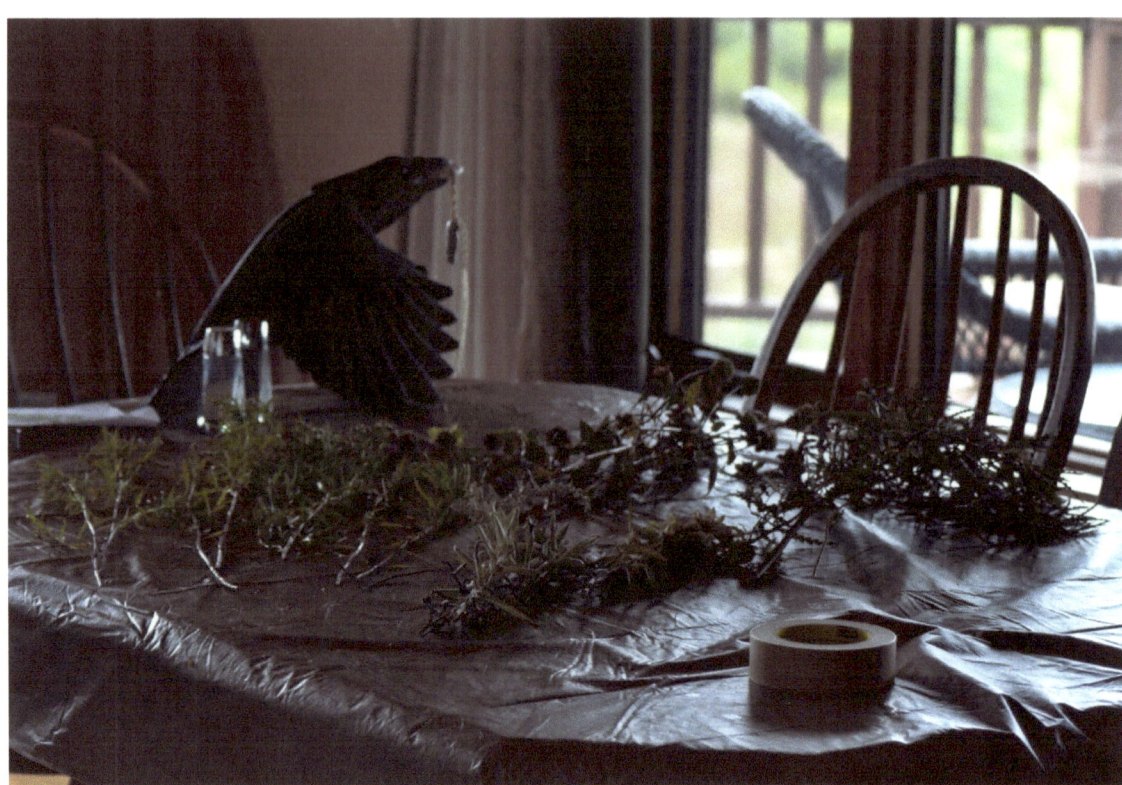

Collecting leaves and flower heads for teas, sage for smudging, prairie cord grass for weaving.

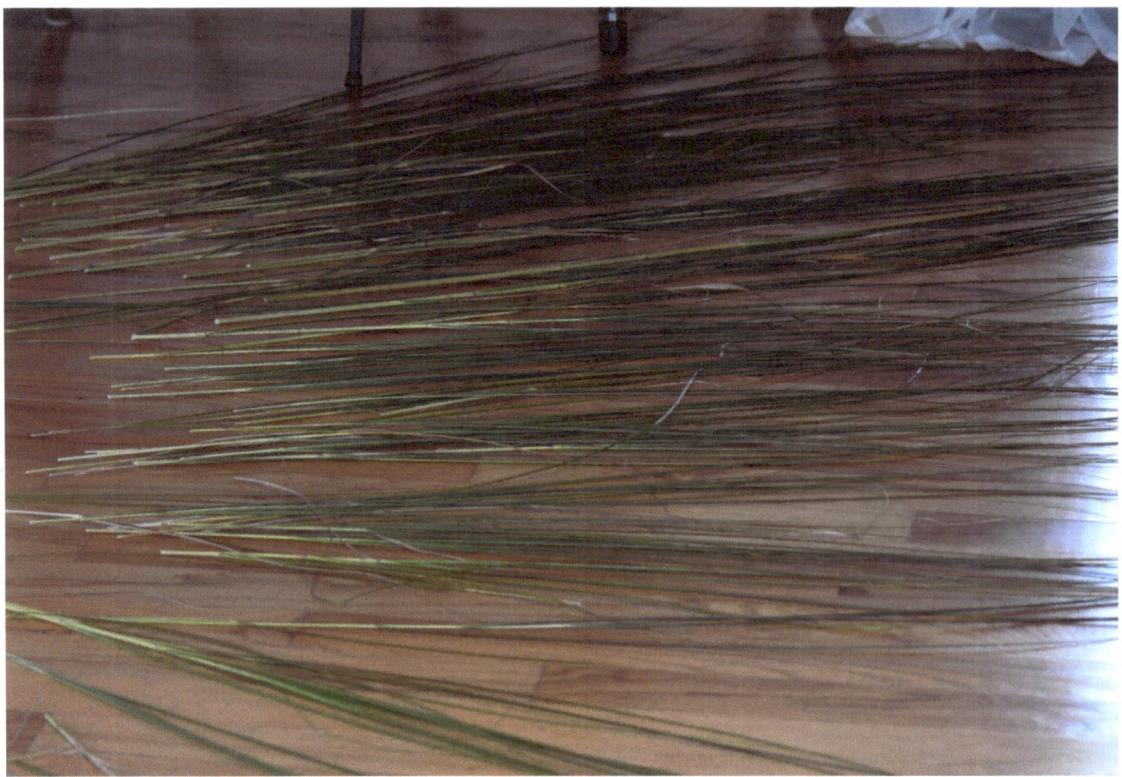

Wet bobcat (June 2014) crossing the meadow and creek, a route seen taken often when it rains.

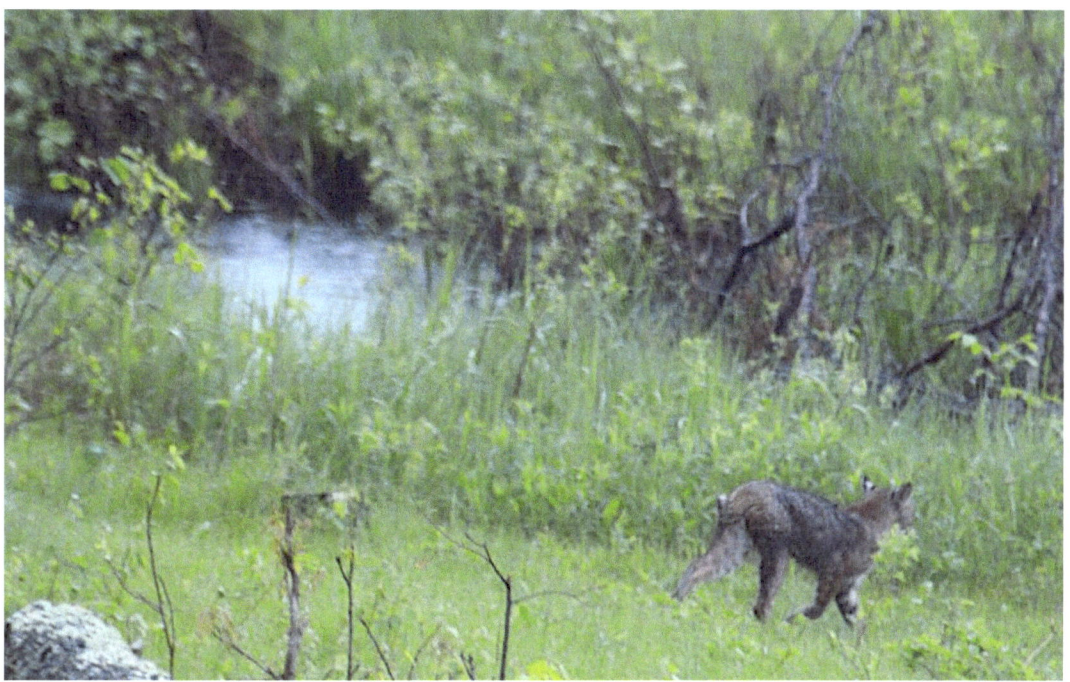

Tom turkey displaying (2010) for a female on the rise just east from the bench at *Station 1.*

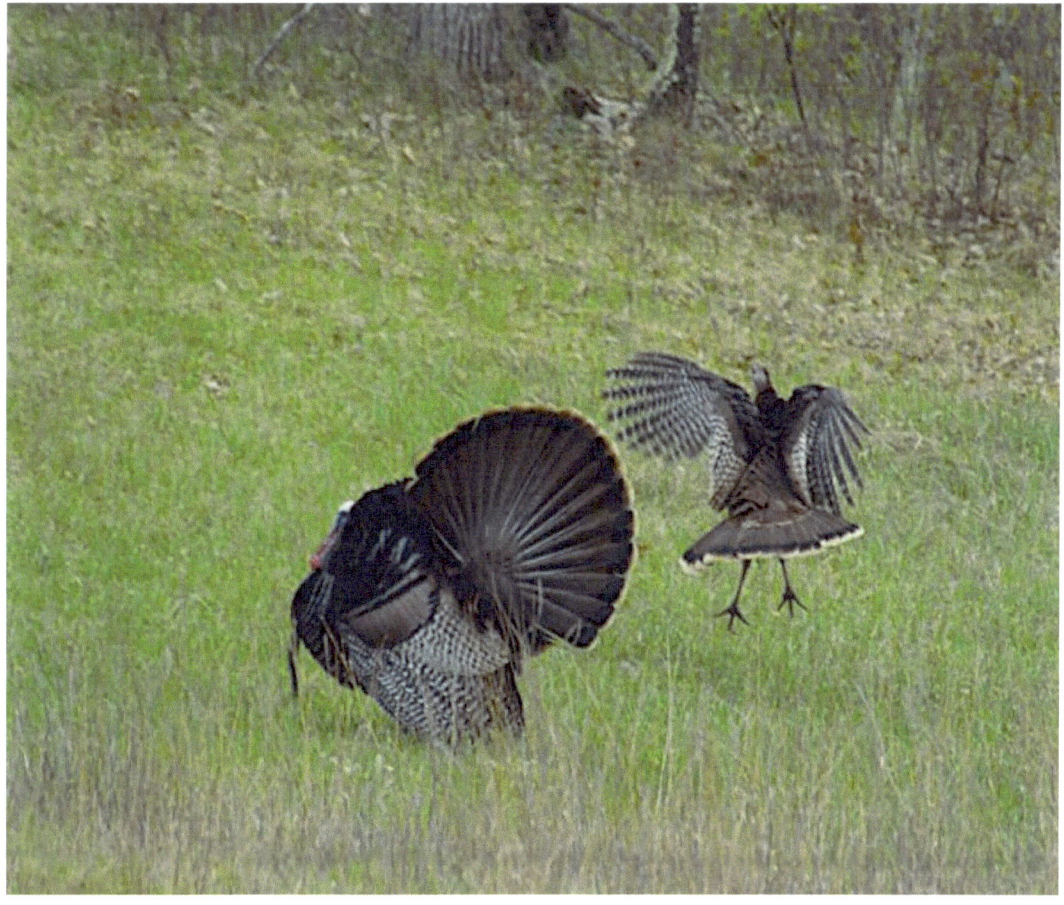

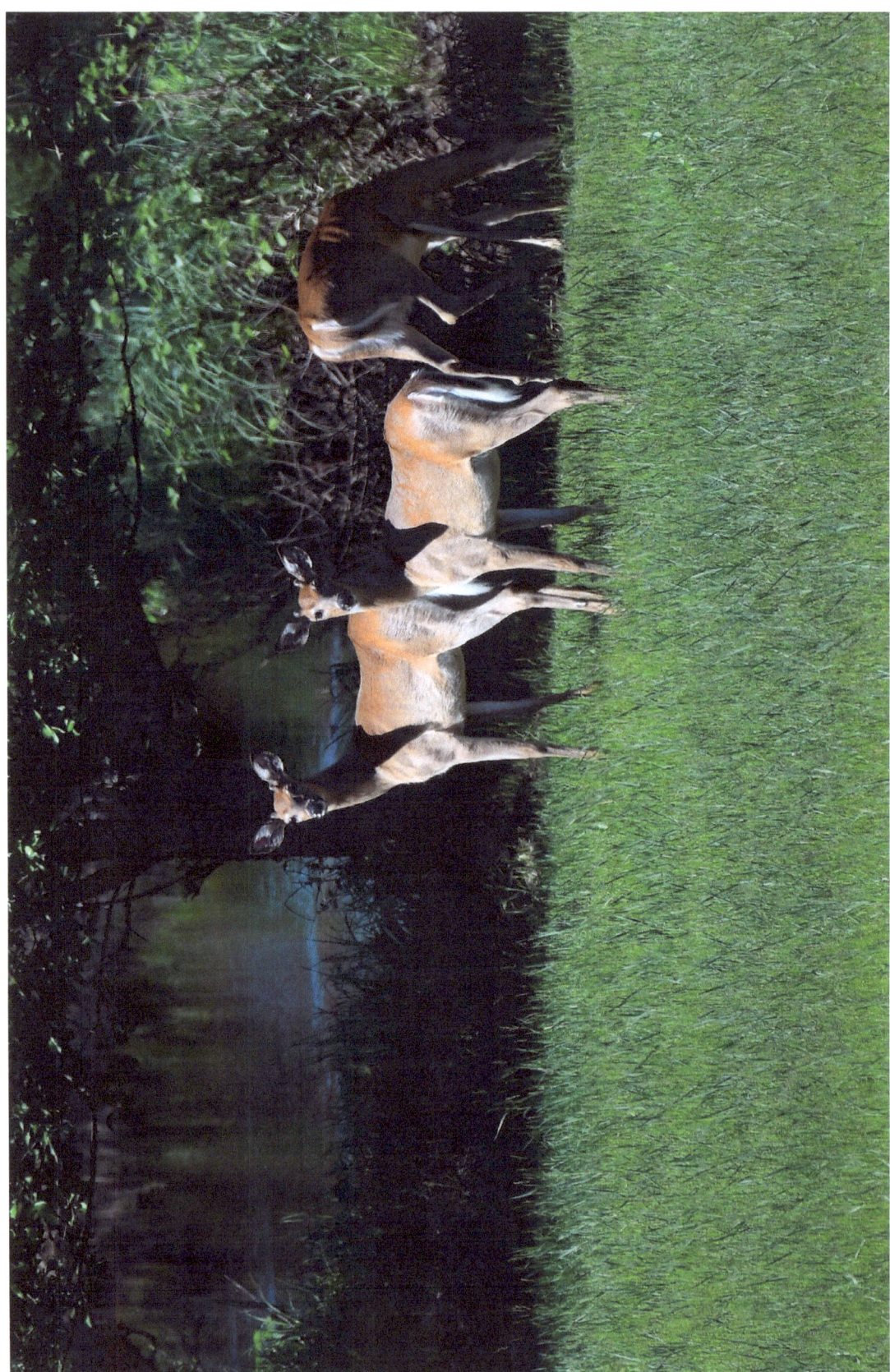

Doe with twin fawns under the apple tree by the creek.

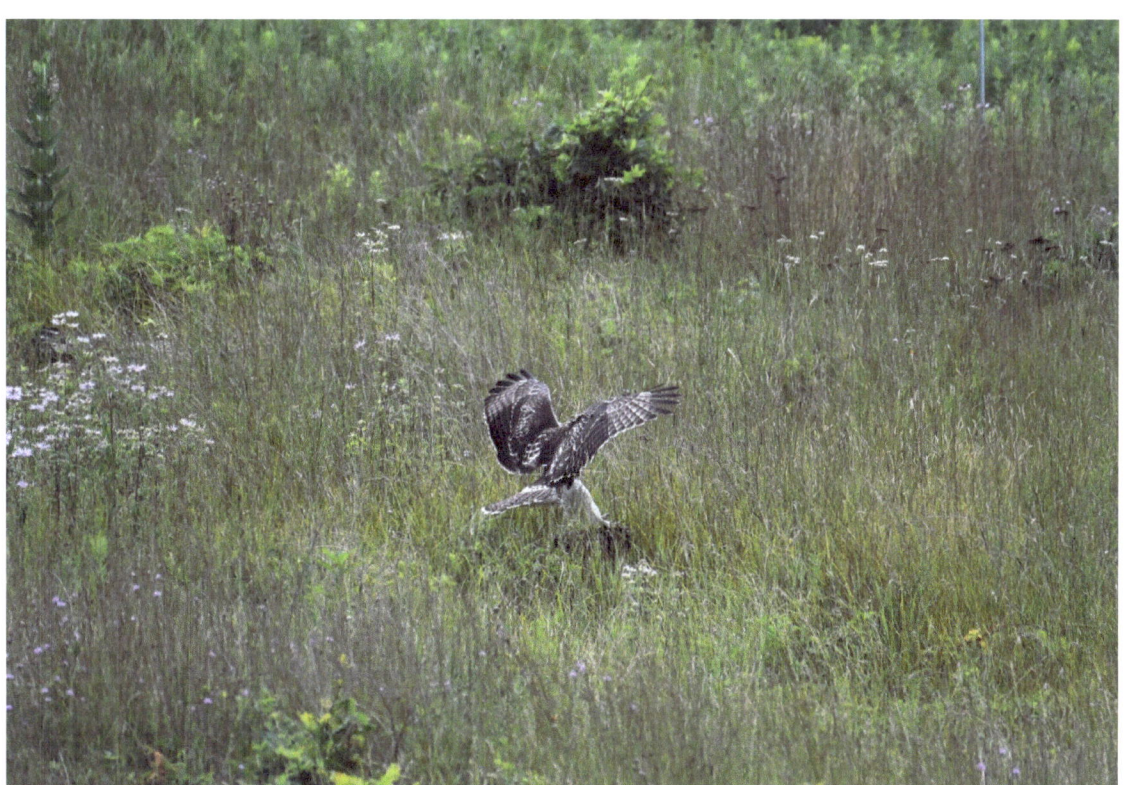

Young fledgling red-tail hawk (August, 2019).

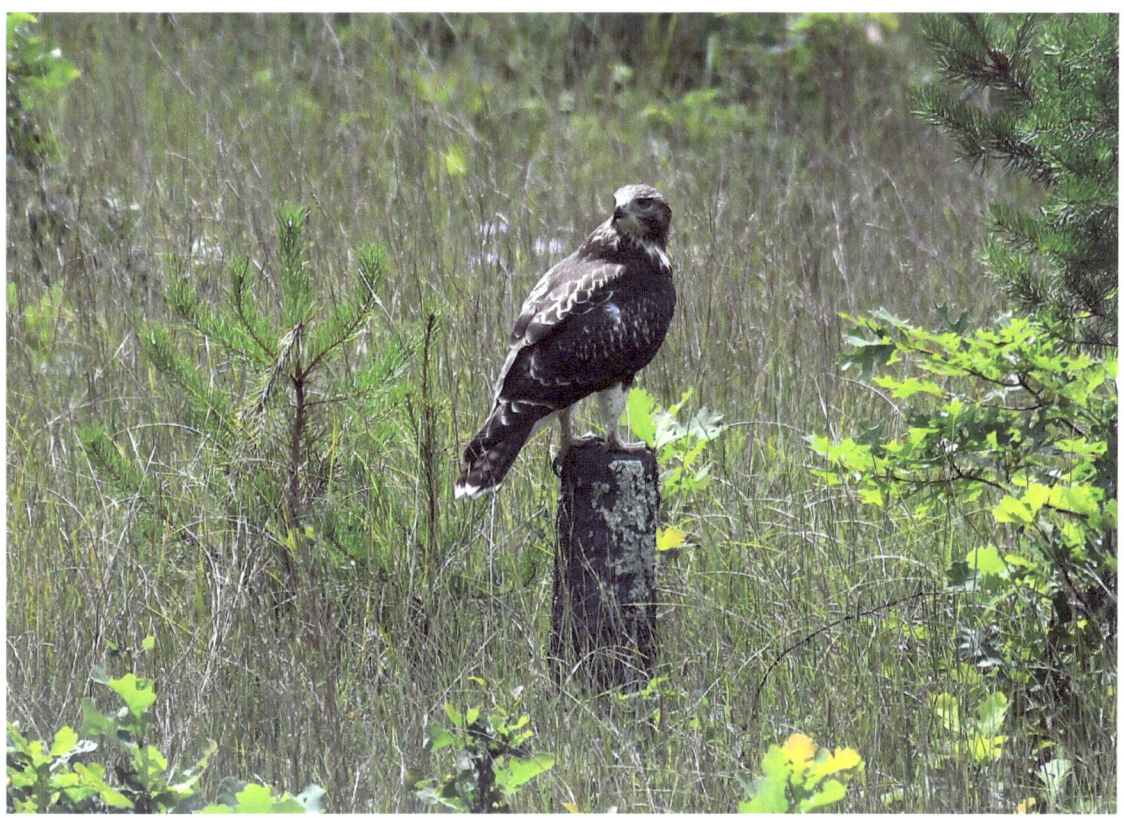

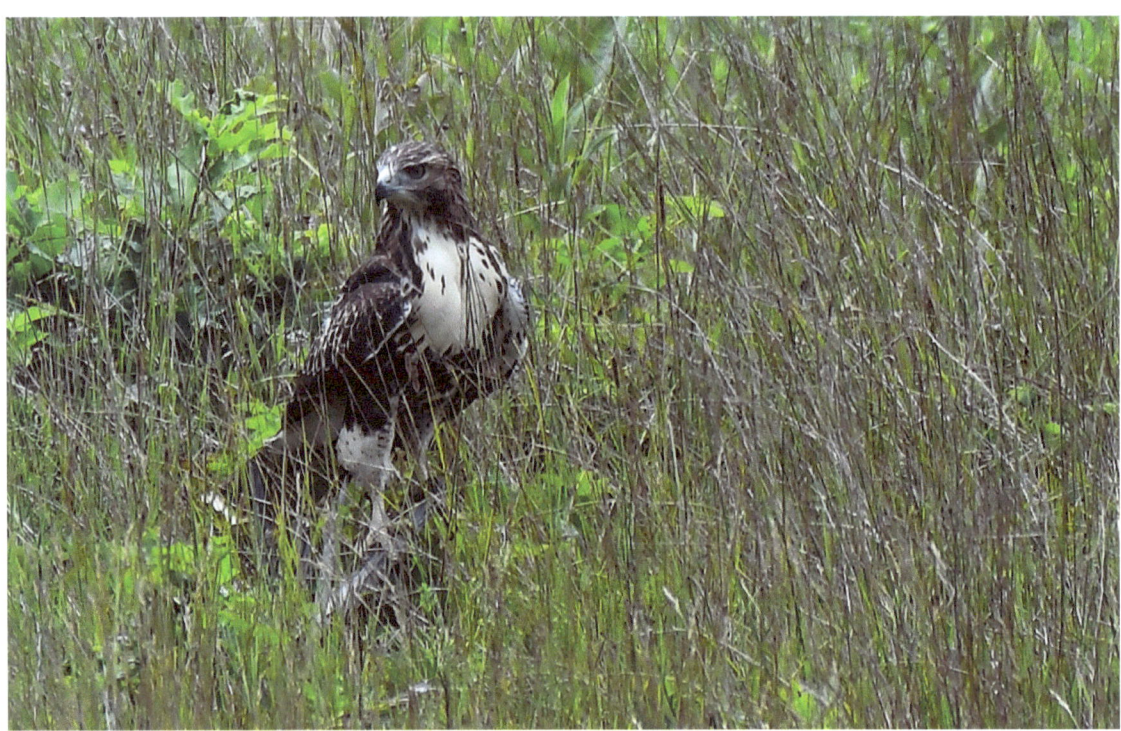

Red-tailed hawk on a stump and then flying under the apple tree by the creek.

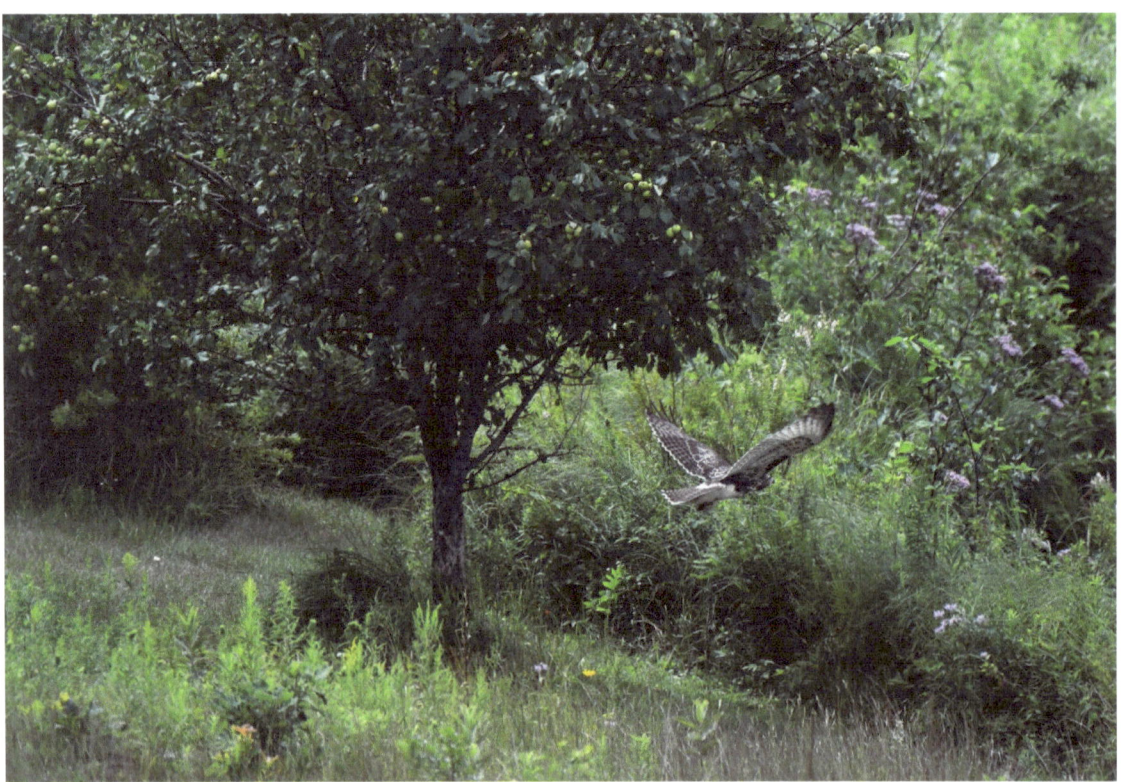

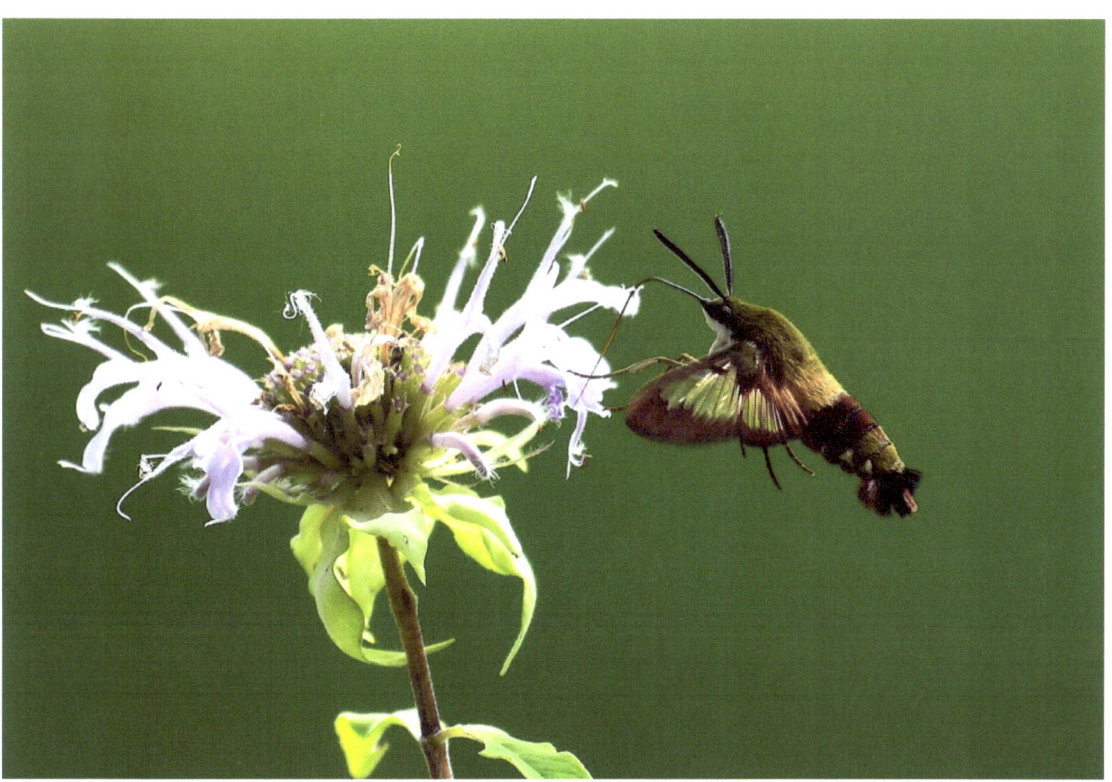

Hummingbird moth (Clearwing moth) on bergamot.

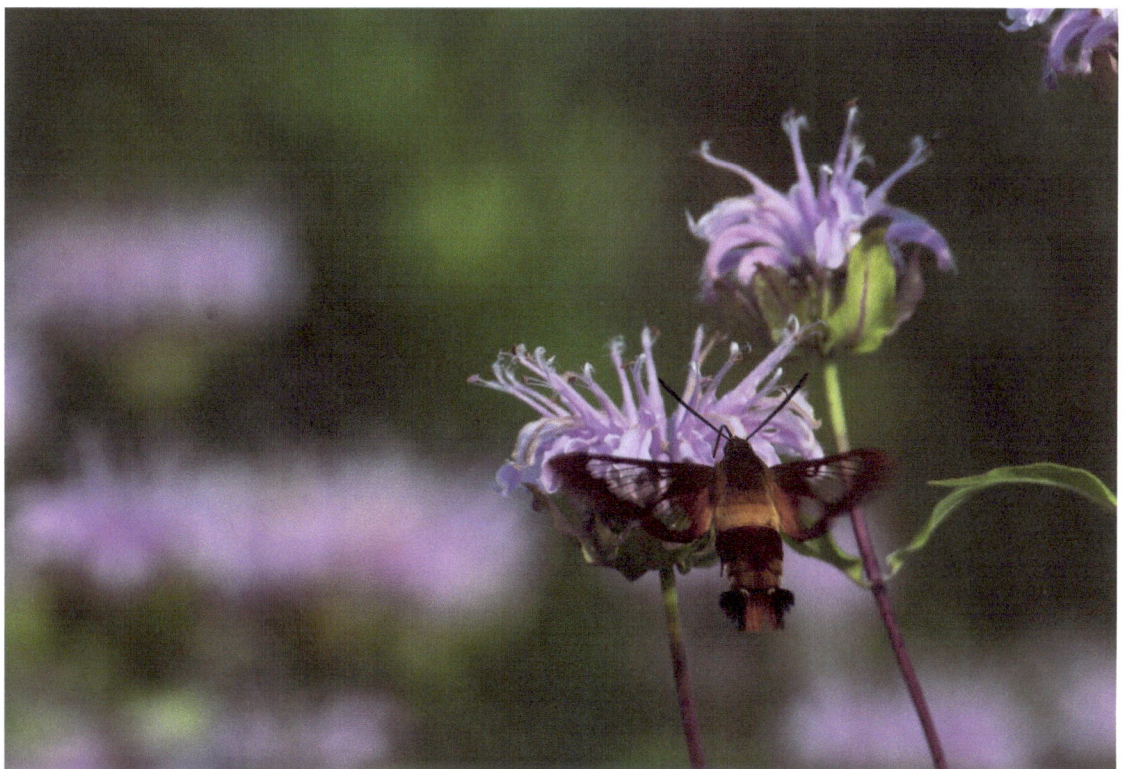

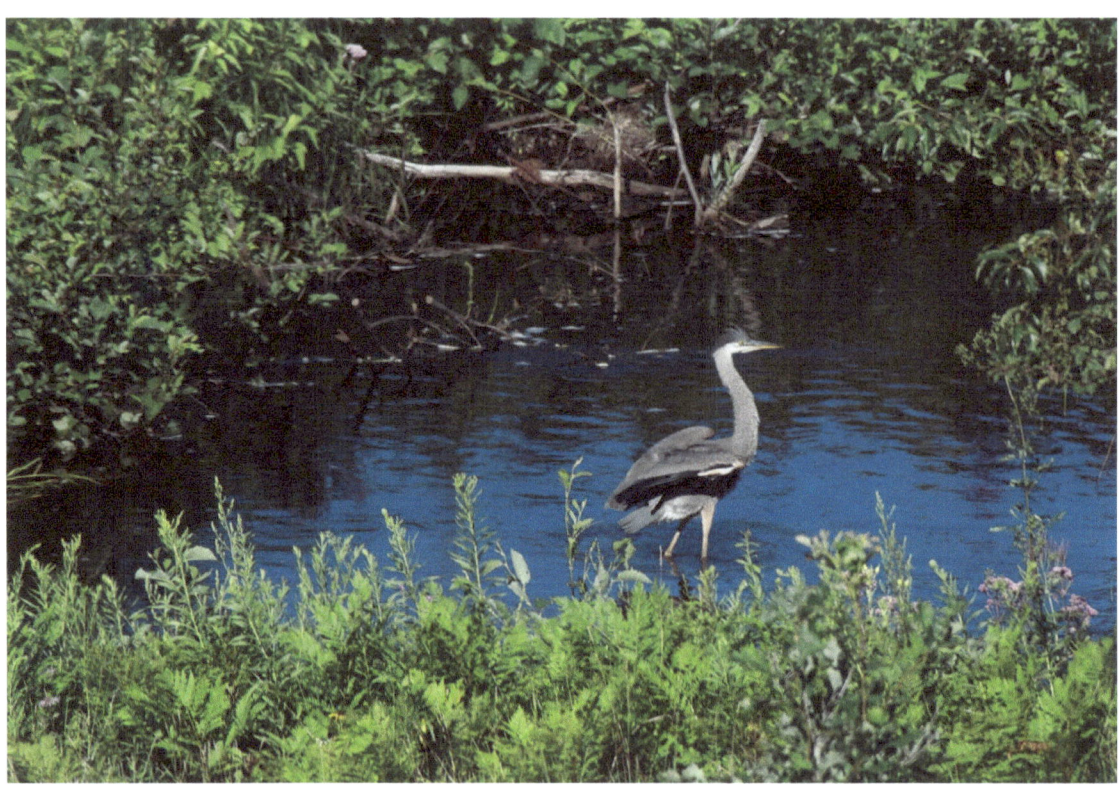

Heron fishing in creek (2014).

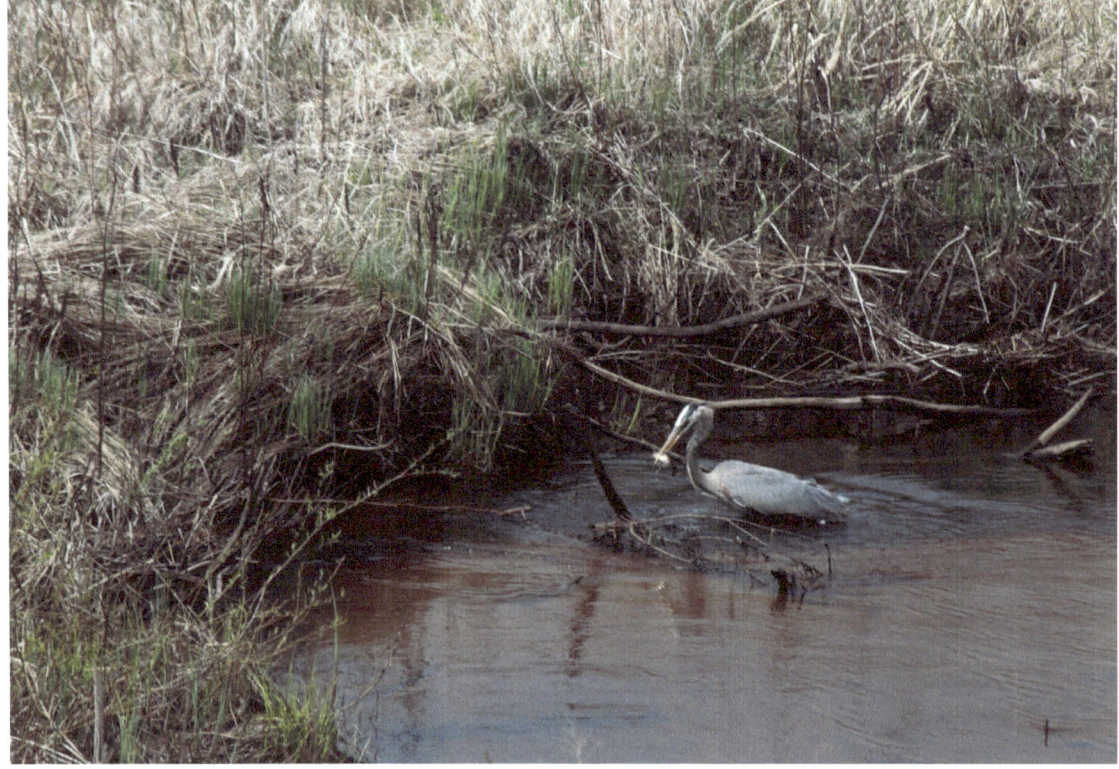

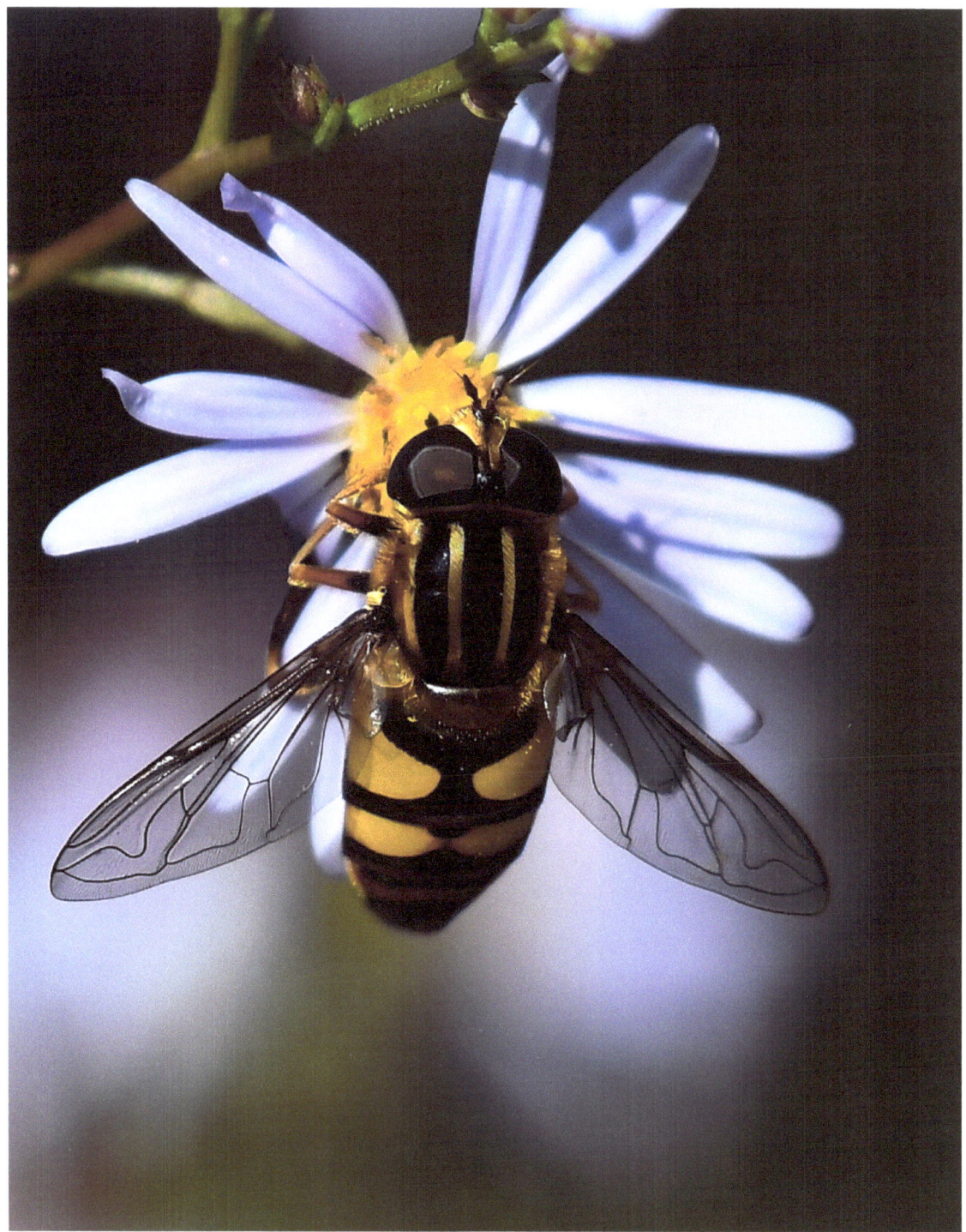

*Helophilus fasciatus* Hoverfly, also called flower fly or syrphid fly: Eggs are laid in clutches on vegetation overhanging ponds. The rat-tailed larvae fall into the pond where they develop. Larvae are insectivores that prey on aphids, thrips, and other plant-sucking insects.

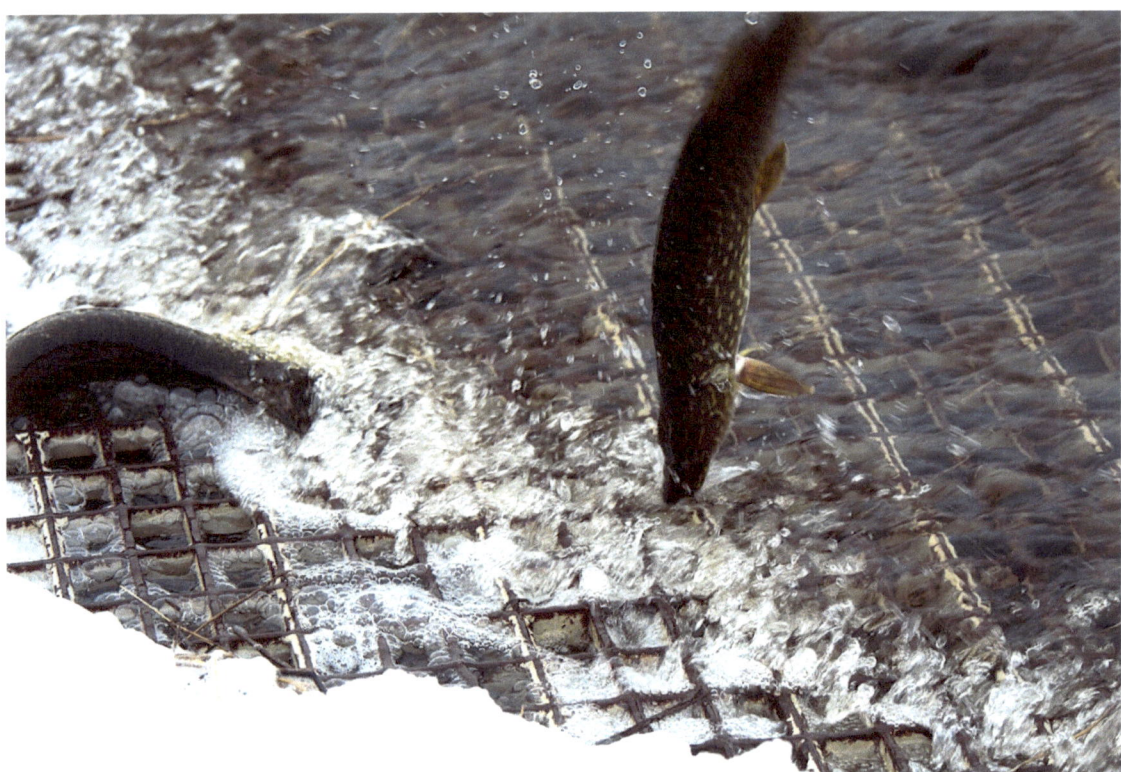

Spring northern pike spawning run up Hay creek – caught as water level suddenly drops.

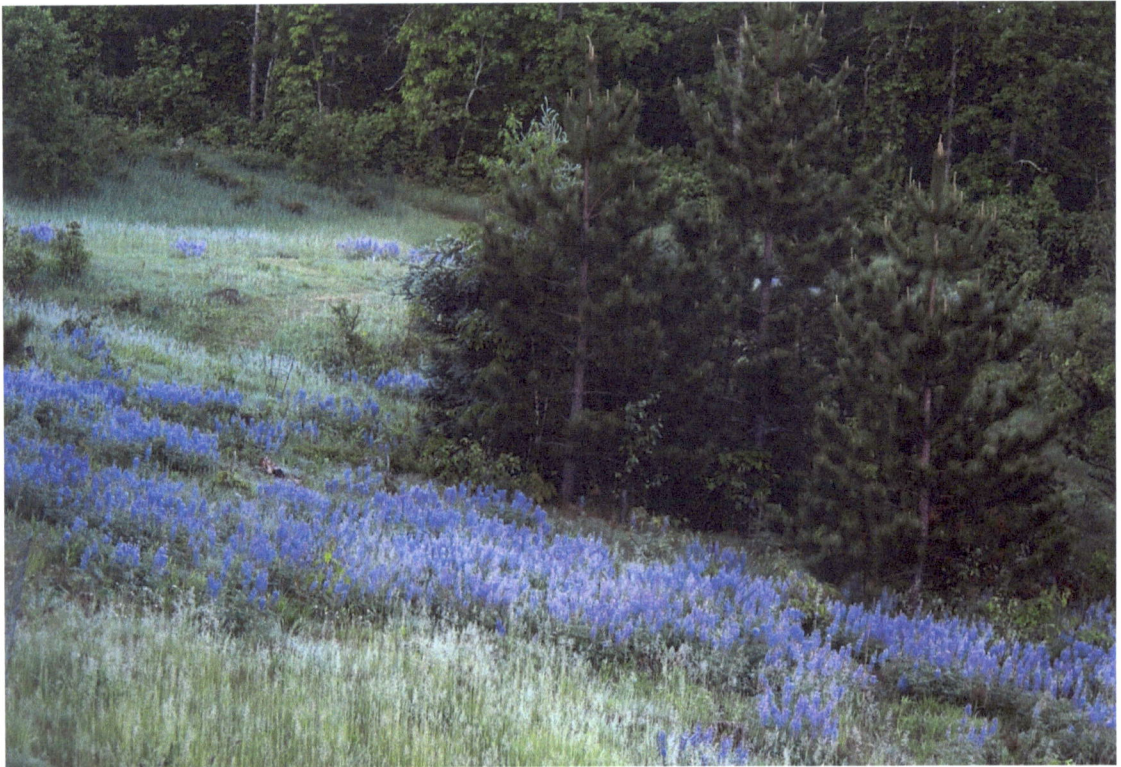

Early June lupine in flower.

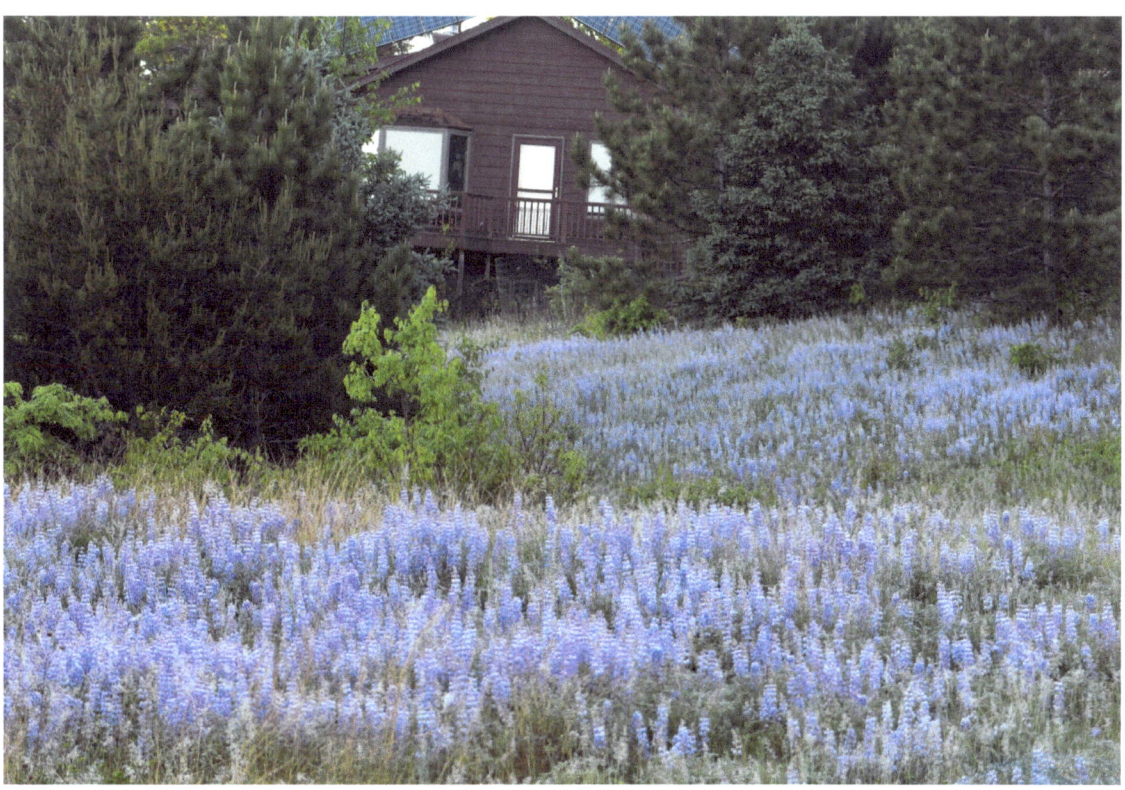

Early June lupine north of *Station 1*, with whitetail doe after she had just dropped her fawns.

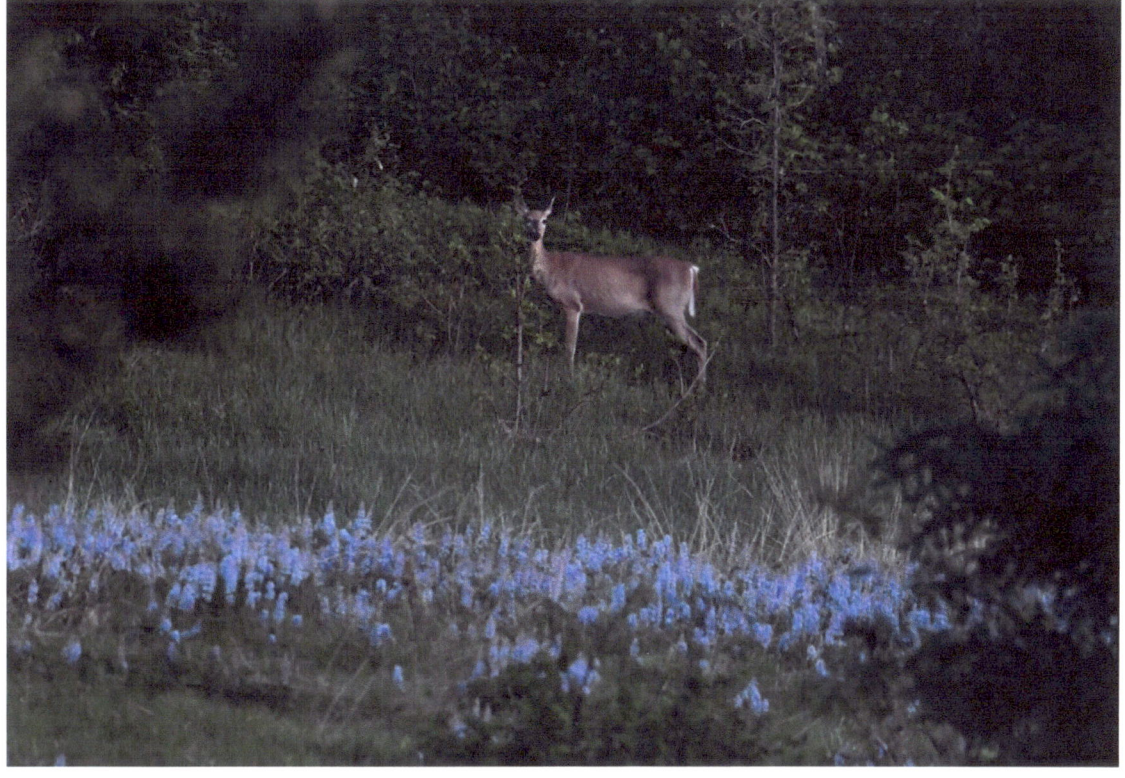

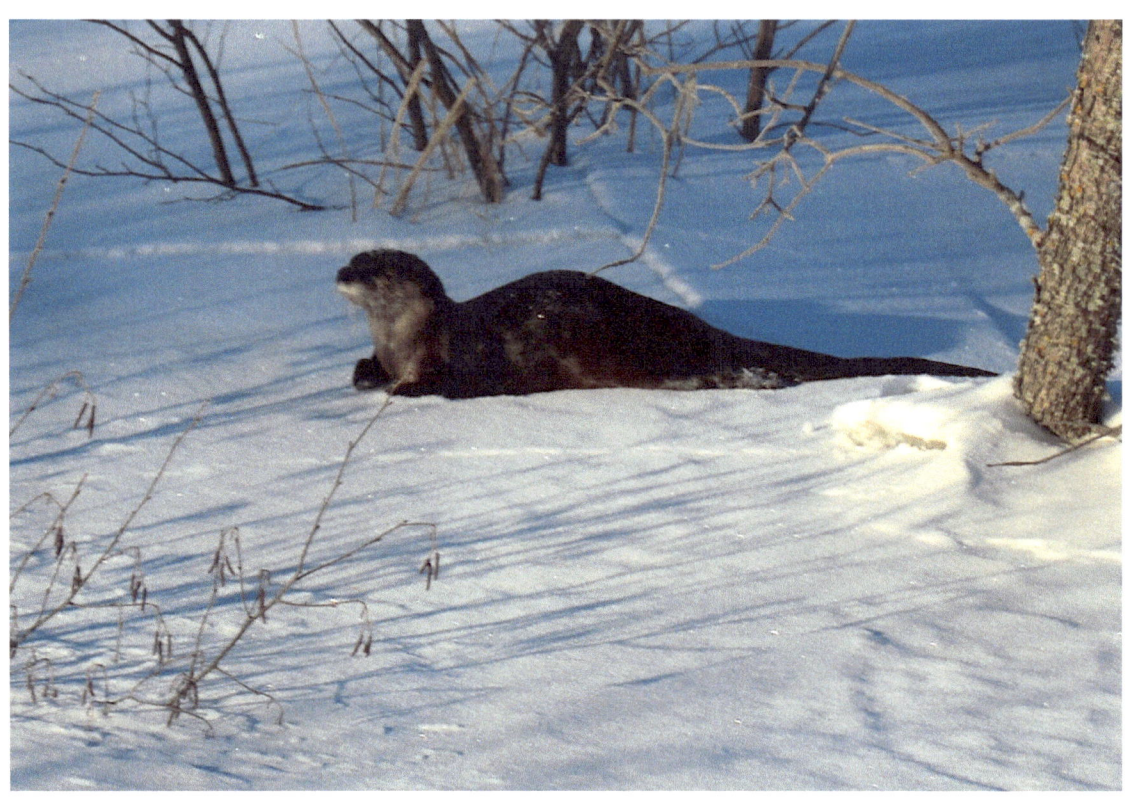

Otter move up and down the creek through all seasons, including winter, feeding on minnows, trout, crayfish and clams.

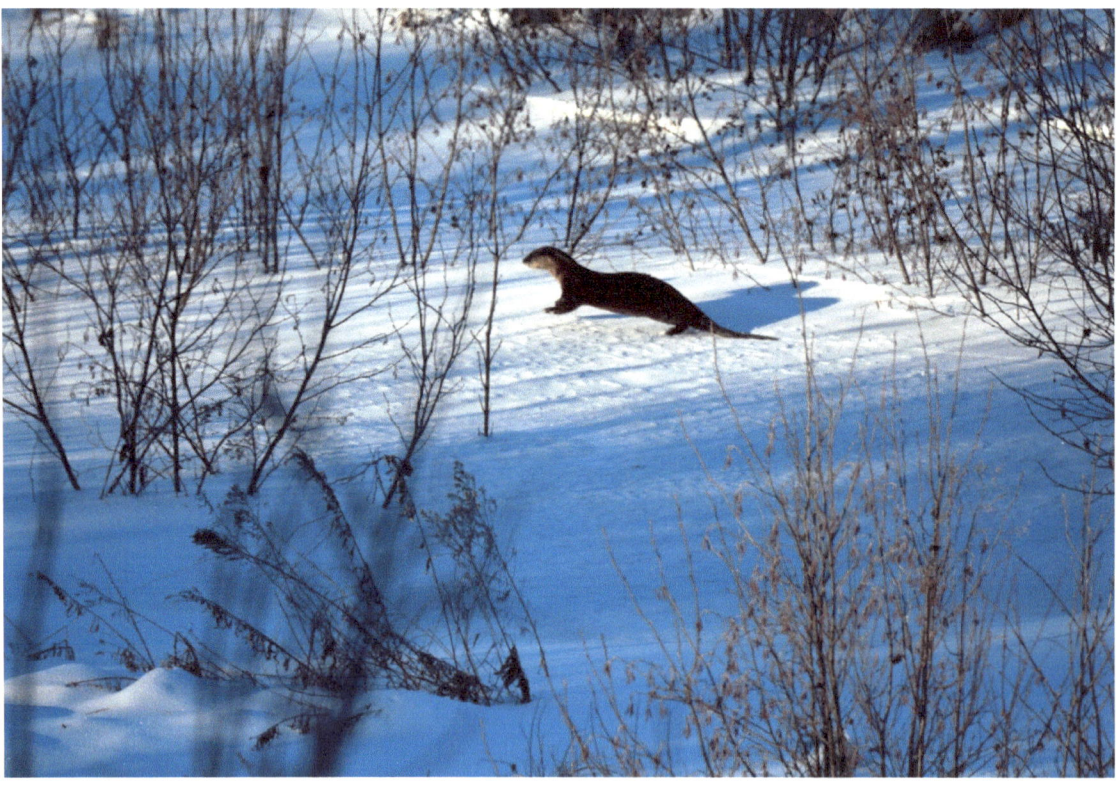

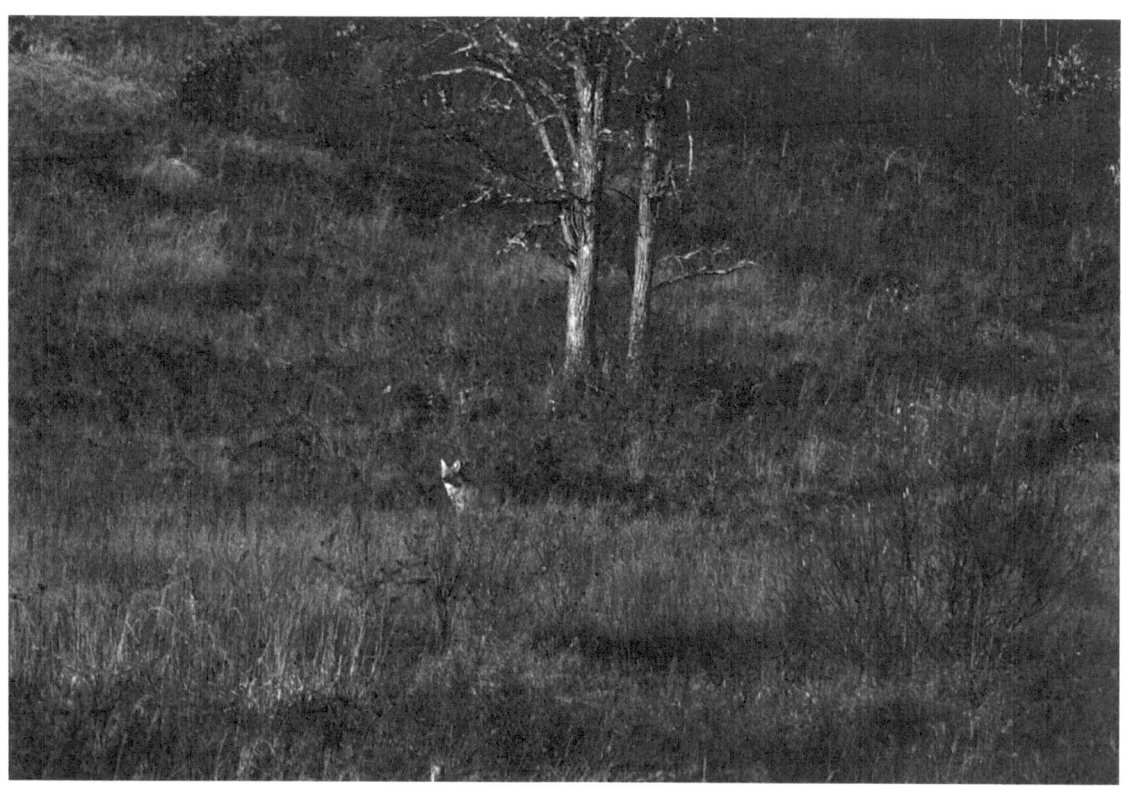

Coyote stalking just across the other side of the creek.

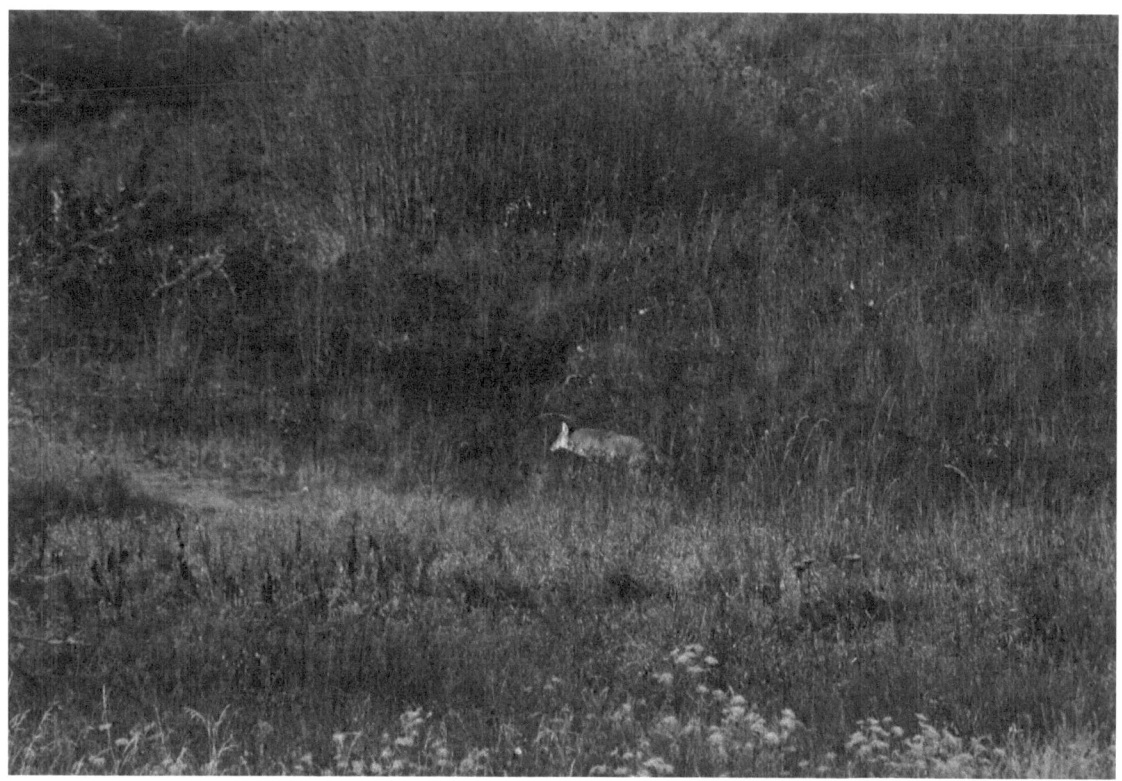

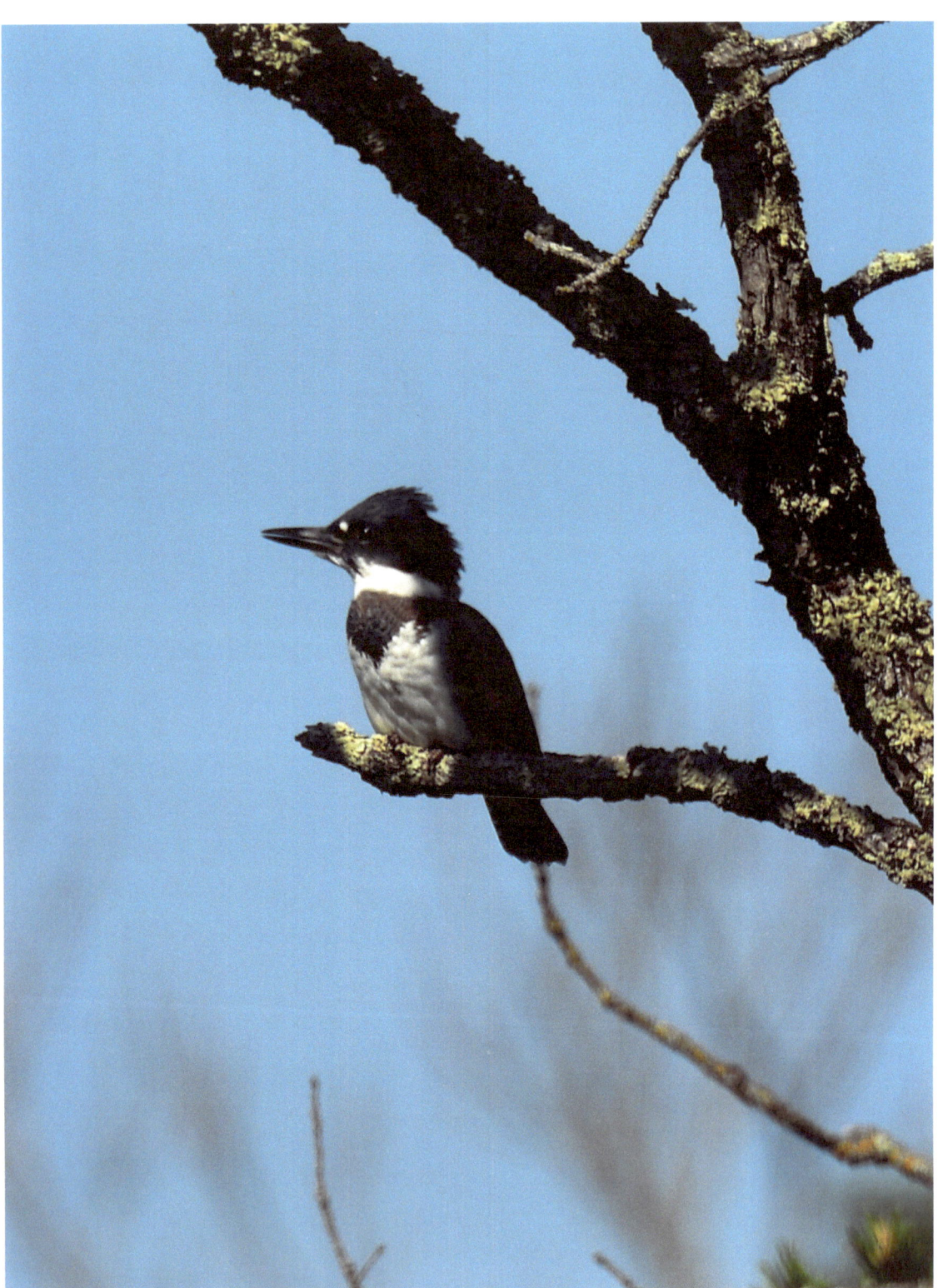

Belted kingfisher fishing from a snag above the creek.

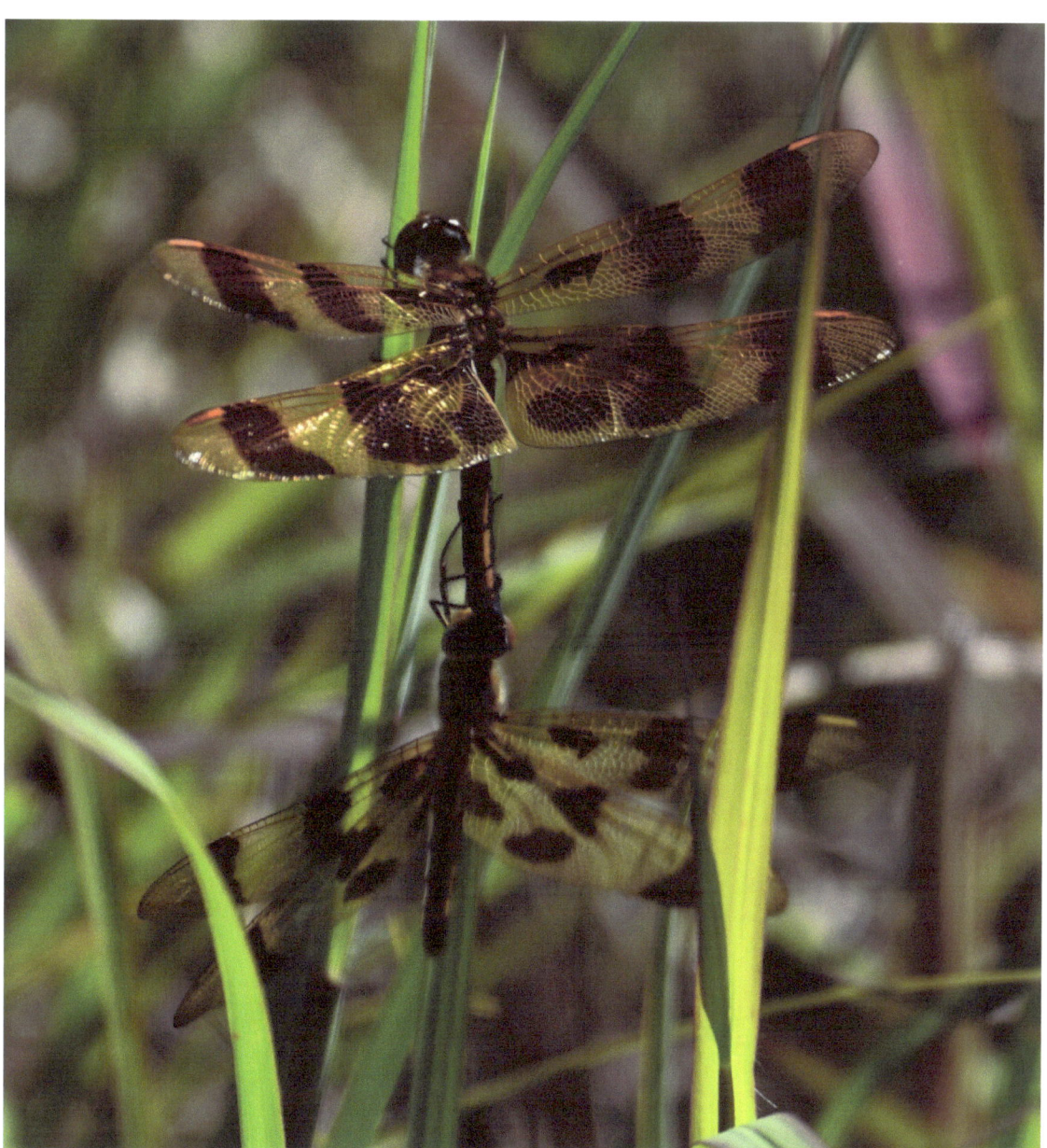

Dragonflies along the creek.

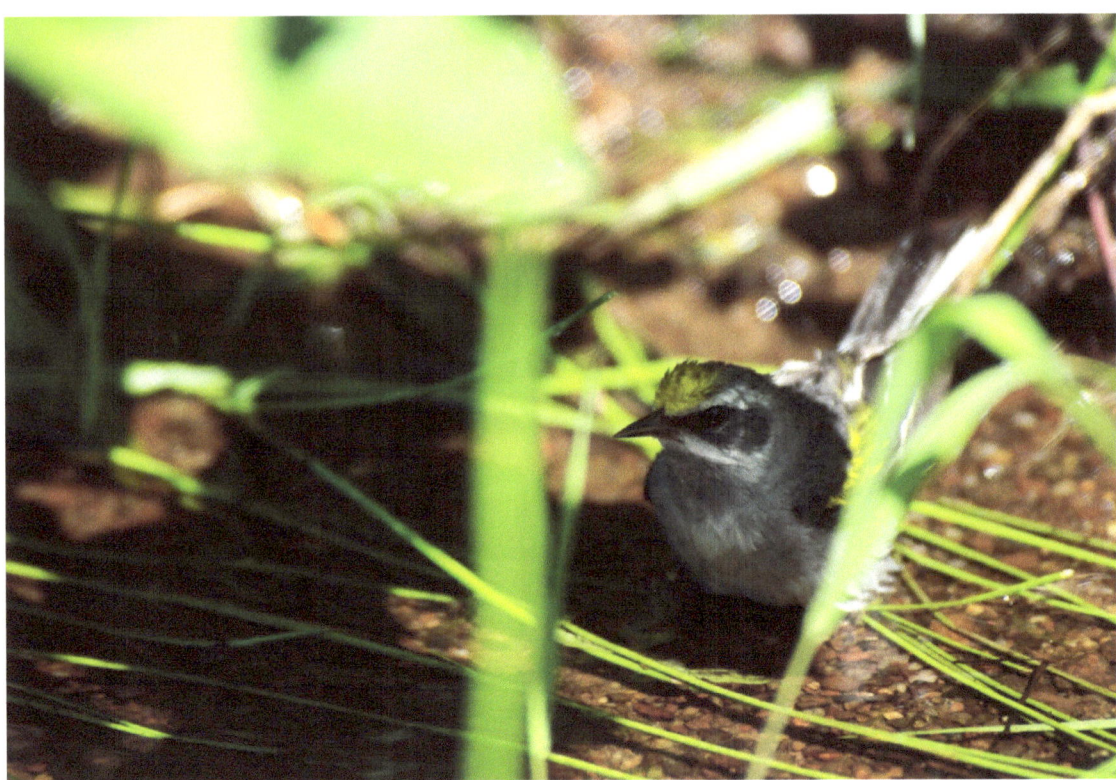

Golden-winged warbler taking a bath in the shallow part of the creek under some alder.

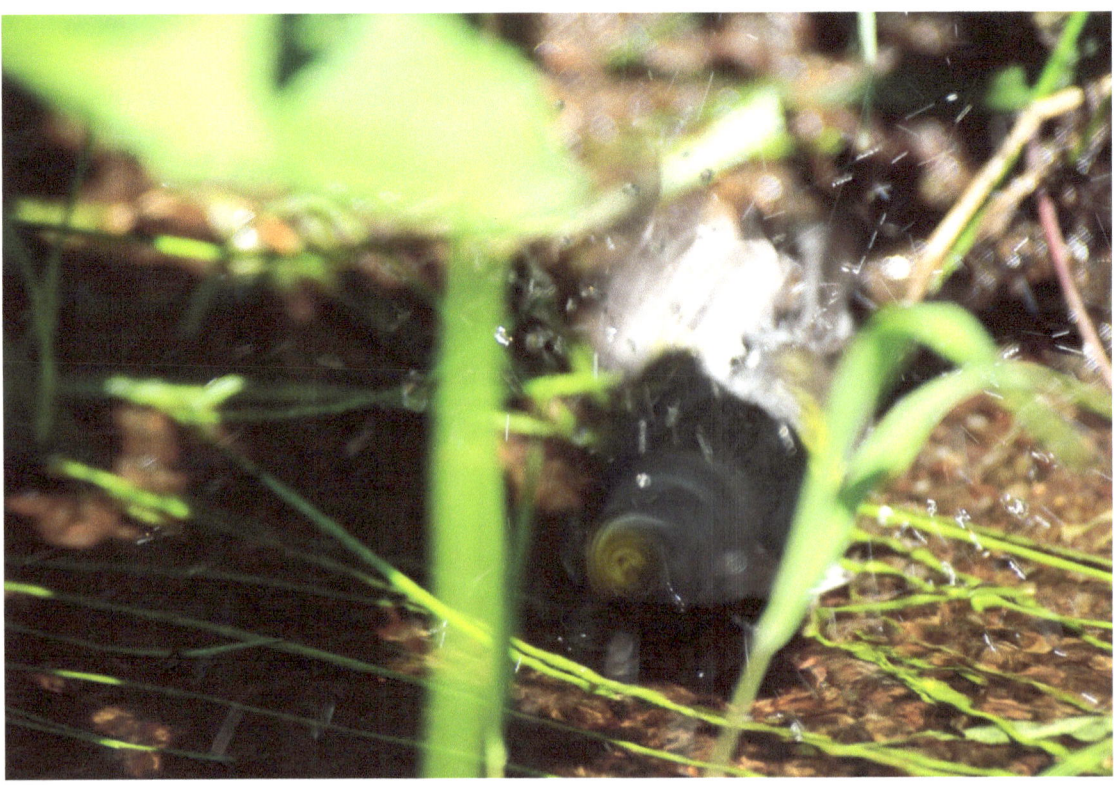

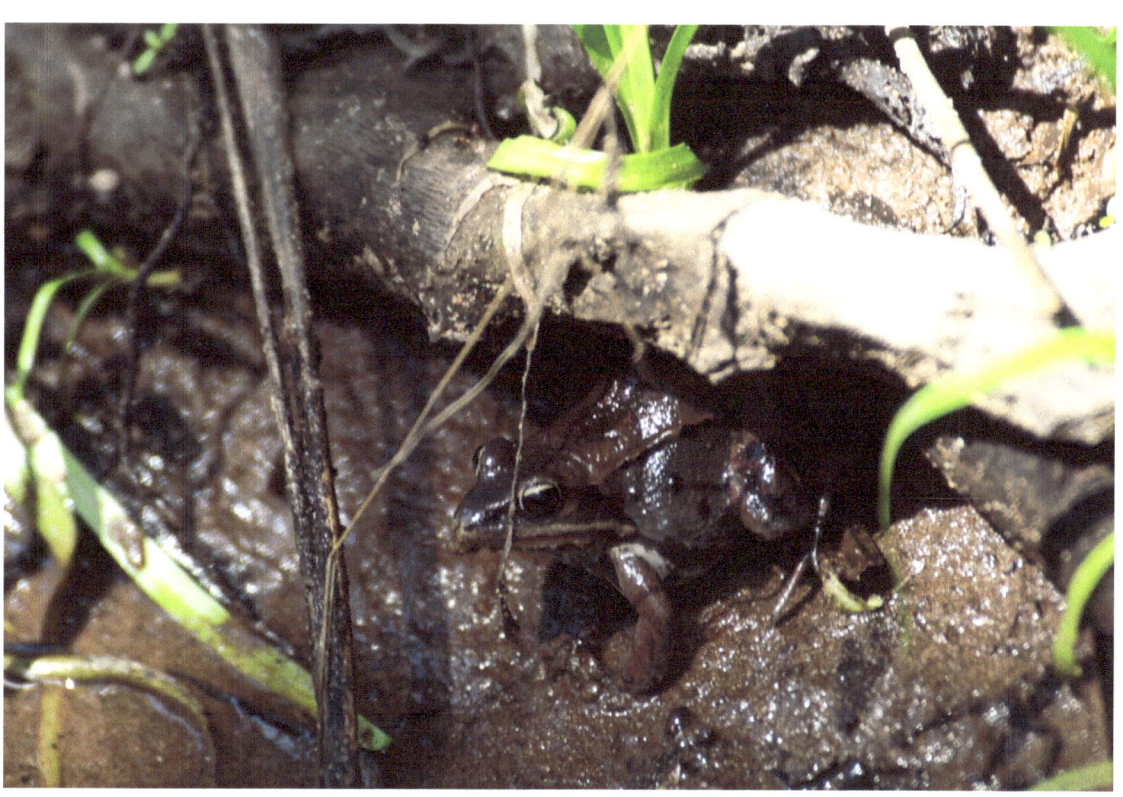

Wood frog (above) under root along creek; tree frog (below) on propane tank next to creek.

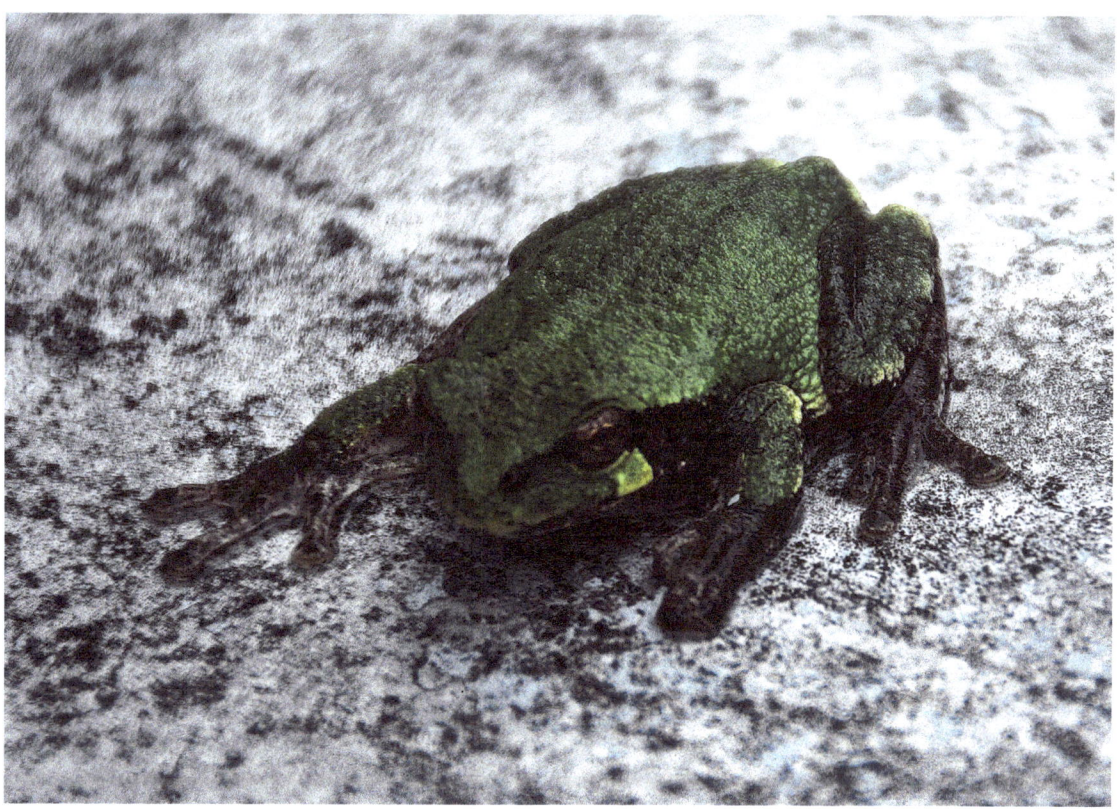

## **Family Story:** *Selected Journal Entries* – 1800's; 1984-2018

You have now seen the surrounding terrain of *Station1*, seen and heard the story of Turtle from both its own perspective (of sorts), from the viewpoint of Damian's efforts to increase Turtle's survival, and from the stored traditional wisdom of his Huron ancestors; that is, accounts of how Turtle signifies the fundament, the land, that was gifted to us out of the waters that were and are everywhere.

In the diaspora to the west from the pressure of the incursions of the Iroquois Confederation (*Haudenosaunee*) and its English suppliers of arms from the northeastern part of the Great Lakes watershed, the Huron moved into prairies and savannas of Wisconsin bringing with them foraging, horticultural and hunting traditions native to the oak savannas of Georgian Bay. The descriptions and illustrations of such effort from the traditional Huron perspective in the stories of the *Three Sisters*, from the viewpoint of efforts by Damian's grandmother to feed her family of 15 children (and sometimes staying grandchildren) is in the same tradition, as well as the Vraniak family's current efforts to continue those sustainable practices. In their restoration efforts the Vraniak family is attempting to continue and to reclaim ever greater portions of these sustaining cultural traditions by foraging berries, herbs, small scale gardening, harvesting and processing, fishing and hunting (turkey, deer), as well as storing up these berry, fruit and meat provisions for the winter. This has been especially relevant during the current 2020-2021 Covid-19 pandemic, as it has been for so many.

Yet, it is challenging indeed to attempt to restore the land, waters and wildlife, while trying to continue and reclaim family-based practices of sustainable sustenance, as well as making effort to work in community to help other families become healthier in a similar fashion. The following pages offer you a day-to-day and year-to-year glimpse of Damian's efforts to do these activities simultaneously. Increasingly over the past several decades, Damian's work with American Indian and Alaska Native children and families, became one with his efforts upon the land his family calls home, until that work invited healers (medicine people), women (abused) who are mothers and grandmothers, families (environmental education), groups (church, youth leaders, tribal mental health staff), and organizations (Boy Scouts, National Park Service) and community members (annual tours) directly to visit and participate here with the Vraniaks at their home.

In the form of the selected journal entries, letters and writings from previous publications written by Damian over the past forty years, you may gather some sense of what it is like to attempt to do these four things – *environmental restoration, sustainable subsistence, cultural reclamation, and community sharing*, simultaneously, as a part of a complex, comprehensive, cohesive and coherent sustained effort. Following these journal excerpts, penetration into the Sacred will be considered, without which such challenging effort would be impossible.

Metis bison hunters' quotidian is highlighted through the extensive Michif French written legacy of Turtle Mountain historian ChWeUm (William Jr.) Davis (1845-1937). Davis's biography anchors a Metis national memory, weaving stories and events from both sides of the Medicine Line. (Émilie Pigeon, 2017) [CHWeUm notes the deaths of Damian's grandmother Alice's grandmother and great grandmother in the following excerpts.]

## *The William Davis (ChWeUm) Diaries Tome 1*

| <u>Michif</u> | <u>French</u> | <u>English</u> |
|---|---|---|

Page 32

| 120. Marie Nolin Roger désédé sept 27 an 1915 agé de 72 ans | 120. Marie Nolin Roger décédée le 27 septembre 1915 âgée de 72 ans. | 120. Marie Nolin Roger died September 27 1915 aged 72 years. |

Page 41 & 42

| 168. Margerite Pieti désédé fev 7 an 1907 agé de 92 ans | 168. Marguerite Petit décédée le 7 aout 1907 âgé de 92 ans. | 168. Marguerite Petit died August 7 1907 aged 92 |

Page 67 & 68

Mars 12 an 1918 Otawittakosikke Laloieuse seur de Che Chewekijik Chef fimme de Cadote métise ala eu un garson avec la dite et ils seson sipari Cadote apri son garson avec lui et il se maria avec margerite picard et son garson est mort a la barrier encanana en 1874 a 75

> Le 12 mars 1918 Otawittakosikke Lalouise, sœur de Che Chewekijik Chef femme de Cadotte, métisse, eut un garçon avec le dit [Cadotte] et ils se sont séparés. Cadotte prit son garçon avec lui et se maria avec Marguerite Picard et son garçon est mort à la barrière encanana [?] entre 1874 et 75.

>> March 12 1918 Otawittakosikke Lalouise, sister of Che Chewekijik Chief, wife of Cadotte, Métis, had a son with the said [Cadotte] and they separated. Cadotte took his son with him and married Marguerite Picard and his son died at the encanana barrier between 1874 and 75.

Page 74

1916Fete Ste Ann silebri a Belcourt N Dak novaine jeullet 22 au 30 an 1916 pridicateur rev J T Rochon le jour de la Fête an croi qu'il y à au ou tour de 6000 personne autour de 500 voiture autour de 200 300 otomobil autour de 400 personne qui zon sui la prosession autour de 1800 comminion en prezense de 6 pretre

> Fête [de] Ste Anne célébrée à Belcourt N Dak neuvaine [du] 22 au 30 juillet 1916. Prédicateur Rev. J T Rochon. Le jour de la Fête, on croit qu'il y a eu environ 6000 personnes, environ 500 voitures, environ 200 [ou] 300 automobiles, environ 400 personnes qui ont suitvit la procession, environ 1800 communions en présence de 6 prêtres.

>> 1916 St Ann's Day celebrated in Belcourt, N Dak. Novena from July 22 to the 30th 1916. Celebrant Rev. J T Rochon. On St Ann's Day, we believe there was a total of 6000 people, about 500 carts, 200 or 300 automobiles, about 400 people who followed the procession, and about 1800 communions in the presence of 6 priests.

Excerpts from (grandfather**) Joseph Vraniak Diary** *(January 1, 1983 – May 11, 1985)*

<u>Sunday</u>        *April 29, 1984*        24 Above        29 Above in Shell Lake

Set new time ahead 1 hour        Home LP Gas 65
Bard disked garden        1 hour labor

<u>Monday</u> *April 30, 1984*        30 Above        Snowing

Schools closed        promise 3 to 8 inches of snow

<u>Wednesday</u>        *January 16, 1985*        qp Above

Letter from Day [Damian] and Anne from Greece, coming home

Excerpt from Dedication for *Maps & Metaphors of the Human Heart:*
        *1,2,3-Mystery Book 2. Parents, Pals, and Partners* (2009)

### Talia's Necklace

Talia, the gold ring on this necklace was present at the conception of your mother [Damian's daughter], at her birth and throughout the years of her childhood. The other ring on this necklace, from your Great Grandmother, is of similar significance. Together these rings, threaded through the beauty of this double chain, represent the presence of an unbroken circle of love passed down the generations ... love that perseveres, protects and provides under the greatest of challenges, a love that is true and truly sustaining. May the love that you come to experience as a child, the love that you offer each person in your life, and perhaps, if you are allowed the opportunity, even the love you gift as a parent and grandparent, may all the love in your life be as present, as true and as enduring as the love witnessed in the gift of these two rings, in the unbroken circle of this necklace of love. Above all else, dear child, especially in the face of whatever great challenges in your life, may this gift remind and help you always to keep love alive in your heart ... and to be true.

### Talia's Bracelet

Talia, in the last days of 1984 I was alone on the bow of a very fast boat moving from an island through the Aegean sea towards Athens, as the dark, dark clouds of a very bad storm came quickly towards us. The wind whipped and the waves had whitecaps, but the ship cut through them cleanly and sharply as we sped toward safe harbor. In the moment that I glanced down into the utterly turquoise water I saw them, and I felt wonder and awe at the beauty of their movement, at their knowing look as they peered into my eyes. Two dolphins, side by side, rode the bow wave like they were flying in the bluest-green sky, effortlessly gliding next to the speeding ship. Next to the birth of your mother, they were the most beautiful sight I had seen in my life. That there could be such gentle, tender grace and such sensuous, stunning power so easily combined in one motion was beyond my imagination. Two moving as one with such utter delight I almost laughed and jumped in for the complete joy I shared with two silvery blue dolphins swimming the Aegean Sea.  Later in the streets of that Grecian city I found this gold bracelet with two dolphins swimming towards one another but forever not touching, yet always and ever together.  I brought it back to your Great Grandmother and she wore it for many years. And now we gift it to you. May you swim your life with such simple grace and elegance in seas stormy and calm and know the beauty that the water of life within you is wedded to the water without, so in the end there is nothing to fear, for we are all one ... and you are Heaven's Dew.

[*Talia* in Hebrew = *"Heaven's Dew"*]

Damian A. Vraniak

Damian's relationship with the land is tied closely with his efforts to meet the needs of American Indian and Alaska Native children. In part, because of the influence of his grandmother, and his experience of his mother becoming one of the first American Indian social worker aides tutoring Indian students in the public schools in the 1960's, he took up a career serving those children and their families.

In the 1970's Damian designed and implemented one of the first gifted programs for American Indian children in the Minneapolis Public Schools (Red Elk Banks; Duane Dunkley, Rosemary Christiansen, Marigold Linton), reviewed the first drafts of Eddie Benton Banai's book *Mishomis* while Eddie was at the Red School House, created and directed one of the first urban mental health centers in a medical clinic (IHB of Mpls; JoAnne Barr and Norrine Smith), held the first state-wide meeting of mental health center directors and tribal representatives, and then worked with Indian Health Service's Indian Children's Program (Al Hiat, Scott Nelson, Bea Medicine). Participating with Carolyn Attneave (advisor to Damian's future wife) in the beginnings of the creation of the *Society of Indian Psychologists* (SIP), in the 1980's Damian would enable SIP to meet at the annual gathering he conceived of and created in Utah. Returning home and working for the LCO tribe, he implemented a mobile multidisciplinary team that shared professionals serving tribal children in the northern part of Wisconsin (Rick St. Germain). Later Damian would help refine a state-wide team coordinated through UW-Madison (WINGS; Arvina Thayer), and finally, after returning from out west in 1989 he would design and direct another such team serving reservations in northern Wisconsin through UW-Eau Claire.

In the mid-1980's Damian was asked to attend a NATO Advance Study Institute regarding Adaptation to Extreme Environments at a conference held in Athens, Greece, that was in the anticipation of creating an international space station. Damian's contribution to the future human factors design of the planned space station was based upon the form and functioning of small traditional winter hunting camps formed by Ojibwe and Cree hunters/trappers in the extreme north.

During his absence from Springbrook in the 1980's Damian designed, secured funding ($1 million), and directed the first five-year longitudinal study of the emotional challenges among American Indian and Native children in North America (*Flower of Two Soils Project*, White Cloud Center, Oregon Health Sciences University, Portland, Oregon) with sites in AZ (Window Rock, Navajo), SD (Pine Ridge, Sioux), Canada (Manitoulin Island and other places) (James Shore, Morley Beiser, Spero Manson, Gerald Mohatt, Judy Kleinfeld, John Redhorse). Afterwards, he and his family moved to Logan, Utah where he designed, secured funding and directed a doctoral program in psychology for American Indian and Alaska Native students. At USU Damian conceived of and initiated a gathering of American Indian psychologists and psychology graduate students that had an academic component (conference proceedings) and social-traditional component (camping and sharing in the mountains at Bear Lake). That gathering has occurred annually for the past 33 years and grown to include other Native healers, including those from Hawaii and New Zealand (Maori), among others.

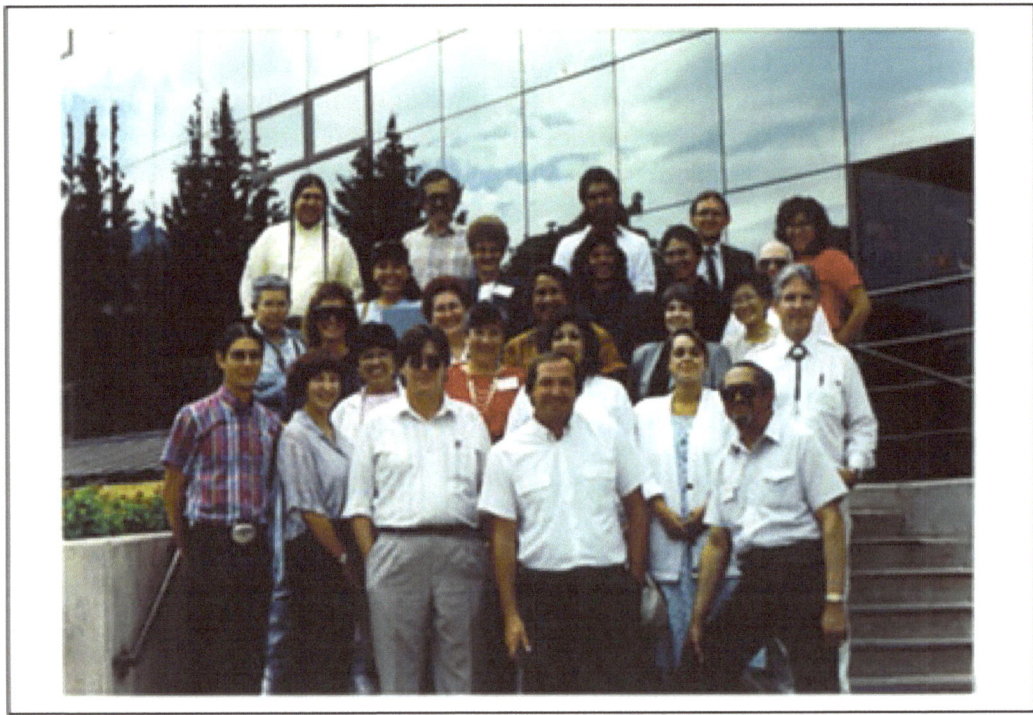

**Photo 2.** First meeting of the Annual Conference of American Indian Psychologists and Psychology Graduate Students at Utah State University, 1987. (Back row: Art Martinez, Paul Dauphinais, Steven Byers, Ed Starr, Mary Nordwall; Next row: Rebecca Crawford, Carolyn Barcus, unidentified woman, unidentified man, Art Blue; Next row: Beatrice Medicine, unidentified woman (sunglasses), unidentified woman, Grace Sage, unidentified woman, unidentified woman; Next row: Kevin Foley, unidentified woman, unidentified woman, Candace Fleming, Linda Dyer, unidentified woman, Scott Nelson; Front row: unidentified man, Damian (McShane) Vraniak, unidentified man.

Returning home to Wisconsin (Madison) eventually led to returning home to Springbrook and integrating these experiences into the culturally relevant design and development of curriculum and training materials for staff of an environmental charter school, culminating in summer programming over several years on Vraniak land in Springbrook, for reservation and non-reservation children.  Damian hosted an annual community prairie tour – this coming year to be its 25th – and invited out students from five different school systems to see, plant and restore. He began a not-for-profit organization (*Prairie FEASSST*), secured grants to do a variety of projects with the land that would be recognized with a regional award, create a Friends group (*Friends of the Namekagon Barrens Wildlife A*rea), becoming its first President; helped begin a recomposed *St. Croix river Association*, begin a new organization called the *Namekagon River Partnership*, sitting on the respective boards of directors. Damian also began a special project bringing older and younger people together on the landscape along the river (*Mashkawis, River Elders*), hosted a series of meetings at his home along the Namekagon River on the St. Croix River National Scenic Riverway between the National Park Service and the Boy Scouts *Order of the Arrow* in order to bring 300 young men to do projects along the river, and many other teachings, trainings and sharings. Selected entries from Damian's various journals illustrate this interwoven journey upon the landscape…

Journal Entry: *September 7, 1992*                    *Monday 11:45 pm*

*My son and I discussed what we had done this weekend. In one manner of speaking we built more firebreaks or roadways on the central forty acres in order to be able to burn and further develop prairie grasses and forbs, as well as to make it easier to dig a few ponds. In other words, we scrapped the living covering from the earth we steward, leaving bare the sand and soil which had given nurturance to the living green that had existed upon it.*

*My son and I discussed our feelings about what we had done to the earth, uncomfortable feelings that bothered us in some vague but definite way. We had done something, as Peter said, that we could not retrieve; we had somehow changed the wildness and free beauty into something less so … something more controlled, more contained and more planned.  We had altered the balance between the wild and the civil.*

*The only mitigation to this uneasy sense of injury is the knowledge that green will follow uncovering and burning, and the heartfelt sense of purpose that I am physically and spiritually a part of the water, earth and wood I meet and interact with, and that together we may do a brief dance of beauty, that this dance will be taken up by my son and my son's sons or daughters, and, that, in the end, the wind, water and woodland will caress and hold the earth without our ephemeral touch. In truth, both dances will be once and again forever a living act of love and beauty.*

7-FEB-1994 13:27:24.04                              MAIL
From:  SOC::VRANIAK
To:    EUNICE::"----@publications.wisc.edu"
CC:    VRANIAK
Subj:  today

The last three mornings I have been able to view the sunrise. This is a coming back to a
more natural, daily rhythm for me and has done much to settle my soul.

I missed you at the gym today. I do not know if I will be able to accept your dinner invitation
for this evening; in the late afternoon I am going out to Mt. Horeb to get my seeds and to
explore how they do early seeding and growing indoors. However, I am going to spend a
quiet evening at home later, .... Again, thank you for the invitation ... have a good day.


22-FEB-1994 09:17:41.68                             MAIL
From:  SOC::VRANIAK
To:    MHRC::----
CC:    VRANIAK
Subj:  RE: day of importance

... my day of importance went quite well; I was very pleased. After meeting with two or
three different groups in the morning, I walked into the Dean for Students conference room,
into a meeting with seven or eight women of color (and one guy) ... it was like coming home.
One forgets how comfortable it can be with those of similar background and worldview and
common cause. I get lost in the main culture of the university sometimes and coming back
to the reservation or to a small caring community of ethnic minority folks is like breathing
the fresh air of Maainganagun after the fumes of the city.

...thank for your wishes and thoughts; they made me smile and warmed my heart.   -D


*January 15, 2001*                    Time: 7:30pm

Temperature: 32°F
Sun: overcast
Precipitation: light snow

      One of my clients today described how her mother places carrots in a ten-gallon
container of sand in such a manner that no one carrot touched another. Stored in this
manner the carrots remain fresh all winter in the 'root cellar'. Her mother jars different
berries, as well. She also mentioned an uncle or friend who cans potatoes in a way that
preserves them for a long time and they taste great when opened and prepared however
one prepares potatoes.

      Mom mentioned that Mike Waggoner is the best gardener around, and Barb
(Vraniak) Turpin has had a produce garden and put up vegetables for years. I believe I will
interview [as I did retired educators, medical and mental health professionals] several local
individuals and try to secure their view of the best of the local practices, varieties and
preparations for this climate, soil conditions and geography.

I am truly excited about visiting the local agricultural station in Spooner, area orchids, the ag school in Madison, and in general forage for best practices, as done by those who have been doing so for a long time!!!!


*January 16, 2001*          Time: 8:30pm


Temperature: 17°F
Sun: overcast
Precipitation: light snow


There is a story about how recent cross-breeding of blueberries has resulted in high bush blueberries that are 10-15' tall ??!! Is this true? There is one local berry farm in Shell Lake and another in a county to the south that raises different kinds of berries, which will be good to visit.


*January 17, 2001*          Time: 9:30pm


Temperature: 13°F
Sun: clear
Precipitation: light snow


This was a busy day and I only had time to find a couple of sites concerning beans and book-marking them. Betti's son Scott who lives on Chippewa Trail has acquired some dehydration or freeze-drying equipment and also a small device that tightly wraps and seals with plastic dried foods in such a manner that there is no air in the packet. Betti will ask Scott about the details and get back to me.


*January 19, 2001*          Time: 8:30pm


Temperature: -7°F
Sun: clear
Precipitation: none


I am thinking it will be good to specify each of the garden plants and the number of seeds that will be planted in order to be able to obtain the proper quantities of seed. Indeed, I have already found seed sources for three or four bean varieties that were grown by tribes in the northeast, midwest/plains and west. The other aspect is to draw a graphic depicting where all the varieties of plants will be located, including those sections that will provide next year's seed.


*January 20, 2001*          Time: 9:00pm


Temperature: 0°F
Sun: clear
Precipitation: none

It was almost -20°F this morning at sunrise, but reached +20°F by the afternoon; it was a clear, crisp, beautiful day. Tom Brown Jr.'s book on wild plants is quite helpful since it is based in large part in the pine barrens of NJ. Today I collected sweet fern leaves from the knoll on snowshoe and brewed a nice aromatic cup of tea; the second cup with honey added was tasty as well. I look forward to trying dried fresh leaves in the spring. I should write Tom Brown, Jr. a letter and eventually meet him. It seems appropriate given his relationship with Grandfather and with the pine barrens. [Subsequently, Damian would train with Tom Brown three times for extended periods, twice in NJ and once in CA.]

*January 21, 2001*                    Time: 3:00pm

Temperature: 21°F
Sun: clear
Precipitation: none

A fine clear, sunny day. I felled the aspen just to the north of the walkway up the hill; just a few more aspen to come down and the area to the south and east of the house should be primarily pine. Discovering some field guides and naturalist writings with regards to the New Jersey pine barrens suggests that I should explore the other primary local geographic areas where pine and fire and sandy soils have occurred in conjunction with one another and seek any literatures (historical, ecological, current) that develop knowledge of such ecological terrain.

*December 28, 2002*                    cloudy in the am with light
Saturday   6 pm                        snow, mid-30's sun in pm

Picked up mail and went for a 2 mile walk.

Four adult men on sand road with bows, five standing back in woods.

Mid-day gathered flats into back of truck and seeded lupine, hyssop (x3), onion (x3), cup plant, compass plant, prairie dock and others and then placed on bedroom deck.

Toward dusk the solar array still faced northeast although the sun shone brightly in the southwest. Using the extension brush I placed a rag on the west side of the small device which orients the array and the array then moved to the east, then the south and then oriented correctly to the southwest. This evening tried to burn remaining brush pile with little success.

*Hope with a good measure of discipline will accomplish much.*

*January 4, 2003*                    cloudy with brief flurries
Saturday   10 pm                      20's

Went for a walk down the sand road in the morning. A goshawk flew up a few feet from me. Feeding on a rabbit the goshawk probably did not see me until the last minute. The last time

67

I saw a goshawk was in the late 1970's while living on the reservation (Chief Lake) under similar circumstances, it having killed a snowshoe rabbit in winter. Moved the new file cabinet into the guest room and that cabinet into the library. Mapped disturbance planting matrix. Answered questions by a reporter on the telephone regarding 'after holiday blues'.

*A sudden surprise is either a path to wonder or to suffering. Be prepared for either, for both are gifts to be received with humility and gratitude. The loosening of laughter and tears is always a prelude to new opportunities to learn and to love.*

*January 5, 2003*                                   cloudy with brief flurries  
Sunday   8 pm                                      20's

Woke late and went for a walk on the woodland trails, taking pictures and then onto the islands. Sideoats, blue and hairy grama are all coming along nicely.

Read a bit of Weaver's 50-year study ... needle grass among the first to send up shoots and livestock love it so much it is often eaten out of an area.

Put up wood duck house opposite the cabin on a dead jackpine on the edge of the pond..

Cut down three jackpine leaning out over the channel.

Walked ... on new back loop.

Talked with Mom about her angiogram tomorrow and about Snooks' bone cancer.

Played new word game after dinner.

*Whether life seems short or long, each moment is as precious as the gift of love.*

*January 7, 2003*                                         sunny  
Tuesday   9 pm                                      40's, near 50

Did the Cat's-eye and lifted early in the morning, came back and had eggs and rice. Most of the day was spent finishing revising the preface and overview for Book III, it came out quite well! U of Nebraska Press is interested in the story books and we will see if they like them. This evening watched Barb's son Grant play for Spooner against Hayward in basketball after dinner at Subway.

*There is a wonderful flow in living that you can catch briefly for a few moments ... cherish those moments.*

Excerpt from ***Prairie Relations***: *Book One: Seasons, Signs and Flowering Plants of the Prairie and Savanna* (2004)

[shared as the Plenary (closing) Speaker at the 19th North American Prairie Conference, University of Wisconsin – Madison in Madison, WI August 8-12, 2004]

"It was such a simple act, planting flowers with my grandmother when I was small. The sunlight fell softly on our shoulders and arms; the soil was warm to the touch. With the sun gently behind and above, the earth welcoming beneath and below, my grandmother kneeled next to me … we kneeled together, carefully parting the soil, gently placing the young plants and covering their roots. This seemed my first true prayer. I was too young to know about grace, but kneeling in the soil with my grandmother I learned deeply of comfort.  The land is now and always a warm and welcoming hearth, and the memory of her kind and caring heart is comfort for me still.

However, now there is a crisis of comfort and caring in my community as such contact with the land and with family is being lost. The crisis calls forth a response from each one of us who has been so fortunately gifted in our experience. This is my response.

As I share such words as these with you they are not meant to be another way for you to be a spectator, for you only to read once again the shared expressions of those who have had direct experience of prairie and savanna. To be touched by the expressions of others is necessary and good, yet it is less than choosing to touch the land and the life of the land yourself, and to be touched by them directly, in turn. For words are not warmth and concepts are not caring.

Many of you already know that information is not knowledge, and that knowledge is not wisdom. More importantly, ideas are not relationships … if each of us does not experience contact with the land directly, engage the life that lives upon the land with tender respect and caring ourselves, then mere words and stories will not call forth a sufficient response to the crisis we face.

While television and radio, and, yes, even books are sensory in nature, they are not whole, for they do not require us to respond and reply in relationship; thus they are sedentary, secondary and vicarious.

In my response to this situation I have been doing prairie and pine barrens/savanna restoration since 1975, with the land upon which my family has lived for generations. In a very literal sense I have regularly knelt upon the earth with children and youth in much the same manner as my grandmother knelt carefully and prayer-fully with me.

In the past two decades I have involved tribal youth and high school students in my restoration efforts as a way of helping them to recover a more intimate relationship with the land and with their families. In the process of sharing with them the geological and cultural history of the land, I have shared the unique traditional stories of the origins and uses of prairie plants, as well as the varied (and sometimes opposing) history of my family's stewardship of the forests, grasslands and wetlands in the Dakotas, Minnesota, Wisconsin, and the Great Lakes provinces of Canada, during the past 500 years.

So it is that over the past twenty-five years I have watched this deepening crisis of caring, as deteriorating families and communities have undermined the ability of children to grow and thrive well. Many of us have worked against these worsening currents and contexts, trying to help children and couples survive, become healthier.

During this period there also has been an expanding crisis of ecological connection and consideration, as the use and development of the land increasingly destroys its future vitality and providence. Some of us have worked against this narrow exploitation for economic profit, trying to illustrate by example how the land might be restored and enhanced to benefit future generations. In my effort to express the crucial relationships between and among these layers, I have found hope for the children of my community and focus for my work by mapping the following layers of potential for change:

*Cultural Rehabilitation  -  restoring a community's identity           (synchrony)*
*Family Renewal       -  reviving and reclaiming life's intimacy     (harmony)*
*Ecological Restoration   -   recovering the land's integrity      (balance)*

One of my primary experiences has been that family life can be revived and reclaimed when the family is once again involved, as a family, in those traditions that historically were determined to be a part of their grandparents' and great-grandparents' relationship with the land, especially sustainable subsistence activities. Indeed, if done in an informed manner, a variety of foraging and gardening *efforts can involve restoring the land as a fundamental method of uncovering caring … caring for the land can lead to a renewal of loving one another well.* If a family, by exploring its own history of relationship with the land and with one another, can share that process of discovery and recovery with a few other families, then the possibility of restoring a sense of common purpose and identity in the community is increased.

This need only occur on a very small scale to have a considerable impact upon family, neighborhood and community life – planting some flowers, picking a few native berries, gathering some eggs from the one hen, helping to lamb, making apple sauce, offering a recipe for venison stew or smoked fish – and, most importantly, sharing with one another the stories of how great-grandma and grandpa did it.

My mother tells the story of her early contact with prairie grasses, early in the last century, as an example of recalling such activities: *Dad would have all fifteen of us kids get gunny sacks and wet them in the pond. We would make a large circle around the grassy meadow and he would light last year's dead grasses. When the fire got close to anyone in the circle we would beat it with our wet sacks. We did this to improve the forage for the animals, as the young shoots would come up green and succulent.*

In this manner of recalling, this book is a sharing of the stories of my family - stories of the Huron and Menominee, Ojibwe and Cree, Assiniboine and Ho-chunk, and the stories my family's friends and neighbors who were traders, explorers, writers, naturalists and scientists. It is also a sharing of pictures, of visual images of the flowers that have come from the seeds I have planted, of the grasses I have burned and of the animals like the deer and the rabbit who have eaten those forbs and grasses, and whom I have eaten. When I die and I am food for the flowers I have cared for, these animals will eat me as well, completing a very natural and sacred circle of nourishing stories.

May these words and pictures touch you simply and deeply, and then move you to engage directly in the experience of the land. My hope and prayer is to generate in you an impulse toward the contact which will bring attachment, much more than persuade you to think new abstract thoughts or bigger ideas. May your hands feel the soil and your heart comfort and gratitude!

So, let us begin now. In the following pages a series of traditional tribal stories about the origins and qualities of wildflowers found in prairies and savannas are retold in their seasonal order. The stories and accompanying narrative offer the reader guidance in restoring integrity and balance to the land and recovering intimacy and harmony in our relationships. It is suggested that the restoration of endangered ecologies and the re-vitalization of deteriorating individual and family life may inform and support one another; that is, care, respect and positive relationship with the land may increase balance within ourselves and the harmony between us.

The land itself is the most compelling aspect of the narratives. The land is so providential in its beauty and so generous in its loving abundance; it is so alive in its presence, if we open our eyes and hearts to its presence and its essence:

*Upon the Prairie*

*To walk upon the land alone, but in the footsteps of those who have gone before us, is to learn to sense the beauty of before and the lasting scenes of beauty yet available to us now. This is to come to recognize the reality we share with our ancestors and with God.*

71

*To share water with one another, even so much as to share the journey of sperm and egg – a most intimate joining of water with water – is to share the songs of love. This is to realize intimate relationship with each other.*

*To share the wind, the very air, is to breathe together the shared stories of living that are true. We represent the relations of beauty with love and share this truth with all others.*

*In the fire which devours all, we cease and allow all to burn away, until only essence remains. This is to rest in the silence of the sacred in order to recover and recompose and, eventually, to begin anew, and complete once and forever again the circle of the spirit-which-moves-through-the-all-of-everything."*

And so, after the loss of his wife, Damian and his children would travel up north, to the place he was born and grew up, to the land his grandparents shared with him, at least once a month, often every other weekend or for extended periods in the summer, where he would find solace in restoring the wetlands, prairie and savanna over the next 25 years, coming to live here after both children graduated from high school.

*February 19, 2005*
Saturday
0 F  crystal clear,   snow on the ground

A night full of dreams. Sun sparkling off the snow and the sky a bright blue. The day begins fresh and new.

*Lord, thank you for the beauty of your creation and the surprising wonder of this new day.*

*March 17, 2005*
Thursday, 5:10 am
 3 F  clear,  snow on the ground

I woke up about 1-2 am last night with my neck and left pec pain ... the vicadin worked for a while at least. The early morning was not wasted, however, as I was able to articulate 'braided corridors' and c-CARE (citizen, couple, class, club, county, corporate conservation and restoration efforts) and map out a 4-year plan to plant lupine for karner blue butterflies in a manner that links Crex, Namekagon and Douglas Co Wildlife refuge Barrens. Exciting !!!

*Lord, bless my efforts to restore the landscape and our healthy relations with it and one another.*

*March 21, 2005*　　　　　　　11 F  clear,  melting snow
Monday, 5:15 am

The boxes for the library at UND are packed and will picked up at 3 pm today. Peter is indeed going to Denver Health Medical Center for his residency and Brook took the job with the Corporate Executive Board of the SAT's and will locate in Washington, D.C. Today I will draft the Friends of Bradley Brook charter and revise the draft of the <u>Pine Barrens, Oak Savanna Corridor Mapping and Restoration proposal</u>. It is as if I have finally gotten to where I would like to have begun in 1989 … it only took 16 years, as along as I had been married to Anne.

*Lord, please forgive my slow, faltering way upon the path that you have offered me. Guide my steps so that now they might be straight and true.*

*March 24, 2005*　　　　　　　32 F  cloudy,  melting ice and snow
Thursday, 6:45 am

I burned the low meadow last night, just before the dance party. The fire burned the sedges and blue joint grass down to about an inch of the soil, which is still wet and/or frozen. This will help reduce risk when Jim Reimer and others come out to burn in earnest later in the spring.

*Approaching Easter, Lord, and it is your sacrifice and suffering that humbles me in gratitude.*

*March 25, 2005*　　　　　　　18 F  clear,  melting ice and snow
Thursday, 5:05 am

The moon is full and bright in the sky, as we celebrate our Lord's gift of suffering. Yesterday I stopped by and spoke with Ernie Lein, who knew all of my aunts and uncles, who worked for Pat for several years. He talked about how Hwy 24 went across Bradley Brook and became the first signatory [to the Friends group]. What a great conversation and it was his 85th birthday yesterday! Also had an interesting talk with Dick Pfister; he showed me his 800 acres and what he is doing with it, after relating the story of acquiring it from an old farmer who chose to give it to him instead of his kids, who then died the next week. Stories of the heart's connection to the land ….

*Lord, to place the heart upon the path in spite of inevitable suffering entails such caring courage … strengthen me!*

*March 27, 2005*　　　　　　　20 F  clear,  melting ice and snow only remaining in woods
Thursday, 7:25 am

It is Easter; we are forgiven and death is vanguished … such mercy and compassion calls forth awe, wonder, humility and joy. The geese are calling loudly each morning. The front pond is open, yet there is still ice in the channels and back ponds. Bucky and I piled the downed aspen by the cabin, to be burned at a later date. Eagles are feasting on uncovered deer along the roadsides; I have seen two kestrels and Nancy has seen a marsh hawk gliding along the creek and low meadow. It is spring.

*Lord, Lord, Lord … our hearts rise as you have risen and we sing the joy of a song everlasting …*


*March 28, 2005*              34 F  clear,  melting ice and snow only remaining in woods
Monday, 8:50 am

The first red-winged blackbird arrived today and I thought I heard a cardinal calling. The kingfisher came by and two deer crossed my path on my early walk. Most seeds have germinated in the flats at the dance studio. Spring is beginning and early migrants will be arriving daily.

*Lord, thank you for the warming sun in this new season.*


*March 27, 2005*              48 F  cloudy
Tuesday, 4:50 am

The first pair of doves, a crane calling, wood ducks in the front pond, a cardinal calling yesterday, signal the beginning of spring in earnest. Last afternoon Josie and I selected a boulder which Thompsons will place between 63 and the railroad tracks near Bradley Brook at the outskirts of Hayward, upon which we will put a plaque relating to our restoration effort. Today I go to Crex Meadows to talk at the sharptail grouse conference. Tonight it is supposed to rain, with the possibility of thunder. Some say thunder is necessary for helping the frost to go out quickly.

*Lord, thank you for the rain, for the opportunities to share with others the beauty, love and truth of your creation.*


*March 28, 2005*              48 F  cloudy
Wednesday, 5:25 am

On my way to Crex … first meadowlark of the season … at Crex … trumpeter swans, bald eagle nesting, wood ducks, geese, cranes, marsh hawk, buteos, first bluebird. The DNR professionals managing sharptails started with young researchers who had few answers to the wrong questions, rather than beginning with the elders who might have asked the best questions in relation which to focus our attention. I was to be the last speaker and the second to the last speaker went over by 45 minutes, meaning I began when the gathering was to end for the day and go to supper … my attempt to shorten and extemporaneously do my piece left me frustrated and disappointed. It has been a while since I have spoken to a large group to my satisfaction, in spite of less than optimal contexts and situations.

*Lord, what am I to do, here at the end?*

*March 29, 2005*
Wednesday, 6:25 am
34 F  cloudy          new snow on the ground, melting, very windy

The red leaves of the northern red oaks are bright against the new fallen snow that is fast melting. The past is honored as movement toward the future proceeds apace. What we hold onto and what melts away is often a bittersweet experience, when both are present, if only for a moment.

*Lord, may your gifts balance the losses we so poignantly experience.*

*April 2, 2005*          22 F  clear      little snow, creek waters coming up through bridge
Saturday, 6:15 am

There is still no communication from Jim Evrard, the person inviting me to speak at the gathering of Barrens managers ... no thank you, nothing. Courtesy has indeed left the world bereft of considerate manners.

Bluebirds have arrived. Today I rototill the garden and a few patches where more native forb seeds will be placed. Hopefully a couple of teens can come out and continue to help pile logs and brush.

*Lord, comfort those who pray for the pope.*

*April 3, 2005*      24 F  clear    little snow, creek waters still coming up through bridge
Sunday, 6:25 am

The Pope died yesterday. I rototilled the garden and the new planting area behind the cabin. Visiting Paul Kraemer just out of Hayward, he offered me a small trailer-load of 7-year old dried pig manure that I placed in the sandier part of the garden. Today the kids come and help complete piles of debris between 2 and 5 pm. This morning I will seed several areas – behind the cabin and some of the small brush-pile burn areas in the back 40 savanna. We move our clocks ahead today, which means it will still be light when we eat dinner and go to bed. It is indeed spring.

*Lord, thank you so very much for the beauty, the sounds and sights, of spring!*

*April 5, 2005*          46 F  clear              snow gone , creek waters have dropped more
Tuesday, 6:15 am

It was warmer than usual last night I once I woke it was difficult to return to sleep. Yesterday I saw my first killdeer (although I had heard one a couple of days earlier) and a phoebe hit the picture window in the dining room and flew off. The day before yesterday a wood duck or merganser exited the nesting box at the cabin pond. Prairie smoke plants on the knoll are greening. My meeting with Ted [Gostmoski] yesterday went quite well and after a stroll around the wolf trail, we detailed the pine barrens mapping and lupine planting proposal.

*Lord, thank you for this spring without surgeries and a cast!*


*April 7, 2005*　　　　26 F  clear　　　　snow gone, creek waters have dropped more
Thursday, 5:45 am

The swallows are back checking out the martin house, but do not seem to stay. Mallards are mating; mergansers were diving in the creek pool by the bridge; a bear took down the bird feeder; bald eagles, broad winged hawks, marsh hawk all pass over the meadows. I finally cut sown the jack pine from which I fell … there is now only a stump remaining.

Work on *Maps and Metaphors* is going slowly but well. I await Pete's call regarding our trip this spring.

*Lord, please keep me focused on only one or two projects so that I might complete them!*


*April 11, 2005*　　　　54  cloudy　　　creek waters have slightly dropped more
Monday, 825 am

Burned Friday and Saturday evenings. The low meadow and the east hill of the cabin pond burned, as a bit of a wind picked things up and made them more exciting than I would have liked. I talked with Peter about a mountain hiking trip in CO after he gets set up in Denver … now I will have to get in better shape!

*Lord, please be with Peter as he tries to recover from his exhaustion.*


*April 13, 2005*　　　　28 F  clear　　　creek waters have dropped significantly
Wednesday, 6:55 am

I cut some of the brush on the east hill of the cabin pond, biked and hiked yesterday. Pete is suggesting canoeing the White or Albany Rivers in Ontario and then hiking, rather than hiking in the mountains of Colorado; we will talk today. Talked with Pam Rasmussen of Xcel Energy and TPE [The Prairie Enthusiasts] and she will be supportive of our pine barrens corridor proposal to the DNR. Radio show this morning … and so on … very busy!!!

*Lord, please keep all those we love safe in these transitions and travels!*


*2006 March 26*　　　　mid-40's　　　Sunny, wind from SE
Sunday

　　　As I burned a few brush piles and the southern slopes, two buteos circled overhead, much higher up a crane croaked and spiraled, watching the flames, and a bald eagle crossed the river nearby. A lone red wing blackbird arrived, a shrike made its unusual song from a high perch and a bluebird winged by.

*2006 March 27*                     35 F     Sunny and calm
Monday 8:20 am

        The red-winged blackbirds have arrived in force, singing their territories from atop brush and pine. Twenty-some geese in V's headed north while another group circled back to the big island in the river. Then a flock of ducks wheeled, straightened out and went on to parts only they could fathom. Three red squirrels met grandpa's 22 rifle while in the box elder tree next to the cabin, and one was in the live trap placed by the garage door; he gained freedom on the other side of Spring Creek. It is surprising how noisy spring is compared to the silence of winter!

*Appearing in the mind, with one hand fear twists the stomach and with the other squeezes the heart; the only recourse is to let fear go from its primary residence so that it looses its fierce some grip.*

**From:** Damian A Vraniak <maaingan@centurytel.net>
**Date:** April 13, 2006 8:14:24 AM CDT
**To:** Peter Vraniak <dvraniak@hotmail.com>, Peter Vraniak <dpv2001@columbia.edu>
**Subject: bears, kestrels and wolves**

Hi, Pete.

        A couple of days ago the bear finally came out of its den by the cabin and came up to the house for his first meal - a bird feeder; he was long and lanky (about 300 lbs), much thinner than when I saw him enter his den in the fall. Yesterday the kestrels were mating, and today I ran into a wolf on the back 40 savanna trail - she looked at me and I at her and then she trotted off. Spring is here in earnest!

      love,
          Dad

*January 12, 2014*        *4:30 am*         Journal Entry

        Many times have I begun this process of recollection, reflection and recomposition, of remembering, being present and dreaming. And so I begin again.

        The Earth: The Bones of My Ancestors *(Day 1)*

        I am of the earth formed by the bones of my ancestors. Laid down over the millennia, this beautifully fertile essence has come to me directly in my dna and indirectly in the bones that are the words, both oral and written, that have come into being because my ancestors were present upon the earth.

<u>Past:</u> My great grandfather *Nicolas Arendaki* provided for his young wife and new daughter in the Huron way in the fertile ground near what we now call Georgian Bay of Lake Huron. His name means 'Spirit of the Rock' in the language of the Wyandot, the Huron. He helped build the lodges from the oaks, burn the savanna which allowed the planting of the corn, his

community rotating every 40 years or so in a cycle of replenishing the soil. In 1649, when his daughter Katherine Annenontha was not yet one year of age, he laid down his bones in this soil by the great lake named after his people during one of the first battles with the Iroquois, who would shortly destroy the Huron Nation as a community of clans woven together in such sustainable use of the land, in protection of his wife and daughter, his clan and community. He was one of the first chiefs of a Huron clan to become a Christian, and, I suspect, this also contributed to the reason for his dying. There is a picture of a mask made from the soil of that region that looks at me from my wall, as I honor the life and death of my ancestor, Nicholas Arendaki, in some small, but fundamental way.

Present: In the beginning it is a small step. To start writing about my intent to attach to the land in an ever deepening cycle of seasonal living, is to begin to come home truly. Is it possible to align more clearly and cleanly with the land that is *here*, with life that is *close*, in a manner that expresses the natural sequence and order of right relations between the two? This will I attempt as best I may, with humility and gratitude for the opportunity to do so.

The first effort is to begin to be awake and alert and aware of the **parts**:

> What are the elemental parts here? (Describe the constituents –
> > earth, water, air, fire.)
>
> What are the essential participants? (Describe the constituencies-
> > plant and animal life.)
>
> For my living, what is minimally providential? (Determine what parts
> > are nutriment (food and drink).

> When and where are these nutritious and providential essences available?

The second effort is to begin to appreciate my relationship with these **processes**:

> How do I encourage seed and root, sapling and yearling to grow?
> How do I find, collect, prepare and consume each life-giving essence?
> How do I gather and harvest and store each life for future consumption?

> How do save and restore some of each for re-birth and the genesis of a
> > new cycle?

Why will these first and second efforts lead to an effort to understand the primary and most important **principles** of living?

> A definitive contact and experience of the local landscape leads to a deep
> recognition of reality which results in *integrity-through-learning*;
> A close and regular connecting engagement with local life leads to a deep
> realization of relationship which is an *intimacy-through-loving*;
> The informing contributions of these life-giving parts and processes
> expresses  a re-presentation of reality and relationship that may be
> shared with others which is an *identity-through-living*.

> And, finally, there is an exiting of this local life-death-life cycle which allows a
> release and restoration which is an *integration-through-leaving*.

This, then, is the **pattern**:

The Land gives and I am nurtured, *within*, my body becoming what is in me to be;
A generous Life offers Love, *between*, one heart and another, belonging;
And these well-ordered relations are a natural Law, *among* us, that contributes a
mindful believing;

All woven together, there is a final Leaving of scenes, songs and stories, to a silence which is the sacred source which runs *through* it all, making each and every one a part of the whole.

*Future:* This first entry has been so long … tomorrow I will be more brief, simpler, in what I voice of what I dream.


*January 13, 2014*      *11:30 am*     Journal Entry

The Earth: The Bones of My Ancestors *(Day 2)*

My ancestor and great grandfather, *Jean Durand*, came from Doeuil in the ancient province of Saintonge (now part of the Department of Charente-Inferieure), bordered on the north by Poitou and Aunis, to the west by the Atlantic, to the west Guyene and to the east Angoumois. The area then was known for its great fertility of soil, for the esteemed absinthe that grew there, and for the best salt in the world produced there from an astonishing number of salt marshes. Born in the village Doeuil on the river Mignon in 1636, Jean Durand would leave when he turned 21, to travel to the New World in the spring of 1657 on the ship "the Arms of Amsterdam" as an *engagee* of *Antoine Grignon* (another ancestor we will speak of later) and his son Jean, his brother-in-law Pierre Gaigneur and Jacques Masse, to work along the St. Lawrence River between Quebec City and Montreal at Cap Rouge for three years.

There are two etymologies of the name 'Durand'. The first starts from the Latinized form *Duramus* containing two elements: *Dur* – referring to the 'God Thor' and *ramn* – referring to 'raven' in the Old German, combining to be come 'raven of the God Thor". This connection to the *raven* becomes quite important much later in this story of the bones of my ancestors. The patronymic 'Durand' may be understood, as well, to come from the Latin *"durare"* which means 'to last, to endure, support and perservere', a very appropriate naming for this man and this family, indeed! In the times of Jean Durand, names conveying an idea of endurance and fortitude were in great favor, and, of note is the abbreviation of Durante, a name his friends liked to designate for the author of "The Divine Comedy", whom they found far too resolute, and persistent in his attitudes.

Jean Durand would marry the daughter of *Nicholas Arendaki*, **Catherine Annenotha**, when at 13 years of age she came out of the boarding school of the first Catholic nuns (the Ursulines) in the New World, able to speak and write in French, her Native Huron and a smattering of other Native languages she picked up from other Native children at the school. The sons and grandsons of these two would travel back and forth the entire length of the shores of all of the Great Lakes for at least 5 generations as Voyagers in the fur trade, sons who would also marry other Native women in other tribes.

*January 13, 2014*        *11:30 am*        Journal Entry

The Earth: The Bones of My Ancestors *(Day 3)*

### Origins of CADADEAU/CADOT/CADOTTE

Matherin Cadeau (1) dit Poitevin was born about 1590 in France and married Mathurine Menon and then Perrine Larcher.  Matherin's son, Rene Cadot (2) was born in 1620 in Andard, France and married Renee Rusgande.

Rene's son, Mathurin Cadot (3), was born in 1649 in Vendee, Poitou, France and came to the New World. There he worked for several years in the fur trade and made several trips to the upper country.

At age 39 he married **Marie-Catherine Durand**, the daughter of Catherine Annenontha and Jean Durand, who, like her mother, had come through the school of the Ursuline nuns. She was 22 years old. The two settled at Becancour and had six children: Their first, a girl named Marie Jeanne Cadot, was placed with the Ursulines like her grandmother and mother. Their second child, a son named Jean Francois Cadot (4), was born in1693 in Cap-de-Madeline, Quebec, married Marie Joseph Proteau and had six children, five of whom were sons. Augustin Cadotte (5) was born in 1728 and married Marie Joseph Cosset in 1759. Augustin's son *Laurent (6) would marry a Cree woman and live in the Red River region.* Augustin's brother, Jean Baptiste Cadotte would marry Anastasia Equawise at St. Ignace (Mackinac) Michigan. He worked as an interpreter for the fur merchants running the trading post at Sault-Ste. Marie.

In 1764, during the Pontiac war, Jean Baptiste Cadot saved the life of Alexander Henry, who left memoirs of Cadot and together formed a fur trading company in 1765 that extended their boundaries to the mouth of the Saskatchewan River in 1776. In 1775 Cadot and Henry were joined by Joseph and Thomas Frobisher, later by Peter Pond, thus forming the origins of the famous North-west Company.  Henry, who wanted to establish himself in the fur trade, requested that Cadotte, who knew the Indians extremely well, became his partner for "M. Cadotte enjoyed a powerful influence over their conduct. They considered M. Cadotte as their chief; and he was not only my friend, but also a friend to the English. It was by him that the Chipeways [sic] of Lake Superior were prevented from joining Pontiac. *"Cadotte's "powerful influence" stemmed in no small way from the fact that like so many of his compatriotes he lived among the Indians and had married one of them. "His Ojibway wife appears to have been a woman of great energy and force of character, as she is noted to this day for the influence she held over her relations - the principal chiefs of the tribe; and the hardy, fearless manner, in which, accompanied only by Canadian 'Coureurs du bois' to propel her canoes, she made long journeys to distant villages of her people to further the interests of her husband."* (Tobola, 1 4, Henry, 1 49; Tobola, 16).

[Note: When he is 9 years old *Laurent's* uncle, Jean-Baptiste Cadotte and Alexander Henry are joined by Joseph and Thomas Frobisher (and later by Peter Pond), forming an organization which can be considered the origin of North-West Fur Trading Company. His two slightly older cousins Jean-Baptiste (born 1761) and Michel (born in 1764) married into the Ojibwe communities and were central in the Sault-Mackinac-Lapointe fur trade. As this is a central "flow-through" or staging area either toward Green Bay or toward the Red River region west of Lake Superior, it is perhaps not surprising that the young *Laurent* ended up involved in the fur trade and found a Native wife (Suzanne Crise/Cree) and then located out in the Red River region.]

Cadot is one of the most ancient names that came from France during the Middle Ages. It is a Breton name for a person who was small but strong fighter. The name Cadotte is derived from the Old French word *cad*, which means little fighter.

CADOTTE : 'COAT OF ARMS' MOTTO : ' RIEN NE ME TOUCHE ' {Nothing touches me}

*Cadotte*
Canadian spelling, reflecting the local pronunciation, of French Cadot, a nickname meaning 'little dog'. Compare *Cadet.*

*Cadet*
Southern French: nickname from Old Occitan *cadet*, 'small dog', or perhaps from Gascon *capdet*, a term designating the youngest member of a family (however, this term is not recorded in French until the 15th century).

The daughter of Damian's younger brother (his niece), would marry a Cadotte and their children now attend LCO tribal and Hayward public schools. Her sister (his other niece) has become involved in mixed martial arts and embodies the legacy of our Cadot lineage and name. The children of the two sisters will undoubtedly be fierce competitors in the sports they are beginning.

---

As water nourishes, fire may destroy and renew. This is the challenge of children, to learn what is good for growing and what is not, what quenches the thirst and what burns. While each child's story begins in water, it begins anew when the child's feet gain solid purchase upon the earth, and the child begins the movement toward what sustains and away from that which diminishes, becoming well grounded in the various natural and human languages of the land.

In the beginning of this story, at the eastern end of the Great Lakes, the French called the children of white men and Indian women, **chicots** -- **half-burnt stumps** -- given the practice of their fathers, who typically were *coureurs de bois,* for taking a *roture* (a plot of land obtained from a *seigneur* in exchange for rent and dues), and then, rather than cultivating it, cutting the timber (burning the brush and stumps), selling it and finally abandoning the plot for another down river.

At the western end of the Great Lakes, the Ojibwe called such people, *wissakodewikwe (female) or wissakodewinini (male)*, after a commonly used term for a partially burned forest or tree, **wissakode**, for 'They call the half-breeds so, because they are half-dark, half-white, *like a half-burnt piece of wood*, burnt black on one end, and left white on the other'.

As some trees are better able to withstand the fires that kill the forest and promote the prairie, so do some men and women thrive in between the conflicting values and methods of different cultures. Red pine and oak tend to survive burning and provide beautiful open groves under which prairie grasses and forbs flourish, both renewed by frequent low to moderate fires. However, the forest does not intrude where the intense fires of the open prairie prevail, while prairie plants cannot survive the overcrowded density of fully canopied forest. The generational stories of my family that mixed the blood and ways of different peoples, the stories of the **chicots** or **wissakode, the half-burnt people**, may help to describe a manner in which the burning cultural conflicts may renew and open up new landscapes of opportunity rather than only destroy them, much as the fire renews the pine or oak savanna.

*The stories of the half-burnt children* are not only stories of survival in the face of disaster or destruction; they are not just stories of loss and lamentation. The stories of the half-burnt children are also resilient stories of acquiring many languages, of accumulating skills, techniques, information and knowledge from different cultures and integrating them into new configurations of coping and adaptation.  The stories of the half-burnt children are stories of wandering and searching the earth, first for a mate with whom to spend one's life, next for a place beneficent and providential for raising a family, and finally, for sustenance of the soul.

*How were these children raised; who raised them from birth through early infancy and childhood? How were these children educated; how and from whom did most of them learn one or more of their native languages, Latin, and one or more of the European languages? How did these half-burnt youth find partners to marry? How did the young couples support and provide for a family? And how did these half-burnt people endure the rejection and scorn of both Native and European communities?*

Intriguingly, there is another meaning of the French word *chicot* that illuminates these questions: The tree is now called the Kentucky coffee tree (*gymnociadus diocus*) and has been placed in the subfamily Caesalpinioideae of the legume family Fabaceae, native to Cananda, the Midwest, and the Upper South of North America. A 10-year-old sapling will stand about 4 meters (13 feet) tall. Its branches are stout, pithy, and blunt; roots are fibrous. The fairly short-lived, healthy trees living from 100 to 150 years *and* sheds its leaves early during the fall and appears bare for up to 6 months.

Because of the absence of smaller branches and its later leafing, the French in Canada named it **Chicot**, "stubby". The expanding leaves are conspicuous because of the varied colors of the leaflets; the youngest are bright pink, while those which are older vary from green to bronze, variation much like the coloring of the half-burnt children.

Winter twigs are very stout and dark reddish brown to green brown in color; the pith is very thick and salmon pink to brown in color. The terminal bud is absent,

82

and the lateral buds are small, bronze in color, and appear to be partially sunken beneath the bark of the twig.

Being a legume, the tree has pods six to ten inches (150–250 mm) long, one and one-half to two inches wide, somewhat curved, with thickened margins, dark reddish brown with slight glaucous bloom, crowned with remnant of the styles. Stalks an inch or two long. Seeds six to nine, surrounded by a thick layer of dark, sweet pulp.

The tree's taproot in proportion is like a carrot. A seedling tree grows many times in root length to its growth upward in height. The taproot makes the tree somewhat difficult to transplant. Being in the Legume family the roots fix nitrogen in the soil. It is tolerant of poor soils, has extreme drought tolerance, and is not vulnerable to serious insect infestations or disease problems.

The entire life cycle of Kentucky Coffee-tree is a relict of processes and environments driven by extinct large mammals. A number of tropical legumes with similar seed pods are successfully dispersed by agents such as elephants in West Africa and rhinoceroses in South Asia. The Chicot may have evolved its unique seeds, which seem unpalatable and even toxic to native fauna, specifically for the now-extinct mastodon-assisted dispersal. Thus, the coffee tree is considered an example of evolutionary anachronism. The tough, leathery seed pods are too difficult for many animals to chew through (in addition to being poisonous) and they are too heavy for either wind or water dispersal. It is thus believed that the tree would have been browsed upon by now-extinct mammalian megafauna who ate the pods and nicked the seeds with their large teeth, aiding in germination. This behavior is seen among African elephants eating *Fabaceae* relatives in Africa. Because of this, its prehistoric range may have been much larger than it has been in historical times. Today, in the wild, it only grows well in wetlands, and it is thought that only in such wet conditions can the seedpods rot away to allow germination in the absence of large herbivores.

The tree's native range is limited, occurring from Southern Ontario, Canada and in the United States from Kentucky (where it was first encountered by Europeans) and western Pennsylvania in the east, to Kansas, eastern Nebraska, and southeastern South Dakota in the west, to southern Wisconsin and Michigan in the north, and to northern Louisiana in the south. It is planted as an urban shade tree across the United States and eastern Canada, including California. *Gymnocladus dioicus* is used as a street tree as far north as Montréal, Québec. It resists well harsh winters and de-icing salts. The wood is used both by cabinetmakers and carpenters. It has very little sapwood.

This tree usually occurs as widely dispersed individuals or small colonial groups with interconnected root systems. This tree is found in floodplains and river valleys but is also sometimes seen on rocky hillsides and limestone woods. In the northeastern part of its range, seemingly natural groves of this tree are actually associated with known prehistoric village sites.

The beans of the tree were eaten, after roasting, in the *Meskwaki* (Fox), *Hocak* (Winnebago), and *Pawnee* tribal cultures. The Meskwaki also drank the roasted ground seeds in a hot beverage similar to coffee. The common name "*coffeetree*" derives from this latter use of the roasted seeds, which was imitated by settlers because it seemed a substitute for coffee, especially in times of poverty, similar to chicory. The European colonialists, however, considered it inferior to "real" coffee:

In addition to use as a food, the seeds of Kentucky coffeetree were used by Native Americans for ceremonial and recreational purposes. Seeds were used as dice in games of chance that were common in eastern tribes. The seeds were also used in jewelry. The importance of Kentucky coffeetree to Native Americans undoubtedly contributed to its dispersal.

A correlation exists between current extant stands of Kentucky Coffee-tree and former Native American and Aboriginal settlements; thus, it is possible to infer that these cultures played a significant role in the perpetuation of the species and in shaping the tree's current distribution (Van Natta, 2009). It is hypothesized that many of the floodplain populations of Kentucky Coffeetree occurring in North America originated from abandoned human settlements of Native Americans, Aboriginal peoples and early European pioneers where the seeds were used as game pieces and as a coffee substitute (after roasting to detoxify). Some occurrences on Walpole Island First Nation are known to be found near former Anishinabeg homesteads. Canadian occurrences are noted to follow known travel routes used historically by Aboriginal peoples, which may in part explain the species presence in floodplains, as streams were natural corridors of movement for Aboriginal peoples. Other traditional uses include jewelry, music, and medicine.

Coffee-trees are toxic to livestock, many were likely historically removed by farmers. Although rarely used industrially, Kentucky coffee-trees are rot resistant and occasionally used in the U.S. for railway ties, fence-posts, and in construction.

The *Omaha* used the outer covering of the root in hemorrhage, particularly from the nose or during childbirth. The root was used also when the kidneys failed to act. Their native name for the tree was *non'titahi*. The root, powdered and mixed with water, was administered to women during protracted labor. The pulp from the tree could be used to combat fever and to treat headaches, or as a laxative. The Omaha would mix bark of Kentucky coffee-tree and gayfeather (Liatris aspera Michx.) to use as an appetizer and tonic when mixed with crushed buffalo-gourd. The pulp was also used as a treatment for insanity and the leaves could be seeped as a tea-like drink.

The most significant use of beans from the Kentucky coffee-tree was for ceremonial and recreational purposes. Beans from the Kentucky coffee tree were used as dice in a game that was found in nearly every pre-colonial culture in some shape or form, explicitly among 130 different tribes. The game itself was given many names, including squaw dice, women's dice, bowl-and-dice, platter, hubbub, *Paquessen,* or simply called dice. While different forms of the game can be found across the United States, the most common variation of the dice game in the Great Lakes region was played with a bowl or basket, up to eight dice or sticks, and a hide or blanket.

To play the game, a hide or blanket was spread out on the ground and a pair or group of players sat around it. Two sides were needed, but the number of people on each side could be as few as one or as many as could fit around the playing area. The number of games played was decided by the players if the game was played for leisure; a dream or vision would otherwise dictate the number of games necessary: either 4, 8, or 12. Each player took turns tossing the dice by either throwing them upward out of a bowl and catching them again, or by throwing them against a hide or blanket that was held perpendicular to the ground and allowing them to fall, where they were scored. The score of each roll was determined by counting the number of dice of one color and assigning points based on a scoring system. Tribes across the U.S. had different methods of scoring, but the overall objective was the same: to receive the most points. Players kept track of scores using decorated sticks or beans, and the winner was the first to reach a set number.

Native Americans often placed wagers on such games, and spectators became involved by placing side bets (Oxendine 1983). While most Indians played because of social customs and not to gain possessions, by the 19th and 20th century such games were relatively uncommon because most early colonists to North America sought to stop such "evil" practices. While betting would have occurred when the game was played for recreation, the most significant implications of the game occur as it was played to fulfill a dream obligation.

The *Potawatomi* version of the dice game was played mostly in winter by women (although it wasn't uncommon for men to play as well), in place of double ball (a game also played by women, similar to lacrosse). Such games were played not simply for recreation, but "to honor the spirits and to cure the sick," as such ceremonial activities in *Menominee Music.*

The custom of fasting in order to receive a dream is common to many tribes. The dream promises certain benefits and makes certain requirements in order that the benefits may be received. The requirements differ among tribes, and the *Menominee* believe that they must play certain games in order to receive the benefits of two classes of dreams. If a woman dreams of the spirit women in the east, she must play either the bowl-and-dice (*akä'-sianûk'*) or the double-ball (*kowitci'isowûk*) game at definite times and in a prescribed manner, according to the directions received in the dream. Similar traditions held with the *Sioux* and *Chippewa*. In most cases, the playing of ceremonial bowl-and-dice games was said to provide healing or alleviate trouble or anxiety.

Winnebago (*Hočąk*) women also played the game and tell a story of its origins: According to Thundercloud, a Winnebago informant, there are four spirit women playing the bowl-and-dice game in the northern sky, and the eight stars in a circle (constellation known as the Northern Crown) are their dice. Once these stars dropped down to the earth and became the dice with which the Indian women play the game. Early in the morning, when the sky is red, the spirit women are playing their dice game, and the color in the sky is the color on their faces.

Colonists, again, viewed many of these practices as deplorable, which can account for the dwindling of such games by the 19th century. One such view can be observed in an account of the *Hurons* given by Father Brebeuf in 1636:

*There are three kinds of games particularly in vogue with this people; cross, platter, and straw. The first two are, they say, supreme for the health. Does not that excite our pity? Lo, a poor sick person, whose body is hot with fever, whose soul foresees the end of his days, and a miserable sorcerer orders for him as the only cooling remedy, a game of cross. Sometimes it is the invalid himself who may perhaps have dreamed that he will die unless the country engages in a game of cross for his health. Then, if he has ever so little credit, you will see those who can best play at cross arrayed, village against village, in a beautiful field, and to increase the excitement, they will wager with each other their beaver skins and their necklaces of porcelain beads. (Thwaites 1901)*

Because of the nature of the game, and the cultural and spiritual significances associated with it, games could continue for long periods of time. Sioux women often became completely absorbed in the game, 'sometimes playing all day and all night at a single sitting'. Other games continued for three or four days. The length of these games shows not only its popularity as a recreation, but also the significant role it played in Native American spirituality and culture.

Variant forms of the dice game can be found in nearly every Native American Culture across the United States. While the premise was basically the same, the tools used to play it were equally as numerous. The implements with which they were played were considered sacred and could not be sold. They were often decorated with sacred symbols that were supposed to bring luck to the player. Men, women, and children all played the game, but it is most often cited as a game for elderly women. The type of bowl or basket used in the dice game was dependent on available materials, spiritual evocations, or personal preference. For instance, a turtle shell could be used in accordance with a dream. If no such obligations existed, carved wooden bowls, woven baskets, or pottery were used to toss and catch the dice.

The most intriguing aspect of the bowl-and-dice game, however – and probably the most significant concerning the range of Kentucky coffee tree – was the type of material used to create the dice. Native Americans played with two-sided dice. These flat dice were colored or had decorative markings on one side, but the

86

opposite side was plain. There were made of bone, shells, split cane, wood, peach or plum pits, stone, pottery, and a variety of other materials. The *Menominee* used plum stones as dice, along with antler, beaver or muskrat teeth, and pieces of wood. The Chippewa also used plum stones (they called the game, in fact, *plum stones*), and both men and women played. The plum stones were carved to represent various images – a fish, a hand, a man, a canoe – the object being to make the figures stand upright". The *Dakota* also use a similar name for their version of the game.

Because Kentucky coffee-tree seeds are impermeable to water and require scarification to germinate, the act of carving or cutting the seeds by Native Americans for use in bowl-and-dice games would have created conditions beneficial to germination should the seeds become lost or discarded.

Music was another significant aspect of Native American culture that may have utilized Kentucky coffee tree seeds. Among the instruments described by Densmore in her book *Menominee Music* are drums, rattles, flutes, and whistles, not to mention songs of voice and dance. *Iroquois* living on the shores of Cayuga and Seneca Lakes used Kentucky coffee tree seeds in rattles. The two types of rattles used by the Menominee consisted of a hollow gourd filled with seeds or pebbles, and the second type a "doctor's rattle," as it was used by a doctor when treating the sick.

Finally, The Walpole Island Heritage Center in Ontario, Canada, comments on the appeal of Kentucky coffee tree seeds as beads in rustic jewelry. The center points out that "they are known as "hully-gullies" and are sometimes carried by children as a good luck charm." Walpole Island First Nation is comprised of six islands totaling 22,400 hectares in the St Clair River delta from Detroit. According to the World Wildlife Fund, the territory contains *seven of the most diverse tall grass prairie and oak savannah sites remaining in Canada.* These ecosystems, once abundant in the region, but now exceeding rare, have survived here for the simple reason that the practice of burning has been carried on by the *Ottawa, Ojibway, and Pottawatomi* tribes of the delta virtually without interruption from pre-contact times down to the present. Indeed, the history of burning on the island, the knowledge and attitudes of the local people, and the methods they use in burning have established the islands as a rare example of a central North American grasslands landscape where the ancient practice of burning has been maintained. Historically, burning has occurred on the island since pre-European settlement and was originally performed by young hunters to clear lands and maintain conditions suitable for farming and hunting. The burning off of trees and brush served to fertilize garden plots and enhance wildlife habitat. Burning also kept marsh areas open and free of dense undergrowth. Muskrats and migrating ducks attracted to these burned areas provided a major food source and source of income for hunters on the island. This practice continues today, with burning still carried out in ways that are more traditional than scientific. *In Canada, Kentucky Coffee-tree is found only in southern Ontario.* Of 33 known native populations, 23 are considered extant, with an estimated total population of fewer than 500 mature native trees. It is designated

Threatened in Canada under the Species at Risk Act (SARA). *Most of these are found at Walpole.*

Why be concerned with such a lengthy story about a term used pejoratively by French settlers in the New World in the 1600's to describe the half-breed (*chicot* – 'half-burned stumps') children of French fathers and Native mothers? Perhaps to suggest that the term might have been viewed differently by Damian's Huron/French ancestors and their children, given the much deeper recreational, ecological and spiritual relationship with the being so-named, that the French thought was just a short, squat tree to be removed because it interfered with animal husbandry as a result of its poisonous seeds. So it is that the *Chicot* tree and the *Chicot* people shared many more important characteristics and associations than the colonial settlers suggested in their naming.

---

*The stories of the marriages and journeys of Damian's ancestors and cultures eventually encircled the Great Lakes. Beginning near Quebec one family group took the northern route toward the Dakotas and the other branch of the family took the southern route toward Green Bay. Both branches reconnected in the meeting and marriage of my grandparents in northwestern Wisconsin, where Damian was born.*

Such is the firmament upon which my family traveled and lived for generations:

1) Upon the region of what is called the CANADIAN PRECAMBRIAN SHIELD, around 3 billion years old ... When the Greenland section is included, the Shield is approximately circular, bounded on the northeast by the northeast edge of Greenland, with Hudson Bay in the middle. It covers much of Greenland, Labrador, most of Quebec north of the St. Lawrence River, much of Ontario including northern sections of the southern peninsula between the Great Lakes, the Adirondack Mountains of northern New York, the northernmost part of Lower Michigan and all of Upper Michigan, northern Wisconsin, northeastern Minnesota, the central/northern portions of Manitoba away from Hudson Bay, northern Saskatchewan, a small portion of northeastern Alberta, and the mainland northern Canadian territories to the east of a line extended north from the Saskatchewan/Alberta border (Northwest Territories and Nunavut). In total, it covers approximately 8,000,000 km$^2$ (3,088,817 sq mi). It covers even more area and stretches to the Western Cordillera in the west and Appalachians in the east, but the formations are still underground. The underlying rock structure does include Hudson Bay and the submerged area between North America and Greenland;

2) along the MIDCONTINENTAL RIFT of basalt, over 1 billion years old, a rift that began and stopped, almost splitting North America in two, whose bulwarks of dark basalt can be seen along views on the St, Croix River system; and 3) through the thin layered soils along most of the Great Lakes overlaying this rock that are called ALVARS, one of the rarest ecosystems in the world.

One can appreciate how *Richard Shelton* tells this part of the story, about stones:

The Stones

I love to go out on summer nights and watch the stones grow.
I think they grow better here in the desert, where it is warm and dry,
than almost anywhere.  Or perhaps it is only that they young ones are
more active here.

Young stones tend to move about more than their elders consider
good for them.  Most young stone have a secret desire which their parents
had before them but have forgotten ages ago. And because this desire
involves water, it is never mentioned. The older stones disapprove of
water and say, "Water is a gadfly who never stays in one place long
enough to learn anything," but the young stones try to work themselves
into a position, slowly and without their elders noticing it, in which a
sizable stream of water during a summer storm might catch them broadside
and unknowing, so to speak, and push them along over a slope or down
an arroyo.  In spite of the danger this involves, they want to travel and see
something of the world and settle in a new place, far from home, where
they can raise their own dynasties away from the domination of their parents.

And although family ties are very strong among stones,
many have succeeded; and they carry scars to prove to their children
that they once went on a journey, helter-skelter and high water, and
traveled perhaps fifteen feet, an incredible distance.  As they grow older,
they cease to brag about such clandestine adventures.

It is true that old stones get to be very conservative.  They
remain comfortably where they are and often get fat.  Fatness,
as a matter of face, is a mark of distinction.

And on summer nights after all the young stones are asleep,
the elders turn to a serious and frightening subject - the moon,
which is always spoken of  in whispers.  "See how it glows and
whips across the sky, always changing its shape," one says.   And
another says, "Feel how it pulls at us, urging us to follow."  And a
third whispers, "Its a stone gone mad."

So it is that we try to perceive and understand the earth upon which we
tread. To do so, we follow the footstep of those who have gone before us, geological,
plant, animal and ancestral to see how it works, how it goes. And yet, for the most
part it is all too big, too much of a mystery to grasp and comprehend. We cannot
really wrap our minds around it because it is too large and we are in it, and we are
very small within this enormous realm we live.

**Letter Number 4:** *May 21, 2016*

Dear Talia,

So much has happened this month, it is hard to know where to start! The National Park Service came out and burned just under 100 acres of our land, all the way to the river. The flames were high and the smoke billowing, at times. The next day, there were 7 sandhill cranes who flew in and feasted upon bugs and seeds. Now, two weeks later, the grass is greening and the Indian paintbrush and lupine are beginning to bloom. It is beautiful.

The swallows are nesting in the middle 'bluebird' box, the robins have a nest high in the spruce tree by the shed, the eastern wood phoebes have added to the nest under the deck, and mama whistlesneak (thirteen-striped ground squirrel) is running around very pregnant! Mama geese and mallards have disappeared, presumably sitting on their eggs. Both bald eagles and a golden eagle have been hanging about, one spending much time in the big, old pine tree that your mother used to swing in. We have seen no fawns, yet. The turtles should begin laying eggs soon, within the solar-electrified fence that protect their nests from predators (raccoon, mink, badger).

I have purchased another parcel of land to the east. We now have land along about 1 mile of shoreline of the Namekagon River, a National Wild and Scenic River managed by the National Park Service. On days with little wind, we hear the laughter and shouts from kids and adults canoeing and tubing the river from the deck. What delightful sounds to go with the frogs and birds.

The re-staining of the main house is almost finished and looks great!  Repair of the lower deck led to finding that the posts bearing up the upper deck and roof had rotted, so we also repaired them and all is as good as new.

For my birthday I had fresh lobster (our local market now has a special section that flies it in fresh seafood), venison sirloin, mashed potatoes and fresh asparagus. It was delicious! Dessert included a dark chocolate, cherry and whipped cream birthday cake with frozen yogurt ... I am still happily full. With more than 40 birthday wishes from family and friends, it was a joyful day.

At 10 weeks of age tomorrow, Daybreak continues to sleep all night every so often and seems to have found his hands to handle things. His gurgling and babbling smiles seem spray early morning sunshine right into our open hearts. Christina is tending to Otter Haven, our guesthouse, with the first guests, a young family with two children, arriving next weekend, with the summer mostly booked into September. She will be busy!

I had a wonderful conversation with a 90-year old Catholic priest who knew my father, Damian Joseph Vraniak , and his brother Jerry Vraniak, when all three were in high school at St. Procopius in Chicago, before 'big Day' went into the Air Force in World War II. Wonderful stories!! And my cousin, Barb (Vraniak) Turpin, who lives just a few miles down the road, just dropped off my grandparents' – Joseph & Mary Vraniak - large, colorful, fancy marriage certificate, written in Slovic, among other mementos and pictures ... how precious.

I am sad to say, that while we will continue to write to you, since we are unsure whether you are receiving these letters and photos, we will hold onto them for you if and

90

whenever your Mom or Dad or you express that you would like to read them. There is so much more to share, and the writings will continue for you and they will be here when you wish to have them.

Love you,

Grandpa Day & Christina

*Abundance       - To create space, time and energy for more than for oneself -*

Counting the number of snapping turtle, wood turtle and spiny-nosed hatchlings that came out of the fifteen or so protected nests was not as much fun as seeing my young two and a half year old son Daybreak find another little hatchling 'spiny' crawling toward the creek down the driveway or watching my wife Christina carry some 36 little 'snappers' from their nest exit and joyously releasing them into the creek. It really was not a lot of effort to put up the wooden structure to protect the nests on the pile of sand next to the creek nor did it take much time to place small cages over the newly laid eggs on the side of the 'sand hill' halfway up the trail to the knoll after watching the female turtles lay them. The consequences of using these two small spaces of sand and taking a little time and energy resulted in nearly 300 turtle hatchlings reaching the creek that flows into the river this year, as opposed to maybe ten or twenty hatchlings luckily avoiding predators digging up the eggs in the nests before they exited. What abundance now occurs each year with the little space, time and energy our family gifts to turtles.

Since I was planting a few little apple saplings, I thought I might plant a few more ... and then plant yet a few more the next year and the next, as well as perhaps a few plum trees and not cut down the small chokecherry trees beginning to grow in the meadow openings along this side of the creek. Now there are twenty apple trees, a few plum trees and several chokecherry trees nicely maturing, producing fruit. My goodness, it did not take much space, time or effortful energy to do this, only a bit of patience and forbearance to let growth occur over time. Again this year, we have frozen enough apple pies (about 15) and applesauce (many quarts) and made enough jam (60 jars) to have some delicious desserts every week through the fall and winter, well into next year. Yet, there is so much abundance that as many apples and plums as we use, the bears and deer will eat some as well, increasing the ease in which they make it through the winter. And in the past few days I have seen as many as twenty migrating bluebirds and/or cedar waxwings, and robins, in the large chokecherry tree by the shed, eating the remaining chokecherries after our harvest. Such shared abundance makes their long journeys southward much easier, I would guess.

Deepening and extending the ponds was a larger effort, but while harvesting wild rice each year it was not hard to throw some into the ponds and channels, in the lagoon of the creek just before it enters the river, or along a couple bends of the river itself. This year about five goslings survived and six or seven ducklings, as the broods of geese and mallards nested along the banks. Now, and next year, the waterfowl, muskrats, and yes, even the wading deer, will enjoy the same rice we enjoy. Sharing our abundance really is not that difficult and does not take extraordinary space, time or effort, just a willingness to share and the generosity to do so.

Many years ago I collected milkweed seeds. It was so easy; there were so many. And the silk reflecting light was so beautifully shimmering. To let them go flying across the land by the hundreds and to spread the ones slipped off their silk, sowing milk-to-come for caterpillars was childlike, innocent fun. And now the fragrant perfume of blossoming milkweed and the sight of majestic monarchs gifts such a small, previous investment in supplying food for a non-human resident and visitor. And so it was also with lupine and sand coreopsis – plentiful gifting of seed from each plant offered easy opportunity to spread and increase such abundance originally shared.

When we visited the boys great grandparents they gave us some of their garden surplus in the form of potatoes, tomatoes and strawberry-rubarb jam, mentioning their other granddaughter brought them some of her homemade blackberry jam, who also, on a later visit brought us one of the musk melon from her garden, while we gifted apples, jam and pie to each of them. Many of us in our rural communities share our abundance with one another, with friends, family and neighbors, without any need for return, except for the expressions of delicious delight on their faces. However, beyond bird feeders, how many of us create and share our abundance with our non-human friends, family and neighbors without expectation of getting something in return (venison sirloins, a bear rug, a stuffed mount), other than the satisfaction of encouraging the survival and existence of these members of our wild family? It is not really that hard; it just a little surplus of space, time and energy which we might to choose to share in generosity of spirit and personal resource.

Journal Entry: *September 1, 2018  4:47 am*

*Bear and Child*

My 2½ year old son, Daybreak, runs like a fawn – beautiful, random, up and down, fast as the wind, sudden turns and leaps about. Easily and smoothly high-stepping down the trail, he is about the size of a fawn. He is, literally, like a fawn, gorgeous. His handsome, nine-month old brother is just about walking and will follow in his prancing footsteps, I am sure.

We reside on about 250 acres along a wild and scenic river, with spring-fed ponds, two trout streams, prairie, and savanna. Basically, we live in a national park and have all the plants and animals you might find in such a special and diverse set of habitats, especially every mammal you might think of – fox, coyote, badger, marmot, ground squirrel, deer, skunk, raccoon, porcupine and once in a while, wolf, as well as the passing through cougar. Yet, of all these neighbors it is the resident bears that most concern me.

Now, please do understand that I know something of bears. My maternal *Huron* ancestors hunted them with dogs before 1600. My grandfather brought the first bear dogs into Wisconsin in the 1930's and taught all of his fifteen children to hunt bear. One of my uncles told me just yesterday that he and his son have eighteen bait stations out for the guests they have to begin the bear season this coming week. However, one of my best friends, who I just lowered into her grave within the past year or two, was Bear Clan, and I do not eat, nor do I hunt bear. And typically I have one to three bears denning on this land where we live, often at least one female who bears young at the end of January or beginning of February. A decade ago bear hunters killed an old bear I was quite familiar with for many years, just up on the creek which passes in front of my home, who weighed 650 lbs. I miss his presence.

This coming spring my sons, Daybreak and Arendaki (named after his Huron ancestor), will be 3 years and 1½ years old, respectively. The following spring they will be 4 and 2 ½ years old. Already Daybreak has led folks along the trails (this year on our twenty-fifth annual prairie walk). He and his brother and mother have collected turtle hatchlings and transported them to the creek, watched does and fawns cavort, chased cottontail rabbits and tracked animals in the sand (he knows the difference between a buck, doe and fawn track). Daybreak has walked over all the miles of trails, presently knows his directions, landmarks (burial rock) and turns, as well as the names (some in Ojibwe) of over 30 mammals and 20 wildflowers ... and each by sight. During the next two springs my two young sons will be all over this rich landscape during the time our bears are coming out of hibernation and are most hungry.

As you may know, a female bear may not eat or drink for as much as six months, as she gives birth inside the winter den, milk is supplied through a combination of the air she breathes and the fat she has accumulated before denning. Not only is she quite hungry, she has hungry cubs to feed. While one of my brothers has been chased up a tree by a bear, I, his much older brother, have been largely left alone, undoubtedly too tough and unpalatable a meal for most any bear. Local dogs have been maimed and eaten by bear. This year a bear feasted on each of the bluebird nests in the boxes I put up last year.  Most relevantly, bear are responsible for 80% of fawn mortality in the spring of each year.

My 2½ year old son, Daybreak, runs like a fawn – beautiful, random, up and down, fast as the wind, sudden turns and leaps about. Easily and smoothly high-stepping down the trail, he is about the size of a fawn. He is, literally, like a fawn, gorgeous. His handsome, nine-month old brother is just about walking and will follow in his prancing footsteps, I am sure.

My sons would be delicious to a bear newly come out of her den with cubs in the spring, this spring, next spring and the spring after that. By the time Daybreak and Arendaki are 6 and 4 years old, respectively, they will capable enough to venture out together without complete adult supervision on the land they know so well, as least for short trips, and for important brief but independent adventures. As delicious as they are beautiful, what am I to do about our close neighbors, the bear, with respect to my young children? While ticks are more dangerous, as are cars and spring high flooding (the boys have already been canoeing and tubing) I must choose between several alternatives with regards to their relationship with bear. What would *you* suggest or advise?

Journal Entry: Sunday, September 2, 2018  12:59 pm

**2020 Christmas Letter**

Dear Family and Friends,

We hope you are well, that your hearts are full and vibrant.

Our life here along the river is forever full and fruitful.  Like many of you have found, there were pleasant surprises in the sweep of this pandemic.  We brought ourselves to staying at home at the end of January, pulling Daybreak from 4K in Birchwood, and reduced grocery and errand trips to twice a month.  Spring and Summer brought a steady stream of intensive endeavors – beginning with pulling up prairie sod to create a garden, and more fully investing in the gardening process.  We restored an overgrown plum orchard and learned more about pruning and organic sprays.  We branched into berry beds, and tended grape vines, and yet learned once again the loss a late frost creates - for such a frost this spring prevented much fruit.  We planted 50 American chestnut seedlings. In all this tending, our hearts smiled at the worthwhile work we could do together because we were home.

In Spring, Damian's mother passed away just before Easter, and later on the day of her funeral, on Good Friday, the four of us walked out to the river.  A doe watched us pass by, and then followed us, nosing near us when we'd stopped at the river.  She came within 10 feet of us, and eventually hoofed off.  Throughout Spring and Summer she made herself comfortable about our home, and even stepped up onto our low deck, pressed her nose to the glass and watched the boys don their coats and hats one morning.  A dear deer.

We had a very successful turtle nesting season, with 30-40 turtles nesting in and about the turtle protection enclosure by our creek, so that over 300 hatchlings making it into the creek in late summer.  This is an annual highlight, and this year we watched and learned that spiny softshell turtles we gather as they emerge from their nests and release in the creek (27 this year) when plopped in the water will burrow in the sand of the creek, completely disappearing on the bottom, eventually to stick an upturned nose out of the sand.  We tracked a good many four footed, furry, and feathered friends in the warm seasons, noting a return of wolves, the presence of otters, coyotes, foxes, and deer, turkeys, various snakes, ducks, hawks, songbirds, eagles, and are learning what it is to be neighbors with a beaver who chews down 90-year old aspen trees and transports branches to lie between the islands for winter fare. And we planted 50 American chestnut trees, with 50 Saskatoon berry shrubs ordered and on the way to plant, as well.

Damian turned 70 this year, and published Volume 4 of *Travailler*.  He is the heart-hum of our home, ever captivating the boys with stories, questions, new news, and ready laughter.  He gives daily lessons to each son in turn about the land and all that live within and upon it.  From these lessons, the boys can identify over 70 mammals, 50 birds, 20 snakes, all the local turtles, and several species of fish, nevermind the bees and insects they now know.  The boys soak him in, responding with questions, and stories, ideas, and laughter of their own.  This year Damian finished brushing the Red Pine Savanna, burned a multitude of brush piles, seeded new trails, and brought all of us into collecting native wildflower seeds.  This was captivating, and we all marveled at the unique packaging, shapes, sizes and surprising quantities of so many native seeds.  As this year ends, Day is crafting a volume about the life on our land, which produced a 2'x4' map that is becoming a bit of a game board, and has sourced a family study from the Bible about animals.

As for me, Christina, the year was rich with learning.  I learned that gardening is a 3-season endeavor, that rich soil is a fascinating gift, and that successful gardening and common sense go hand in hand.  I greatly enjoyed restoring the plum orchard, and hummed a happy tune when it bore fruit.  Tip-toeing up to baby turtles is a yearly delight, as is the arrival of Spring's first hummingbirds.  I have also come to love putting up the year's fruit, vegetables, and venison.  There is sweet satisfaction in the successful, steady labor that bears sustenance, and gifts, for family and friends.  We also enjoyed the simple silliness a good ditty derives.  A good rhyme, set to a simple tune, will often continue in giggles and be set with new lyrics.  Such little ditties have made the boys into singers and songwriters, and blooming comedians - it fills our home with happy tunes.

Daybreak is 4 this year, and has grown a foot, and gained ten pounds in this pandemic!  He has a dramatic imagination, often enriching his rest times by casting a multitude of stuffed animals in the scenes he imagines.  He still loves lines, delighting in the drives past pine plantations because all the trees are in a row.  He is drawn to numbers, plays with addition and subtraction, is an engineer and architect in his own right, and is on the brink of reading.  He's begun this year of 4K virtually through Hayward, and we're glad for daily lessons that offer his voracious mind something to chew on.  He and Arendaki have become best brothers, another gift of the pandemic, and he is a daily help, playmate, and mischief-maker with Arendaki.  I laughed one morning when Daybreak topped the stairs with, "Dad, I got Arendaki dressed" and so he had.  Arendaki burst to the top of those same stairs with, "Daybake got me dwessed!"  That evening at bath time, I found them in each other's undershirts, and smiled at our growing boys.

Arendaki just turned 3, and the rest of his body is steadily catching up to his head.  His year has been full of milestones - he began sleeping through the night this summer, he can capably feed himself with utensils, and he has made it through potty training.  In early winter the boys transitioned to sleeping in the same room on a bunk bed, and with these acquired skills, we're beginning to realize we're past the baby stages, nearly out of toddlerhood!  As Daybreak loves a line, Arendaki loves a circle, a ball, and is ever collecting any small ball he can find.  Something about smooth, round continuity fascinates him; he's already quite drawn to basketballs.  When Arendaki turned 3, he became a runner and a conversationalist.  The day after he turned 3, he took to running our 1/4 mile driveway on our trips to and from the mailbox.  This was a surprise to Daybreak, who is also a happy runner, for suddenly Daybreak didn't have time to dawdle, and couldn't out sprint Arendaki's steady quick trot.  Arendaki also loves his stuffed animals, has his favorites and keeps them close.  When it comes to being outdoors, Arendaki will find a bird anywhere, and is currently very interested in clouds, the sun, the moon, stars, planets, and the cell towers that twinkle in the distance.

While we have missed many a good thing during the pandemic of 2020, we have found our relationships and endeavors surprisingly enriched with so much time together.  We hope your year has had its blessings in disguise too.

Merry Christmas!

Love,

Damian & Christina, Daybreak & Arendaki Vraniak

---

So in this viewing of scenes (photos) from *Station 1*, the songs of Raven and Turtle, traditional ancestral family stories of the Huron and Vraniak family stories of protecting turtles and planting a prairie garden, with journal entries beginning to express the journey of restoration as it unfolded, what gift(s) might be received?

*Not Invading, Occupying and Over-filling (Dominating) a Space, nor only Emptying a Space by Consuming or Devouring (Destroying) What is in it*

It is so difficult for human beings to leave a space empty, so that others may enter. Our actions, our machines, our very words so fill a space, that the presence of any other(s) is disallowed. It is similar for some of our four-footed brothers and sisters: A space devoid of herbivores and deer rush in, eating any and all of their plant relatives. Indeed, it is the same for many of our leaved and branched relations, as any good space that opens up is quickly crowded in by aspen, spotted knapweed or buckthorn.

Our invading spaces so quickly and completely is counterbalanced by the opening up of spaces as we consume one another. As deer overpopulate, wolves move in; as aspen crowd in, so come beaver; as there is any resource – trees, soil, oil, water, land – people rush in to devour. Even more quickly, the earth can open up space in devastating fashion, by flooding, by wind, by earthquake, by fire, by death of the old ones, so that new ones might enter.

In between this rushing in, over filling a space, and violently consuming and devastating to open a space - between invading and devouring – there can be a time that a space may be left empty, entered briefly, intermittently perhaps, while beheld from the margins, from the borders. This, I believe, is what the land and its life seeks to do, to open spaces and extend the time it is empty, so that they may be held in common, entered rhythmically, ... as the plant people, four-footeds, and wingeds dance elegantly with one another, entering into the space provided in grand

96

procession, and then dancing, singing in a harmonious and interwoven weave, broken off, the space left, and new dancers and singers entering to paint different colors, dance different movements, sing different melodies, tell old and new stories.

*A space quietly left open may be entered by that which is amazingly transformative.*

Here, at *Station 1*, see if you can still your body, calm your heart, quiet your mind, empty and open your self to the following proposition:

*The embodied knowledge and life-force (the soul) of my ancestors continues in me and my children, as it does in yours, as it does for Other-than-humans, as well.*

As Damian has suggested, a family is the smallest community through which each being, each person, travels, first as a dance, then as a song, eventually as a story, and, finally, as a prayer. A family lives in a larger version of these forms, as well, as both a family and larger communities of families, clans, and cultural nations mix the light and the darkness, the joy and the grief, the success and the failure, the life and the death, composed by these lived creations. And we carry the hope and despair, the strength and weakness of the history of our families, communities and local cultures, as archived sojourns.

There is a flow of this living repository of journeys, from time immemorial into the present and on into the future that is carried within each being as life is lived. And if they are carried, survived and sustained long enough, well enough, such journeys allow us to come to know the longer, arching paths, the ancient lines that connect the constellations of our ancestors.

*The embodied life-force, knowledge and soul of our ancestors, both human and other-than-human, continues in us and in our children.*

*And the embodied history of the relations among our various families and clans - between the earth and water, wind and fire, among plants, animals and people, across the wild and the civil - is best experienced in the spaces left open to the procession of dances, songs and stories that cherish and celebrate our existence together, that consecrate our respect for those that are different and esteem each life within as itself, each relationship between one and each Other, each set of relations among families, clans and communities, as sacred.*

# The Sacred: *Celebrating & Consecrating Relationship with Spirit and Silence*

Fortunately, there is guidance in what has been passed down the generations as Sacred. Exploration seeking to penetrate a very small part of this Sacredness can be done by reviewing and summarizing Biblical passages (2,571) that are concerned with animals, both wild (1,024) and domestic (1,445), that Damian and his wife have been studying and trying translate into a form for educating their 5-year old and 3-year old sons.

In this exploration and sharing we might come to some better sense of ways to celebrate and consecrate our relations with our animal relatives with whom we share this land and upon whom to a great degree our own survival depends.

Therefore, for each of the 20 stations different passages will be shared, beginning with *Creator, Creation and Creatures* for *Station 1* and then proceeding as follows:

Station 2. Snake and viper,
Station 3. Dove and turtledove,
Station 4. Animals,
Station 5. Insects,
Station 6. Raven, eagle, hawk and owl,
Station 7. Partridge, pigeons and quail,
Station 8. Leopard and lion,
Station 9. Wolf and fox,
Station 10. Bear,
Station 11. Deer, antelope and gazelle,
Station 12. Frog,
Station 13. Fish and whale,
Station 14. Horse, donkey and mule,
Station 15, pig, ox, cow, cattle and camel,
Station 16. Goat, ram and mountain sheep,
Station 17. Sheep and lamb,
Station 18. Birds,
Station 19. Swallow and sparrow,
Station 20. Dragons, beasts and behemoths.

If you chose not to read all the passages and *compilations of verses* for *Station 1* that follow, you may skip to the *summary on page 107* ...

Genesis 1:24

And God said, "Let the land produce living creatures according to their kinds: the livestock, the creatures that move along the ground, and the wild animals, each according to its kind." And it was so.

Genesis 1

In the beginning God created the heavens and the earth. Now the earth was formless and empty, darkness was over the surface of the deep, and the Spirit of God was hovering over the waters.

And God said, "Let there be light," and there was light. God saw that the light was good, and he separated the light from the darkness. God called the light "day," and the darkness he called "night." And there was evening, and there was morning—the first day.

And God said, "Let there be a vault between the waters to separate water from water." So God made the vault and separated the water under the vault from the water above it. And it was so. God called the vault "sky." And there was evening, and there was morning—the second day.

And God said, "Let the water under the sky be gathered to one place, and let dry ground appear." And it was so. God called the dry ground "land," and the gathered waters he called "seas." And God saw that it was good. Then God said, "Let the land produce vegetation: seed-bearing plants and trees on the land that bear fruit with seed in it, according to their various kinds." And it was so. The land produced vegetation: plants bearing seed according to their kinds and trees bearing fruit with seed in it according to their kinds. And God saw that it was good. And there was evening, and there was morning—the third day.

And God said, "Let there be lights in the vault of the sky to separate the day from the night, and let them serve as signs to mark sacred times, and days and years, and let them be lights in the vault of the sky to give light on the earth." And it was so. God made two great lights—the greater light to govern the day and the lesser light to govern the night. He also made the stars. God set them in the vault of the sky to give light on the earth, to govern the day and the night, and to separate light from darkness. And God saw that it was good. And there was evening, and there was morning—the fourth day.

And God said, "Let the water teem with living creatures, and let birds fly above the earth across the vault of the sky." So God created the great creatures of the sea and every living thing with which the water teems and that moves about in it, according to their kinds, and every winged bird according to its kind. And God saw that it was good. God blessed them and said, "Be fruitful and increase in number and fill the water in the seas, and let the birds increase on the earth."  And there was evening, and there was morning—the fifth day.

And God said, "Let the land produce living creatures according to their kinds: the livestock, the creatures that move along the ground, and the wild animals, each according to its kind." And it was so.  God made the wild animals according to their kinds, the livestock according to their kinds, and all the creatures that move along the ground according to their kinds. And God saw that it was good.

Then God said, "Let us make mankind in our image, in our likeness, so that they may rule over the fish in the sea and the birds in the sky, over the livestock and all the wild animals, and over all the creatures that move along the ground."

So God created mankind in his own image, in the image of God he created them; male and female he created them. God blessed them and said to them, "Be fruitful and increase in number; fill the earth and subdue it. Rule over the fish in the sea and the birds in the sky and over every living creature that moves on the ground."

Then God said, "I give you every seed-bearing plant on the face of the whole earth and every tree that has fruit with seed in it. They will be yours for food. And to all the beasts of the earth and all the birds in the sky and all the creatures that move along the ground—everything that has the breath of life in it—I give every green plant for food." And it was so. God saw all that he had made, and it was very good. And there was evening, and there was morning—the sixth day.

## John 1 NIV

In the beginning was the Word, and the Word was with God, and the Word was God. He was with God in the beginning. Through him all things were made; without him nothing was made that has been made.  In him was life, and that life was the light of all mankind. The light shines in the darkness, and the darkness has not overcome it.

There was a man sent from God whose name was John. He came as a witness to testify concerning that light, so that through him all might believe. He himself was not the light; he came only as a witness to the light.

The true light that gives light to everyone was coming into the world. He was in the world, and though the world was made through him, the world did not recognize him. He came to that which was his own, but his own did not receive him. Yet to all who did receive him, to those who believed in his name, he gave the right to become children of God— children born not of natural descent, nor of human decision or a husband's will, but born of God.

The Word became flesh and made his dwelling among us. We have seen his glory, the glory of the one and only Son, who came from the Father, full of grace and truth.

(John testified concerning him. He cried out, saying, "This is the one I spoke about when I said, 'He who comes after me has surpassed me because he was before me.'") Out of his fullness we have all received grace in place of grace already given. For the law was given through Moses; grace and truth came through Jesus Christ. No one has ever seen God, but the one and only Son, who is himself God and is in closest relationship with the Father, has made him known.

### Psalm 19

The heavens declare the glory of God; the skies proclaim the work of his hands. Day after day they pour forth speech; night after night they reveal knowledge. They have no speech, they use no words; no sound is heard from them. Yet their voice goes out into all the earth, their words to the ends of the world.

### Job 12: 7-10

But ask the animals, and they will teach you,
or the birds in the sky, and they will tell you;
or speak to the earth, and it will teach you,
or let the fish in the sea inform you.
Which of all these does not know
that the hand of the Lord has done this?
In his hand is the life of every creature
and the breath of all mankind.


## *Creator, Creation and Creatures* (142 verses)

### Compilation 1: *Creator* (13 verses)

*So it was,* that the Creator first created the heavens and earth, then separated light from darkness, created the sky, and separated water from earth, forming the land. Creator had the land produce vegetation, set the stars in the heavens, let the water teem with living creatures and birds in the air, all to multiply and fill the waters and the skies. Then Creator had the land produce living creatures of all kinds. Finally, at last, Creator made human beings, in the image of Creator. And so it came to be that all the green things were food for all the creatures of breath, and they filled the waters, the skies and the land.

*So it was,* that in the beginning was the Word and the Word was with Creator, through which all things were made. In Creator was all life, the life of humankind, as light in the darkness, and the darkness has not overcome it.

*So it came to be,* that the Word became flesh and the true light came into the world, dwelling among all, full of the light of Creator … the Word was made alive and present.

*So it is,* that the heavens declare the glory of the Creator, pouring out speech without sound across all the land to the ends of the world, proclaiming the work and glory of Creator.

*So it is,* that if you ask the animals of the land or birds in the skies or fish in the waters, those who were here before you, they will teach you; if you speak to the earth, the earth will inform you. For every living being knows the hand of Creator, that Creator is the life of every creature and the breath of all humankind.

*Is it not wise, then, to listen to the Word, as it is voiced in the witness of the creatures of the waters, land and air?*

*So this is what we will do in the following pages, to seek the light-filled glory and truth of the Creator as that Creator infuses all with the life that moves us, infused within the speech of the land and the voices of the creatures who were here before us and with which we live and upon which our life depends.*

## Compilation 2: *Creation* (27 verses)

Since the *creation* of the world Creator's invisible qualities— the eternal power and divine nature—have been clearly seen, being understood from what has been made, so that people are without excuse. However, there are things hidden from us since the *creation* of the world. Yet, nothing in all *creation* is hidden from Creator's sight. Everything is uncovered and laid bare before the eyes of Him to whom we must give account.

Rejoice, Creator will come to judge the earth, the world and the peoples.

The *creation* waits in eager expectation for the children of Creator to be revealed. For the *creation* was subjected to frustration, not by its own choice, but by the will of the one who subjected it, in hope that the *creation* itself will be liberated from its bondage to decay and brought into the freedom and glory of the children of Creator. We know that the whole *creation* has been groaning as in the pains of childbirth right up to the present time.

He was loved before the *creation* of the world; He is the image of the invisible Creator, the firstborn over all *creation*. He was given those who are to be with Him where he is; for he chose us in Him before the *creation* of the world to be holy and blameless in His sight.

Neither height nor depth, nor anything else in all *creation*, will be able to separate us from the love of Creator that is in Him who was loved. Therefore, if anyone is in He who was loved, the new *creation* has come: The old has gone, the new is here! He was chosen before the *creation* of the world, but was revealed in these last times for your sake. Thus, a kingdom was prepared for you since the *creation* of the world.

They will say, "Where is this 'coming' he promised? Ever since our ancestors died, everything goes on as it has since the beginning of *creation*."

Neither circumcision nor uncircumcision means anything; what counts is the new *creation*. One's own *creation*, crafted image, cannot speak. All inhabitants of the earth will worship the beast—all whose names have not been written in the Lamb's book of life, the Lamb who was slain from the *creation* of the world. The beast, which you saw, once was, now is not, and yet will come up out of the Abyss and go to its destruction. The inhabitants of the earth whose names have not been written in the book of life from the *creation* of the world will be astonished when they see the beast, because it once was, now is not, and yet will come.

But when He who was loved came as the holy presence of the good things that are now already here, he went through the greater and more perfect place, the kingdom that is not made with human hands, that is to say, is not a part of this *creation*. Otherwise He who is loved would have had to suffer many times since the *creation* of the world. But He has appeared once for all at the culmination of the ages to do away with the Beast by the sacrifice of Himself.

-- Go out and preach this Word to all *creation*.

## Compilation 3: *Creatures* (69 verses)

How many are your works, Lord! In wisdom you made them all; the earth is full of your *creatures*.

There is the sea, vast and spacious, teeming with *creatures* beyond number— living things both large and small. All *creatures* look to you to give them their food at the proper time. Praise the Lord from the earth, you great sea *creatures* and all ocean depths, wild animals and all cattle, small *creatures* and flying birds,

You must distinguish between the unclean and the clean, between living *creatures* that may be eaten and those that may not be eaten. Do not defile

103

yourselves by any of these *creatures*. Do not make yourselves unclean by means of them or be made unclean by them.

Of all the *creatures* living in the water of the seas and the streams you may eat any that have fins and scales. You have made people like the fish in the sea, like the sea *creatures* that have no ruler.

It was you who crushed the heads of Leviathan and gave it as food to the *creatures* of the desert. Ants are *creatures* of little strength, yet they store up their food in the summer; hyraxes are *creatures* of little power, yet they make their home in the crags.

Look at the land of the Babylonians, this people that is now of no account! The Assyrians have made it a place for desert *creatures*; they raised up their siege towers, they stripped its fortresses bare and turned it into a ruin. All kinds of animals, birds, reptiles and sea *creatures* are being tamed and have been tamed by mankind, .... But these people blaspheme in matters they do not understand. They are like unreasoning animals, *creatures* of instinct, born only to be caught and destroyed, and like animals they too will perish.

But desert *creatures* will lie there, jackals will fill her houses; there the owls will dwell, and there the wild goats will leap about. Desert *creatures* will meet with hyenas, and wild goats will bleat to each other; there the night *creatures* will also lie down and find for themselves places of rest. So desert *creatures* and hyenas will live there, and there the owl will dwell. It will never again be inhabited or lived in from generation to generation.

Flocks and herds will lie down there, *creatures* of every kind. The desert owl and the screech owl will roost on her columns. Their hooting will echo through the windows, rubble will fill the doorways, the beams of cedar will be exposed. They will lick dust like a snake, like *creatures* that crawl on the ground. They will come trembling out of their dens; they will turn in fear to the Lord and will be afraid of you.

In that day I will make a covenant for them with the beasts of the field, the birds in the sky and the *creatures* that move along the ground. Bow and sword and battle I will abolish from the land, so that all may lie down in safety.

Ezekiel 1: 1-28

In my thirtieth year, in the fourth month on the fifth day, while I was among the exiles by the Kebar River, the heavens were opened and I saw visions of God.

I looked, and I saw a windstorm coming out of the north—an immense cloud with flashing lightning and surrounded by brilliant light. The center of the fire looked like glowing metal, and in the fire was what looked like four living *creatures*. In appearance their form was human, but each of them had four faces and four wings. Their legs were straight; their feet were like those of a calf and gleamed like burnished bronze. Under their wings on their four sides they had human hands. All four of them had faces and wings, and the wings of one touched the wings of another. Each one went straight ahead; they did not turn as they moved.

Their faces looked like this: Each of the four had the face of a human being, and on the right side each had the face of a lion, and on the left the face of an ox; each also had the face of an eagle. Such were their faces. They each had two wings spreading out upward, each wing touching that of the *creature* on either side; and each had two other wings covering its body. Each one went straight ahead. Wherever the spirit would go, they would go, without turning as they went. The appearance of the living creatures was like burning coals of fire or like torches. Fire moved back and forth among the creatures; it was bright, and lightning flashed out of it. The **creatures** sped back and forth like flashes of lightning.

As I looked at the living *creatures*, I saw a wheel on the ground beside each *creature* with its four faces. This was the appearance and structure of the wheels: They sparkled like topaz, and all four looked alike. Each appeared to be made like a wheel intersecting a wheel. As they moved, they would go in any one of the four directions the *creatures* faced; the wheels did not change direction as the creatures went. Their rims were high and awesome, and all four rims were full of eyes all around.

When the living *creatures* moved, the wheels beside them moved; and when the living *creatures* rose from the ground, the wheels also rose. Wherever the spirit would go, they would go, and the wheels would rise along with them, because the spirit of the living creatures was in the wheels. When the *creatures* moved, they also moved; when the *creatures* stood still, they also stood still; and when the creatures rose from the ground, the wheels rose along with them, because the spirit of the living creatures was in the wheels.

Spread out above the heads of the living *creatures* was what looked something like a vault, sparkling like crystal, and awesome. Under the vault their wings were stretched out one toward the other, and each had two wings covering its body. When the *creatures* moved, I heard the sound of their wings, like the roar of rushing waters, like the voice of the Almighty, like the tumult of an army. When they stood still, they lowered their wings.

Then there came a voice from above the vault over their heads as they stood with lowered wings. Above the vault over their heads was what looked like a throne of lapis lazuli, and high above on the throne was a figure like that of a man. I saw that from what appeared to be his waist up he looked like glowing metal, as if full of fire, and that from there down he looked like fire; and brilliant light surrounded him. Like the appearance of a rainbow in the clouds on a rainy day, so was the radiance around him.

105

This was the appearance of the likeness of the glory of the Lord. When I saw it, I fell facedown, and I heard the voice of one speaking.

Revelations 4-19

Also in front of the throne there was what looked like a sea of glass, clear as crystal. In the center, around the throne, were four living *creatures*, and they were covered with eyes, in front and in back. Each of the four living *creatures* had six wings and was covered with eyes all around, even under its wings. Day and night they never stop saying: "'Holy, holy, holy is the Lord God Almighty,' who was, and is, and is to come." Whenever the living *creatures* give glory, honor and thanks to him who sits on the throne and who lives forever and ever,

Then I saw a Lamb, looking as if it had been slain, standing at the center of the throne, encircled by the four living *creatures* and the elders. The Lamb had seven horns and seven eyes, which are the seven spirits of God sent out into all the earth.

And when he had taken it, the four living *creatures* and the twenty-four elders fell down before the Lamb. Each one had a harp and they were holding golden bowls full of incense, which are the prayers of God's people.

Then I looked and heard the voice of many angels, numbering thousands upon thousands, and ten thousand times ten thousand. They encircled the throne and the living *creatures* and the elders.

The four living *creatures* said, "Amen," and the elders fell down and worshiped.

I watched as the Lamb opened the first of the seven seals. Then I heard one of the four living *creatures* say in a voice like thunder, "Come!" Then I heard what sounded like a voice among the four living *creatures*, saying, …

All the angels were standing around the throne and around the elders and the four living *creatures*. They fell down on their faces before the throne and worshiped God,

Then one of the four living *creatures* gave to the seven angels seven golden bowls filled with the wrath of God, who lives forever and ever.

… a third of the living *creatures* in the sea died, and a third of the ships were destroyed.

And they sang a new song before the throne and before the four living *creatures* and the elders. No one could learn the song except the 144,000 who had been redeemed from the earth. The twenty-four elders and the four living *creatures* fell down and worshiped God, who was seated on the throne. And they cried: "Amen, Hallelujah!"

*Summary of Bible Verses and Compilations*

In this process of looking at this particular body of wisdom, several interesting apparent features can be specified, including:

1) *Creation and creatures were created before human beings;*

2) *animals were the first to inhabit the landscape;*

3) *it is first stated that animals will be held accountable by their Creator for their actions, as will human beings (stated second);*

4) *by implication, then, animals appear to have some choice in what actions they may take (they have agency), and, indeed, may take many beneficial and/or destructive actions toward one another and in relation to human beings;*

5) *animals can communicate through their actions, through their own language, and, in a rare instance or two, in our language;*

6) *animals may be messengers of the sacred and through which spiritual forces may flow;*

7) *what happens to human beings also happens to animals (often first or simultaneously), linking our fates inexorably together;*

8) *animals are mentioned in far, far more verses than any other human character in the Bible ...*

These and other intriguing patterns will be examined more closely in the coming pages and Stations.

However, Damian's own experience of the declarative Biblical statements indicated in 4) through 7) – his witness of the reality and truth of these statements in specific, concrete events that occurred in his life and the life of his family - will be recounted beginning in the narratives of *Station 2*.

*To make a space within oneself is to still the body, calm the heart, quiet the mind, empty and open the soul to spirit. I never explicitly thought that such space might be filled concretely, directly with the voice of my Creator ...*

DAMIAN ... the voice spoke my name with such clarity and distinctness that, startled out of the deep sleep in the middle of the night, I awoke immediately, completely, and abruptly sat up in bed. The voice was real, but it did not sound outside of me.

The voice was not my own, yet I was a part of it. For the briefest of moments I was confused. 'Yes?' ... 'What is it you want?' ... 'Do you wish me to FOLLOW you?' ... 'Why did you call out my name?' ... questions came unbidden to my mind.

The voice was all of everything. There was only the voice, saying my name, once, as if there were a banner with my name on it that hung in space and the only thing in the universe was that banner. There was nothing else and everything was contained in that voice as it said my name, the whole of the universe in that voice, in my name. It seemed the voice might have intent in saying my name and all intent was in the voice. Although my first startled response was to formulate questions for the voice, I quickly realized that I need not ask any questions, for all questions and answers were in that voice. All certainty.

So simple, so clear, so singularly all of what it was, that the voice seemed the loudest voice I had ever heard, yet the voice spoke my name without yelling, without effort.

And all was black nothingness but for the voice. I do not know how to describe how all was contained in that voice that had said my name, the voice, my name, still resonating within me, as if my name had been spoken once, eternally, ... for all time was contained in that voice.

Now a day later, the penetration of that voice still flows through me, still carries me in some fashion through my reality, as if there was a more real reality through which I truly travel, behind and beyond my 'normal existence'. When I was small I had flying dreams and one of the consequences of this voice saying my name is that I am floating through a reality that is more real than the apparent reality I seem to be in.

I have had remarkable dreams and visions in my life, of happenings that came to be ... of death, of loss, of spirit ... that I have rarely shared. I have experienced remarkable messengers in my life, most of whom I have never spoken of to anyone. Dreams and true dreams, surprising occurrences with meanings passed along to me upon which my life has turned; but this was far beyond such wonderful and amazing happenings with which I have come to be familiar, and, yes, somewhat comfortable in awe when they happen. So much more.

A small part of the all of everything that is that voice, that seems to be staying with me, is a sense of peace, a clarity and comfort, in the saying of my name, that I am a part of that voice, a part of that all, and the rest will come, the rest will come, of course, for I am a part of that voice that is the all of everything.


*February 15, 2017    5:17 am*

What is the *Land*?

It is the pressure, the core grounding the holds us to the planet, the heart that binds us to the *rock* that we tread, our feet drawn ever downward toward the center of the hearth that is our home.

It is the *earth*, disassembled weathered rock, fragmented into pieces in such a manner that water may be held, transported, cleansed. This character and quality of being porous means that clay holds up water, while sand allows water to permeate it. Earth is the compact or open space the permits water and life to flow upon it, within it. Earth is the cavities that we crawl into and through, where we wrestle and rest as life, in our home.

The Land is *soil*, the accumulating life that has lived and died upon its surface. This soil is the repository of organic life deposited, in all its rich diversity, individual after individual, generation after generation, millennia after millennia. Life faltering and failing in its striving upward toward light, falls down upon itself, layer after compacting layer, darkening as it decomposes together with other fallen life. As it deepens in its darkness it enriches future life, untold future generations; life begets life in the nurturing depth of the soil, our home.

The Land is the glowering *liquid fire* belched from beneath the depths into the waters that cool it into the land we call home. This bright, hot flow from below cools and condenses in water and becomes the cold bedrock upon which we stand, run and jump and return to, stilled, having come full circle. Yet even this bedrock catches the light of the sun and warms itself, welcoming the life to come, becoming our home, ever again.

What is the Land? It is the element and essence ever separated from, and married to, water. But that is a previous and the next story. For if the Land is true, it is beautiful, but only if it is wedded to water in love. To understand this, one must come to know the *water carriers* that bear water, that bear life.

*May 5, 2021   4:30 am*

109

## East Loop Stations: Huron in the Oak Savanna (corn)
## & the Burnt-Stump People (*chicot*)

## Station 2

## Station 3

www.ingramcontent.com/pod-product-compliance
Lightning Source LLC
Chambersburg PA
CBHW041456280526

45792CB00004B/1033